Colección Támesis
SERIE A: MONOGRAFÍAS, 297

A COMPANION TO JAVIER MARÍAS

Tamesis

Founding Editors
†J. E. Varey

†Alan Deyermond

General Editor
Stephen M. Hart

Series editor of Fuentes para la historia del teatro en España
Charles Davis

Advisory Board
Andrew M. Beresford
Zoltán Biedermann
Celia Cussen
Efraín Kristal
Jo Labanyi
María E. López
José Antonio Mazzotti
Thea Pitman
Julius Ruiz
Alison Sinclair
Isabel Torres
Noël Valis

DAVID K. HERZBERGER

A COMPANION TO JAVIER MARÍAS

TAMESIS

© David K. Herzberger 2011

All Rights Reserved. Except as permitted under current legislation no part of this work may be photocopied, stored in a retrieval system, published, performed in public, adapted, broadcast, transmitted, recorded or reproduced in any form or by any means, without the prior permission of the copyright owner

The right of David K. Herzberger to be identified as the author of this work has been asserted in accordance with sections 77 and 78 of the Copyright, Designs and Patents Act 1988

First published 2011 by Tamesis, Woodbridge
Paperback edition 2022

ISBN 978 1 85566 230 8 hardback
ISBN 978 1 85566 365 7 paperback

Tamesis is an imprint of Boydell & Brewer Ltd
PO Box 9, Woodbridge, Suffolk IP12 3DF, UK
and of Boydell & Brewer Inc.
668 Mt Hope Avenue, Rochester, NY 14620–2731, USA
website: www.boydellandbrewer.com

A CIP catalogue record for this book is available
from the British Library

The publisher has no responsibility for the continued existence or accuracy of URLs for external or third-party internet websites referred to in this book, and does not guarantee that any content on such websites is, or will remain, accurate or appropriate.

Contents

Foreword		vii
Introduction		1
Chapter I:	Writing in the Newspapers: Everything under the Sun	17
Chapter II:	Two Early Novels: *Los dominios del lobo* and *Travesía del horizonte*	46
Chapter III:	Two Transitional Novels: *El siglo* and *El hombre sentimental*	71
Chapter IV:	On Oxford, Redonda, and the Practice of Reading: *Todas las almas* and *Negra espalda del timepo*	103
Chapter V:	Two Shakespearean Novels	139
Chapter VI:	*Tu rostro mañana*	179
Chapter VII:	Other Writings	212
Suggested Further Reading		229
Bibliography		233
Index		241

Foreword

During the course of preparing this book, in addition to the customary reading of professional criticism on the work of Javier Marías, I sought also to stay abreast of the extensive flow of information about him on various blogs and internet sites. In this way I was able to compile an array of information from many sources offered from diverse points of view. As might be expected, some of what I found was quite useful, providing a detail here or an insight there into Marías's life and works. Marías is a popular figure among casual readers as well as academic scholars, and the content of the various websites generally reflected the diversity of readers and opinions on what is important or not, what is good or bad, about Marías's work.

Before sitting down to write this brief foreword, I entered the name "Javier Marías" one final time into the internet search engine Bing, and clicked on the submit button. As it turns out, my search produced a list of 242,000 entries (an increase of about one hundred over the week before)—not a surprising number given the volume of Marías's writing and the fact that his works have been translated into thirty-six languages. However, I feel compelled here to offer a qualification concerning my internet exploration: I have not read all of the entries listed under Marías's name, and further, it is highly unlikely that I will ever manage to do so. At the same time, I am quite confident that, if I have missed something critical, others will hasten to fill in any significant lacunae.

Although my perusal of internet sites may have fallen somewhat short of completeness, my aim in this book is to provide the most comprehensive reading of Marías's work to date. In fact, as I finish this study, it is the only book to cover all of his major works. I begin with a general introduction to Marías, including a brief overview of his life and his thoughts on a variety of topics, as well as how his writing might fruitfully be viewed in the context of Francoist (1939–1975) and post-Francoist Spain. I touch only briefly in the introduction on a number of thematic and aesthetic elements that inform his writing in general—these are then filled in with greater depth in subsequent chapters. In the past decade and a half Marías has written hundreds of columns for the national press in Spain; chapter I explores the wide range of interests and opinions expressed in these writings, including his thoughts on literature in general and fiction in particular.

The major part of my study, chapters II to V, is devoted to Marías's novels, which I (and nearly all critics) consider the imaginative core of his work. It is clearly the part that has resonated most fully with the public and also received the most intense scrutiny from critics. For the most part, I have studied his novels in chronological order, grouping them in chapters by the common ideas and techniques that characterize them. Only in chapter IV, where I discuss *Todas las almas* (1989) and *Negra espalda del tiempo* (1998), have I deviated from this chronological progression for reasons which I hope will be apparent. In the final chapter I include Marías's short fiction and other non-fictional works—these merit critical attention for how they convey his versatility as a writer, but on the whole have not generated the same level of national or international acclaim.

I wish to thank Elspeth Ferguson of Tamesis, who first suggested this study and arranged for its inclusion in the Companion series. I am grateful to my research assistants, J'leen Saeger, Lucero Flores-Paez, and Jason Wells, for their assistance in tracking down and organizing bibliographic material. A sabbatical leave granted by the University of California, Riverside, allowed me to undertake the early research for this project and conceptualize its development. As always, I am thankful to my wife Sharon for her support in ways both large and small.

Introduction

When Javier Marías was asked in an interview in 2006, "What is your natural state?" he responded with a single word: "Indecision." But he quickly qualified his response, suggesting that another layer needed to be peeled away. "But that doesn't mean I never make decisions," he pointed out. "It means I take my time."[1]

For readers with more than a passing familiarity with his writing and, in particular, with his novels, Marías's observation that he takes his time will come as no surprise. Indeed, for the narrators who tell his stories, and for the readers who navigate the complicated path through them, time and patience are both required and rewarded. A contemplative, even bemused indeterminacy lies at the core of Marías's fiction, which is constructed most often with a meandering style that grows slowly and persistently to configure his textual worlds. Marías admires the precision of language (he is an accomplished translator from English to Spanish), yet he celebrates its elusiveness. He constructs his fiction with lengthy, complex sentences replete with subordinate clauses and distant antecedents; his voluble meditations and stylistic digressions sometimes try the forbearance as well as the confidence of even the most assiduous of readers.

Yet Marías has also shown an extraordinary ability to write directly, to say what he wishes to say with efficiency and candor. Using a style practiced and polished for more than fifteen years in his weekly columns for the national press (with specific deadlines and word quotas), Marías has published hundreds of short pieces that are narrowly focused and remarkably concise. When considering the entirety of his work, therefore, he envisions himself as a writer divided: he is sometimes Marías the "citizen" and other times Marías the "novelist." As he put it in 2006, when responding to a series of questions

---

[1] Sarah Fay, "Javier Marías: The Art of Fiction," Interview with Javier Marías. *The Paris Review*, 179 (2006). http://www.theparisreview.org/interviews/5680/the-art-of-fiction-no-190-javier-Marías. No page numbers. The question about Marías's "natural state" arises in the context of Marías's observation that Joseph Conrad's natural state was "disquiet bordering on anxiety."

appended to the English translation of his novel *Travesía del horizonte* (1972) (*Voyage Along the Horizon*, 2006), "As a citizen I have an opinion about far too many things; for the past eleven years I have been writing a column every Sunday about topics of (generally but not necessarily) current interest, and in this sense I feel very much a part of the world, and quite obligated to become involved in what is happening around me."[2] In contrast, he affirms that, "As a novelist ... I try to steer clear of judgments, moral codes, and, of course, morals at the end of the story" (*Voyage* 181). Marías's manner of writing—tightly forged as a "citizen," elegantly tenuous as a "novelist" —has enabled him to engage the world with rigorous clarity as well as amorphous ambiguity through a wide range of literary and non-literary forms (the novel, short story, essay, newspaper column, and the interview, to provide an incomplete list). As a result, in the whole of his writing he has managed to cover philosophical, social, political, and literary matters both concrete and abstract, from women's rights to political correctness, from Hollywood movies to the art of fiction writing, from the practice of religion to the frustrations of daily life in his native Madrid.

Despite his large and varied body of writing, however, Marías remains hard to define. He is the most widely known and frequently translated of living Spanish writers; he also has borne harsh criticism from critics and intellectuals in Spain for not being authentically Spanish. He has written novels set entirely outside of Spain with no reference to Spanish culture; he has also written novels that offer intimate glimpses into the Spanish Civil War and the Franco regime. Marías respects Spanish writers such as Cervantes, Ramón del Valle-Inclan, and Juan Benet, to name only a few, but he harshly condemns the tradition of the Spanish novel as insufficient and unimaginative. He is an enthusiastic reader of canonical literature from both Europe and the United States, and he finds the grand tradition of the novel to be closely allied with English language authors such as Laurence Sterne, Joseph Conrad, William Faulkner, and Henry James. At the same time, Marías delights in ghosts and ghost stories (Joseph Mankiewicz's movie *The Ghost and Mrs. Muir* is one of his favorites); he is also a cinephile who watched eighty-five movies in six weeks in Paris when he was seventeen years old. He is captivated by films from Hollywood as well as by more artistic productions from Europe, yet he reproaches pretentious filmmaking while lauding the great American directors of the 1940s and 1950s (Mankiewicz, William Wilder, and John Ford are among those he most admires). He finds novels

---

[2] Javier Marías, *Voyage Along the Horizon*, trans. Kristina Cordero (San Francisco: Believer Books, 2006), pp. 180–81.

(and novelists) wholly intent on reproducing external reality to be inept and insipid, even though he asserts in many of his essays that such a purpose, given the inability of language to reproduce anything at all, remains beyond reach.

Marías offers staunch support of democratic principles and Republican Spain; he also wears the crown of King of Redonda.[3] He disdains political correctness, which he believes leads to non-reflective and uninspired action—his own political beliefs seem to frame him as a liberal, a conservative, and a libertarian all bound into one, with delight taken in maligning all political parties. He is an avid football fan with insight into the strategies and traditions of the sport, and follows his home team (Real Madrid) with uncommon energy. He does not use a computer or surf the internet (he writes on an electric typewriter); he does not even own a cell phone. He keeps two apartments in the center of Madrid, each lined with shelves full of rare books, DVDs, and his unique collection of toy soldiers;[4] he writes about Madrid in his columns with humor, affection, and anger as it grows ever more challenging to live amidst the noise and crowds of the city. In his various writings he can show sympathy, even tenderness toward those who suffer misfortune and abuse; he can also be cynical and caustic in his social and intellectual observations, which have drawn the wrath of politicians, writers, and intellectuals from nearly every quarter of Spain.

Javier Marías was born in Madrid on September 20, 1951, the fourth of five sons. His family has clearly played a critical role in his personal and intellectual development throughout his life. His father, Julián Marías (1914–2005), was one of the most prominent Spanish philosophers of the twentieth century; his mother, Dolores Franco (1912–1977), published an important anthology of Spanish literature in 1944 entitled *La preocupación de España en su literatura*, but soon gave up her career aspirations to care for her family. Marías's life as the son of two intellectuals provided him with opportunities for learning that were both unusual and challenging. Shortly after the Civil War his father was falsely accused by his closest friend of anti-Francoist activities (he was indeed opposed to the Franco regime but

---

3   For a lengthy discussion of the Kingdom of Redonda and Marías's relationship with it, see chapter IV on *Todas las almas* and *Negra espalda del tiempo*.

4   Marías often mentions his collection of toy soldiers (of various kinds and from various countries and time periods), especially in relation to their impact on his writing: when he was young he spent many hours making up battle scenes and various scenarios for the soldiers, an activity directly related to his insistence that in order to write stories about the real, one has to be able to imagine it.

hardly a threat to its stability) and was imprisoned by the regime with the threat of execution. Though he gained his freedom after a few months, he was not permitted to hold a university position in Spain, approval of his doctoral thesis was deferred for several years until 1951, and he was prohibited from writing in the Spanish press until the early 1950s. Largely as a result of this on-going punishment by the Franco government, he lived what might be termed an inner exile in Spain for the rest of his life, though he did spend time in the United States, where he was recognized and embraced as a distinguished intellectual and leading disciple of Spanish philosopher José Ortega y Gasset.

Because of his father's difficult standing with the Franco government, Javier spent periods of his early life outside of Spain. As he has commented on more than one occasion, on the day he was born "my father, as he usually puts it, shook my hand and left for the United States for the first time."[5] The family followed him a month later, where he took up the first of two major teaching posts in the United States—at Wellesley College in Massachusetts in 1951, and four years later at Yale University in New Haven, Connecticut. Javier's first memories of childhood are linked to the family residence in New Haven, though during his time there he did not attend American school and, because his parents spoke Spanish at home, he learned very little English. While it would have been possible for him and his family to stay on indefinitely in the United States, and while Spain offered few opportunities (not to mention the threat of further retaliation against him), Julián felt strongly that he could not abandon his country permanently. He wished to raise his children in Spain, but also feared the prospect of prolonged alienation from Spanish culture and language, which he believed over time would diminish the intellectual rigor that he needed to sustain his work. Thus he returned to Spain permanently in 1956. Although he accepted occasional visiting professorships in the United States for short periods, he and his wife both managed to secure regular employment in Madrid in study abroad programs offered by American universities. Javier thus had contact with American students as he was growing up and also began to sharpen his skills in English.

Javier Marías is not a philosopher by education and preference, as he has often reminded interviewers. To be sure, he has generally drawn a sharp distinction between one kind of thinking and writing, demanded by philosophy, and another kind that gives shape to literature. While it may appear in

---

[5] Aida Edemariam, "Words and Meaning." http://www.theage.com.au/news/books/words-and-meanings/2005/07/08/1120704543379.html. No page numbers.

his novels that characters and narrators offer philosophical meditations on a wide range of subjects, instead they undertake what he refers to as "literary thinking"—the kind of speculation and deliberation that only takes place in literature and that, in contrast to philosophy, allows for a single character or narrator to make contradictory assertions, each one implicitly true in the context in which it is made. This type of conflictive thinking forms the cornerstone of Shakespeare's writing, as Marías sees it, as well as that of one of his most influential Spanish mentors, the novelist Juan Benet, whose fictional space and narrative style in works such as *Volverás a Región* (1967) and *Una meditación* (1970) create a world of shadows comprised of ambiguity and incongruity bound up with the oxymoronic.

Marías has never sought to write philosophy, or even to embrace the markings of a philosophical novelist. But he is most certainly the product of an upbringing in which intellectual opportunity abounded, which in turn begot an avid and early interest in literature. He was raised in a household literally overflowing with books and paintings (he has noted that there were so many books and pictures in his home he never saw a plain white wall when he was young). His parents could hardly have provided a more felicitous environment for reading, writing, and perhaps most importantly, for learning how to think critically. Marías's father in particular created an atmosphere at home in which his children were encouraged not only to explore an array of interests but to question and challenge what they had read and what they were told. As Marías recalls in an interview with the BBC, "Recuerdo que cuando discutía o hablaba con mi padre y yo hacía un esfuerzo por razonar, él a menudo decía, 'Ya, ¿qué más?' Y yo decía, '¿y cómo qué más?' Y él decía, 'No acabas de empezar, ¿qué más? Sigue pensando, sigue pensando, sigue pensando …'" ("I remember that when I was debating or speaking with my father and I made an effort to reason, he often would say, 'All right, what else?' And I would say, 'What do you mean what else?' And he would say, 'You've just started, what else? Keep on thinking, keep on thinking, keep on thinking …'").[6]

Nearly the whole of Marías's immediate family, along with several of his more distant relatives, have pursued careers in arts and letters, in some cases gaining broad recognition in popular as well as intellectual circles. His uncle Jesús Franco (known more commonly outside of Spain as Jess Frank), for example, became a prolific film director recognized for both his horror and

---

6 Javier Marías, on-line question and answer session with BBC Estudio Abierto, June 22, 2007. See http://news.bbc.co.uk/hi/Spanish/forums/newsid_6687000/6687353.stm.

sex movies. In fact, it was in his uncle's apartment in Paris where Javier stayed during his movie-watching frenzy in the summer of 1969 and experienced a newly found freedom away from home for the first time. The influence of Javier's mother on his intellectual formation, while largely informal, also resonated during his early years. Throughout her life she shared philosophical conversations and remained deeply immersed in the writing of her husband who, as Javier recalls, never sent off an article for publication without her first reviewing it for him. Hence while she devoted much of her time to raising a family and maintaining the household, she also helped to create an atmosphere in which study and curiosity were nurtured and esteemed. With Javier's brother Miguel as a prominent film critic in Spain, his second oldest brother, Fernando, as an art historian, and his younger brother, Alvaro, as a musician, it is clear that the spirit of arts and letters at home prevailed upon the entire family and shaped many of their later endeavors.[7]

When Javier began to write (though he would not yet publish) in his early teens, he did so with an interest far removed from serious and abstract matters. As he points out, he had read many adventure stories as well as all of the musketeer novels that he could find.[8] He had also been going to the movies two or three times a week and had developed intense interest in the spirited westerns of director John Ford and great actors of the American West such as John Wayne, Gary Cooper, and Jimmy Stewart. In other words, he had danger and peril on his mind. He thus decided to write his own tales of adventure, often imitating the fast-paced action of Alexander Dumas. These were the works of adolescence, of course, never published or archived but nonetheless a formative part of his early practice of writing. Marías denies that at a particular time in his youth he knew he wanted to be a writer. In fact, when pressed, he observes that, "I don't even know that I want to be a writer

---

[7] The first son of Dolores Franco, Julián, died at the age of 3, before Javier was born. Javier has remarked that often when he sees a photograph of his mother he notes an air of melancholy about her. He wonders if perhaps she knew death too intimately and unfairly—her own brother was murdered during the Civil War, and of course the loss of her oldest son seemed to allow the melancholy to settle permanently in her eyes. Marías writes about Julián in *Negra espalda del tiempo*, and also includes a photograph of him in the book.

[8] Marías recalls with fondness the family's summer vacation in Soria in northeastern Spain, where he spent rainy days in the house of family friend Heliodoro Carpintero. It was here, at an early age, where Marías began to devour adventure novels by Erckmann-Chatrian, Paul Feval, Pierre Benoit and John Meade Falkner, writers today who are largely overlooked but for Marías the source of great pleasure in his youth.

now, but I have been publishing for most of my life, so I can't deny that I am one" (Fay, "Interview" np). It is beyond question, however, that he did know one thing with certainty from the very beginning—he did not want to be a Spanish writer. With the publication of his first novel, *Los dominios del lobo*, in 1971, he made his point forcefully, with the entire novel set in the United States and offered as both homage to and parody of Hollywood movies of the 1940s and 1950s on which it is largely based.

Yet the question remains, in this early stage of his writing, why did Marías set out pointedly not to be a Spanish novelist, and what in fact does that mean? First of all, Marías has long held that between Cervantes's *Don Quijote* (1605 and 1615) and Leopoldo Alas's *La Regenta* (1884–1885), Spanish novelists published little that merits attention and wrote nothing of enduring value. Instead, they largely convey in their works a realism of scant depth, resulting in an insubstantial novel of manners and eventually leading to a view of Spanishness rooted in gypsies, passion, violence, and underdevelopment. As Marías has pointed out, it is not the case that his literary background is shaped exclusively by the foreign—he has read extensively in Spanish literature and knows it intimately. However, the deficiency of the novel in Spain strikes him as obvious—as he pointedly notes in an interview in 2000, "We don't have our Herman Melville or Henry James."[9] When he has called attention to this in his columns and in interviews, asserting Spain's impoverished narrative tradition, he has encountered both criticism and condemnation.

However, it is not solely the absence of a grand tradition that compels Marías to turn away from even loosely defined Spanishness in his novels—he also derides the state of the Spanish novel during the period of his own literary formation. During the 1950s and early 1960s the dominant form of the novel in Spain was deeply embedded in the principles of social realism, which grew from the intention to offer an accurate representation of contemporary Spanish society. Later, and even as Marías was publishing his first two novels in the early 1970s, Spanish writers absorbed more experimental techniques of high modern and even postmodern fiction, but continued to write with a deeply felt need to explore the essential nature of Spain and define its authentic nature. To a large degree, this recurrent focus on Spain and Spanishness became nearly an ethical exigency among writers who opposed the Francoist dictatorship. With the regime maintaining strict control over all forms of publishing, with newspapers and the media unable to represent the

---

9 Paul Ingendaay, "Interview with Javier Marías." http://bombsite.com/issues/73/articles/2345, p. 156.

social and political reality of contemporary Spanish life, many novelists argued that the novel should be used as an instrument of explicit representation and of implicit social protest. Thus to write fiction meant to be politically engaged, and the novel was appropriated as a means to reveal and transform the ills of Spanish society.

Social realism in Spain is associated with a number of writers who might have served as natural mentors to Marías and his generation (such as Luis Goytisolo, Jesús Fernández Santos, Rafael Sánchez Ferlosio, and Carmen Martín Gaite, to name only a handful). These writers had remained in Spain following the Civil War rather than opt for exile, and to a large extent had envisioned the entire enterprise of writing as a form of literary transcription. In both interviews and theoretical essays they laid out the fundamental tenets of the novel as they envisioned it in a Spain that desperately required self scrutiny. They asserted that to narrate life is to re-present it in the whole of its authenticity; they affirmed the notion that a literature committed to social action is able to transform the world into something other than it is. But to Marías these writers represented much of what had long been pale and ordinary about the Spanish novel.[10] As we have seen, the use of narrative to challenge political doctrine or to suggest social transformation may be linked to Marías's writing as a "citizen" (i.e., his columns and essays), but not to his identity as a novelist. In his later fiction (beginning primarily with *El siglo* in 1983), social and ethical problems begin to seep into his work and gain a certain prominence, with significant explorations of violence, betrayal, and the role of storytelling in configuring individual and collective histories. But Marías never proposes a fiction of ideas per se. Instead, he writes novels in which ideas can be considered and reconsidered, though never resolved once and for all.

The principles that defined the novel of social realism were both formulated and cast aside during a little more than a decade (from the late 1940s to the early 1960s), and the novels published during this time were closely tied to writers bound up by common experiences of the Civil War and the intellectual antagonisms of postwar authoritarianism. As this novel began to fade from its position of dominance in the Spanish publishing industry, a new and more innovative type of fiction began to gain prominence in Spain—one that

---

[10] It should be pointed out that all of these writers eventually abandoned social realism and took up various styles and techniques that included postmodern fragmentation, existentialism, and even sexual identity and gender formation. To a large extent, however, Spain and its problems continued to form the core of their writing, even for those who have remained active into the twenty-first century.

explored the contingencies of memory and experimented with language and multiple narrative perspectives in which the accurate representation of reality (past and present) was perceived as problematic, even impossible. Works as diverse as Miguel Delibes's *Cinco horas con Mario* (1966), Camilo José Cela's *San Camilo, 1936* (1969), and Luis Goytisolo's *Recuento* (1973), among many others, stand prominently within what is often referred to as the "new novel" in Spain. Yet what linked this fiction to the novel of social realism, and what continued to make it objectionable to Marías, was its fundamental commitment to conveying Spanish reality as a form of contestatory writing set against Francoism. Thus, as occurs with social realism, Marías's early works stand unpropped against these novels, which remain intent on scrutinizing the nation even as they propose multiple truths in their dissent from Francoist perspectives and the traditions of what can be asserted as authentically Spanish.

Marías published two novels in the early 1970s—*Los dominios del lobo* (1971) and *Travesía del horizonte* (1972). While *Dominios* grew largely from Hollywood and American literature, *Travesía* can be linked to the long tradition of adventure fiction—the influence of the seafaring novel and of Joseph Conrad and Robert Louis Stevenson clearly moves to the fore in *Travesía*. As with his first novel, Marías sets out to write a work that cannot be located within the novelistic tradition of Spain. Although a few of the constitutive elements of *Travesía* work their way into his later fiction (most prominently, uncertainty of plot), the work stands largely outside the mainstream of what his fiction will become in nearly all of the novels that follow. In fact, the publication of *Travesía* marks a key turning point for Marías and his writing of fiction—not because of a deep personal or existential crisis that pushes him in one direction or another, but rather because he steps back (though not completely away) from writing fiction and begins to focus on translation. Although he published a hybrid text of brief narratives, poetry, and dramatic dialogue in 1978 entitled *El monarca del tiempo*, as well as a handful of short stories during this period, he does not produce a new full-length novel until *El siglo* in 1983.

Marías's work as a translator closely pertains to his writing of fiction in a number of important ways.[11] First of all, it has compelled him to scrutinize language and the mechanics of writing at close range. In other words, while he had always understood that words constituted the raw material of his craft as a writer, he now appreciated their preciseness as well as their ambiguity,

---

[11] For a list of Marías's most significant translations, see the Bibliography at the end of this study.

their capacity to represent as well as their propensity to distort. Most importantly, Marías perceives (and asserts) that translation cannot be considered a work of re-production—words in one language cannot be replicated as words in another without both gaining and losing some part of their cultural and contextual meaning. Further, as Marías has pointed out on many occasions, there are bad and good translations of texts, as well as incorrect ones. Despite his accomplishments as a translator, however—he has translated major novelists and poets into Spanish from England and the United States and in 1979 was awarded the national translation prize in Spain for his rendition into Spanish of *Tristram Shandy*—translation remains somewhat of a mystery and a paradox for him. On the one hand, he views the translated work as a source of profound bewilderment. Echoing the words of Argentine writer Jorge Luis Borges, Marías wonders how it is possible, when a text has lost everything about it in its original form—its words, its sounds, rhythms—that it remains to some degree the same. The new text is clearly different, but also authentic. As he puts it, "Only pedantic people, or specialists, scholars, would say they haven't read *Anna Karenina* because they never read it in Russian" (Ingendaay, "Interview" 155).

On the other hand, translation does not entail mimicry across languages—a literate reader with a dictionary might then be defined as a translator. For Marías translation requires the ability to read closely and to conceptualize broadly. Translators are privileged readers, as Marías himself has observed, because they read with greater care and diligence than most. Equally important (and for Marías the novelist, utterly critical), the translator is also a privileged writer. And with canonical texts in particular (such as those by Sterne, Faulkner, Nabokov, Stevenson, Dinesen, to name only a few of the authors whose works Marías has translated), the privilege demands creative choice, understood as rewriting what has already been written in its original form. As he puts it, "If you rewrite high literature in an acceptable way ... [y]ou can say that you're capable of renouncing your own style, adopting someone else's, yet the wording is always yours. ... Every single word in my Spanish translation of *Tristram Shandy* was thought of by me, was meditated on and chosen. In that sense I can say that it is my best text. Because I wrote each and every word of it, and of course it is much better than anything I've written myself, originally" (Ingendaay, "Interview" 154–55).

Sterne's masterpiece is of course "much better" than what most writers have published, and for Marías it stands above all others as his preferred work of fiction. But his reading and rewriting of *Tristram Shandy*, and of the many other works that he has translated, also serve to enhance his literary education. He has integrated into his novels various elements of what he has apprehended from others in style, technique, structure, and ideas. Yet clearly, as in his work as a translator, his novels should not be perceived as an effect of imitation. Indeed, his fiction is highly deliberate and carefully crafted but also regularly digressive, even peripatetic.[12] His insistence on imagining the real, shapes texts that configure our perception of the world rather than duplicate what the world in its current configuration may be able to offer.

The question remains, however, where do his novels stand in relation to the immediate context in which they are produced? Are his novels similar to other novels written over the past thirty years? When writing his early fiction, as we have seen, Marías firmly and persistently denounced the novel of postwar Spain for its obsession with the social reality of the time. Furthermore, he eschewed a large part of novelistic tradition in Spain for its general insipidness. Beginning in the early 1980s, however, the Spanish novel seems less connected either to tradition or to a shared set of literary norms that characterized much of its development during the Franco years. For novelists who came of age during this time and who began to publish in the 1970s (shortly before and after Franco's death in 1975), and even for older novelists who had previously opted to focus on the present reality of Spain, perhaps the most critical unifying characteristic within fiction over the past three decades has stemmed from their desire to recover past time—in particular the recent past of the Civil War and of the Franco years—that had been encumbered by the ideological posturing of the regime from its inception in 1939.

At the same time, however, a strong countervailing impetus to forget the past, or at least to disremember it, emerges during the transition to democracy in the late 1970s and 1980s. The tension between the two positions cuts deeply across the grain of Spanish culture as a whole, and also exerts a discernible influence on Spanish fiction of the time. On the one hand, Spanish democracy was born amid a collective agreement (both institutional and cultural) to forget much of what had occurred during the years of the dictatorship. Rather than dig deeply into the government that had ruled the nation with varying degrees of harshness over forty years, and rather than seek punishment for those who committed crimes during the Civil War, leaders of the new democracy opted for reconciliation over retribution (or as many would have it, over justice). This was not an uncontroversial decision,

---

12 Marías explains the meandering nature of his novels as being a result of the way he writes. As he explains to Sarah Fay in his interview in *The Paris Review*, "I work without a map. I work only with a compass, which means that I know more or less where I am going. It's not that I just wander nonsensically in a totally whimsical way. I probably find the same river and the same desert and the same cliffs and the same precipice that the other writers find, but I find them unexpectedly. I like not to know everything."

of course, and the policy of forgetting (countered by the necessity of remembering) has continued to inform political discourse in Spain at the turn of the twenty-first century.[13] Yet memory itself could not be legislated or negotiated away completely, and in memoirs and other narrative forms, especially the novel, recovering the past became a functional way to explore and expose personal and historical injustice and to work through the trauma often associated with it. Memory had already gained a prominent role in the late Francoist period and the years immediately following his death in novels such as Juan Goytisolo's *Señas de identidad* (1966), Juan Benet's *Volverás a Región* (1967), and Carmen Martín Gaite's *El cuarto de atrás* (1978). It grew even more visible during the 1980s and 1990s in works as diverse as Tomasa Cuevas's *Cárcel de mujeres* (1985), a collection of narratives by women who had resisted fascism in the Civil War; Josefina Aldecoa's novelistic trilogy, *Historia de una maestro* (1990), *Mujeres de negro* (1994), and *La fuerza del destino* (1997), which relates the memories of a teacher in Spain from the early twentieth century through the death of Franco and the transition to democracy; and Antonio Muñoz Molina's novel *El jinete polaco* (1991), which evokes the long-suppressed memories of the narrator concerning his family and the Civil War.

At the same time that the national memory was shaken and torn by the deep tensions between forgetting and remembering, Spain as a whole emerged in Europe during the 1980s and 1990s at the forefront of countercultural expression. Obsessed with youth, newness, and change, Spaniards seemed to reach a general consensus that Spanish identity as defined by the Franco regime (summed up neatly in the phrase "One nation, one race, one religion") was no longer operative. Cultural and linguistic heterogeneity, once scorned and suppressed, soon became one of the cornerstones of the new democracy. In the book industry, the eagerness for novelty and cultural openness generated rapid growth and the promotion of novels published in regional languages (Galician, Catalan, and Basque), in addition to an increase in the number of works published in Spanish. The national literary prize was

---

[13] Amid much debate, and not a small amount of rancor, La Ley de Memoria Histórica (The Historical Memory Law) was passed by the Spanish Parliament in October of 2007. Among its many provisions, it sought "to remember" the past in a variety of ways. For example, it proposed to compensate victims of injustices during the Civil War, to help shed light on atrocities committed by both sides during the conflict, and to aid in the exhumation of bodies in mass graves for purposes of identification. It also rejected the legitimacy of trials held by the Franco government against political opponents, and provided for the removal of images of Franco and his regime from public buildings and spaces.

awarded in 1989 for the first time to a novel written in Basque (Bernardo Atxaga's *Obabakoak*), and what once was considered postmodern experimentation in the writing of fiction gained traction as a standard component of many of the novels of the time. Indeed, writers as diverse as Antonio Muñoz Molina (*Beatus Ille*, 1986, and *Sefarad*, 2001), Cristina Fernández Cubas (*El año de gracia*, 1994), José María Merino (*La lógica del vampiro*, 1990, and L*os invisibles*, 2000), and Juan José Millás (*La soledad era esto*, 1994), have disencumbered their work of canonical restraints and traditional Spanish themes to produce innovative novels pertinent to the cultural mainstream of Europe.

Writers associated with what is commonly called Generation X have also gained recognition since the late 1980s. Born toward the end of the 1960s and the early years of the 1970s, novelists such as Belén Gopegui, José Ángel Mañas, Ray Loriga, and Lucía Etxebarria, to name only a few, have intentionally set out to sever all bonds with Spanish history both recent and far removed. Self-identified with a sub-culture that values the present over the past, they stand radically outside the group of postwar writers who were ideologically driven by resistance to the Franco regime. Indeed, they generally proceed in their writing as if Franco had never existed. They frame their novels within postmodern techniques of narrative fragmentation, political disengagement, and disorder, and often locate their characters amid a youth culture shaped by drugs, random violence, and permissive sex. Nonetheless, while often designated by critics as a loose community of writers, their coincident chronological emergence in democratic Spain is not accompanied by a common generational vision or shared set of literary norms, as occurred with writers during the decades of the Franco regime and early post-Franco democracy, and with the novel of memory of the 1980s and 1990s.

Marías's place in this disordered novelistic landscape might best be defined by his perception of himself first offered in the early 1970s—he remains an outlier whose manner of writing continues to link him primarily to canonical British and American authors who wrote primarily in English (though the French novelist Marcel Proust also stands among the writers for whom Marías has expressed deep admiration). Yet there is no small irony to the trajectory that Marías has forged in his writing. For while he frequently references other writers (Shakespeare remains among those to whom he turns repeatedly, with two of his novels, a collection of short stories, and a book of columns bearing titles from the dramatist's plays),[14] he has shaped a narrative during the past three decades that is built at least in part on intertextual

---

14 The two novels are *Corazón tan blanco* (*A Heart so White*), from *Macbeth*; *Mañana en la batalla piensa en mí* (*Tomorrow in the Battle Think on Me*), from *Richard III*. The

connections with his own works. Characters, narrators, plots, spaces, and times recur in Marías's novels to create a textual world that begins to grow ever more familiar to readers of his fiction. For example, the narrator and main character of *Todas las almas*, who teaches at Oxford, reappears as the narrator of the three-volume novel *Tu rostro mañana*. Some amount of time has passed since his stay in Oxford, and he now lives in London, where he works for a mysterious company on counter-intelligence matters and state security. Furthermore, beginning in 1986, all of Marías's narrators in one way or another earn their living by using the words of others—an opera singer in *El hombre sentimental*, a professor of translation in *Todas las almas*, an interpreter in *Corazón tan blanco*, a ghostwriter in *Mañana en la batalla piensa en mí*, an interpreter of the stories of others in *Tu rostro mañana*. Marías's selection of such narrators—the perspective that they offer and the limits to what they know—provides recognizable markings in his novels and creates certain expectations among readers who have grown familiar with the strategies that he employs. At the same time, however, we are never allowed the soft comfort of determinate meanings or unambiguous resolutions. Marías's complex style, his meditative digressions, his intricate structures continue to underpin his fiction at every turn.

What has steadily moved to prominence in shaping Marías's novels over the past two decades is an increasing autobiographical component and a felt need to integrate Spain (if not Spanishness) into his writing. It is important to understand, however, that while Marías's fiction at times is directly related to aspects of his own life—for example, the narrator of *Todas las almas* teaches literature and translation at Oxford University, as did Marías; the narrator's father in *Tu rostro mañana*, like Marías's real-life father, was betrayed by his best friend—his novels should not be read as either accurate representations of his past or as philosophical reflections on it. To be sure, what he has seen and done in his life infiltrates his narrative in individual and multiple works. *Negra espalda del tiempo*, for example, was written as a hybrid narrative/novel, with extensive autobiographical materials, largely to counter what Marías viewed as misguided biographical readings of *Todas las almas*. While *Negra* indeed fills in gaps and builds new layers upon the autobiographical elements that help to shape *Todas* (for example, Marías inserts information about his family, reveals new facts about his Kingdom of Redonda, and offers extensive biographical material about the writer John Gawsworth), the theo-

collection of short stories, *Cuando fui mortal* (*When I Was Mortal*) also comes from *Richard III*; the collection of columns, *Seré amado cuando falte* (literally, *I Shall be Loved When I am Lacked*) derives from the somewhat lesser known tragedy *Coriolanus*.

retical foundation of the work points to the necessary corruption and transformation of the autobiographical by the very process of narration through which it becomes known and available to the reader in the first place.

Marías has always insisted that as a writer of fiction he bears no ethical responsibility to represent the real. Instead, as he has asserted from the outset, he simply needs to imagine it. He advocates this not because he finds language to be insufficient in relation to reality, or the world to be too complex for narration. Instead, he envisions language as both instrument and material that shapes and configures. But importantly, language for Marías does not consist of words cobbled together with the purpose of conveying one idea or another. Rather, language (and its structure) is used to create stories. And it is his constant awareness of stories and the practice of storytelling in the broadest sense that permeates every aspect of his writing. Above all other considerations, as we shall see in the remainder of this study, storytelling stands at the intersection of all of his fiction. Marías perceives the world through stories, and in turn he draws upon them to explain how he understands the world. It is the rapport between the two (seeing through stories and using stories), in a continuous looping back of one upon the other, that in the end sustains his writing. It defines his engagement with the world in which he lives, as well as the world as he is able to imagine it.

I

Writing in the Newspapers: Everything under the Sun

Although Marías published short essays in the Spanish press and wrote articles for newspapers as early as 1976,[1] it was not until December of 1994, when he agreed to undertake what he has called his "tareas dominicales" ("Sunday tasks") for the magazine *El Semanal*, that he began to write a regular weekly column.[2] For Marías, who had drolly embraced writing as a way to avoid holding a regular job bound by a fixed work schedule, the commitment to meet a deadline, and to be paid for doing so, seemed somewhat odd as well as potentially treacherous. He noted in November of 1996, while writing his one-hundred-fourth column for *El Semanal*, that he was still befuddled by his initial decision to write every week and somewhat amused by his perseverance over the previous two years. As he put it to his readers in "La infancia recuperada" ("Childhood Recovered"), "En principio estaba en contra de escribir a fecha fija, y era más bien partidario de hacerlo sólo cuando verdaderamente tuviera ganas, algo que comentar y tiempo para ello. Bueno, aún estoy en contra de lo que vengo haciendo desde hace dos años ante ustedes ..." ("In the beginning, I was opposed to writing to meet a deadline; I was instead inclined to do it only when I truly felt like it, when I had something to say and time for it. Well, I am still opposed to what I have been doing for the last two years in front of all of you ...") (*Mano de sombra* 331). He also confessed in the same piece to the dilemma that many writers have confronted, even when writing without the pressure of a deadline: "hay muchos días en que no sé de qué diablos hablar" ("there are many days when I don't know what the devil to talk about") (*Mano de sombra* 331).

---

[1] Marías's article "El terreno sin confines" was published on May 9, 1976, in the *Diario de Barcelona*. It appears in his collection of articles, *Vida del fantasma* (Madrid: Ediciones El País), first published in 1995. See the revised edition published by Alfaguara in 2001, pp. 417–20.

[2] Javier Marías, "Nota previa," in *Mano de sombra* (Madrid: Alfaguara, 1997), p. 13.

But as Marías himself also pointed out, he has cultivated his narrative voice and sustained his weekly writing despite reservations about his ability and desire to do so. Since 1994 his articles have given public shape to his opinions on a wide range of topics and to various aspects of his personal life, with a tone and temperament that vary from cynical, biting, and humorous to serious, intellectual, and compassionate. It is important to understand, however, that it is precisely his passion and intellectual commitment, above all to the unfettered conveyance of ideas, that led to sharp discord in his work at *El Semanal* and compelled him to leave the magazine nearly eight years after writing his first article. While Marías's participation in the magazine was generally felicitous, where he and fellow novelist Arturo Pérez-Reverte shared space and ideas and often engaged one another with humor over topics ranging from book signings to the nature of their fictional characters, Marías resigned his position in December of 2002 when the editors censored a piece he wrote criticizing the Catholic Church.

The incident with *El Semanal* created not a small amount of personal and intellectual distress for the magazine and for Marías. Following sharp protest by the author over the decision to prohibit his work, the editors relented and approved the piece for publication in the second week of 2003. A short time later, however, they once again disallowed it, even though they had assured Marías that his article would appear. Marías's commitment to the free expression of opinions in this instance was contextually pertinent and historically significant: first, he argued the broad ethical and specific legal principle that a democracy must necessarily embrace open discussion; and second, he framed his position within the urgency demanded by the contemporary history of Spain, where the Franco regime not long before had effectively restricted public debate and virtually crushed dissent for nearly forty years. As he explains in his essay on the censorship of his article and his departure from *El Semanal*:

> Lo he hecho [poner fin a mis colaboraciones] con pena. ... También lo he hecho con amargura: siempre la provoca tener que irse de un sitio por culpa de la censura (que, entre otras cosas, es algo ilegal en nuestro país); más aún si dicha censura se ejerce contra una opinión *personal* acerca de la Iglesia Católica y de las religiones, como si aún estuviéramos bajo un régimen confesional, y como si no hubiéramos padecido durante demasiados años censuras de la misma índole, todos y cada uno de los habitantes de nuestro país.
>
> I have done it [ended my collaboration] with sorrow. ... I have also done it with bitterness: to have to leave a place because of censorship (which, among other things, is illegal in our country) always provokes bitterness;

even more so if such censorship is exercised against a *personal* opinion about the Catholic Church and about religions in general, as if we were still under a confessional regime, and as if every and each one of the inhabitants of our country had not suffered censorship of the same kind for too many years. ("Una explicación y un adiós," *Harán de mí un criminal* 314)[3]

Marías's condemnation of *El Semanal* for restricting his right to write, however, did not compel him to renounce his work as a columnist. Indeed, he missed only a few weeks of writing before signing on with the well-known newspaper *El País*. But his rejection of censorship in 2002 marks a critical juncture, for it affirmed his refusal to speak with a voice controlled by others. It also signaled his understanding that, in the column-writing business, other circumstances would inevitably arise in which he might be asked to moderate or expunge ideas from his articles that vexed particular groups or organizations, and it conveyed to the publishers and to his readers that he would not tolerate what he perceived as unseemly interference.

To read Marías's columns is to understand why he reacted so forcefully to the censorship imposed by *El Semanal*: very little remains outside the broad sweep of his interests, and his scrutiny of nearly all aspects of the social, cultural, and political fabric of contemporary life can be harsh. He has explored in his work topics so divergent that they resist summary: from reality TV (he seems forever surprised at what people will reveal about themselves for short-lived fame) to the denial of a liver transplant to an Englishman who brought on his illness through excessive drinking (he believes it was immoral to deny the transplant); from the jury system instituted in Spain in 1994 (he opposes it as illogical and untenable) to automobile anti-theft alarms (he rails against the frequency with which they are activated in the middle of the night in Madrid); from the numerous articles on football (he is a devoted fan of Real Madrid) to his somewhat grumpy celebration of Christmas (he generally shuts himself in his apartment and watches movie videos).[4]

---

[3] Javier Marías, *Harán de mí un criminal* (Madrid: Alfaguara, 2003). For a detailed account of this incident from Marías's perspective, see four pieces collected in this volume: "La casa en semiorden" (pp. 309–12); "Una explicación y un adios" (pp. 313–14); "Posdata" (pp. 315–16); "*Un inédito censurado*: Creed en nosotros a cambio" (pp. 317–19). It should also be noted that Marías's time away from writing a column was short-lived. On February 16, 2003, he began to publish a weekly column for *El País Semanal*, and continues to write for the supplement today.

[4] See, respectively, "La fama de la fama," in *Mano de sombra*, pp. 99–201; "Mala noticia miserable," in *Vida del fantasma*, pp. 329–34; "Emblema y caso," in *Vida del fantasma*, pp. 33–35; "Ladrones mayores," in *Mano de sombra*, pp. 36–38; see also, for

Marías's Christmas-time movie watching of course suits him well. He is an accomplished cinephile (his brother Miguel works professionally as a movie critic), and he often writes about movies in his columns. Indeed, it is not possible to understand Marías's novels in general (and his insistence in particular on framing life in stories) without taking into account his passion for movies. His first novel, *Los dominios del lobo* (1971), grows explicitly from detective and *noir* movies of the 1940s and 1950s,[5] while his later novels also bear many of the markings of film. As Miguel Marías notes in the preface to *Donde todo ha sucedido: Al salir del cine* (2005), a collection of articles written by his brother between 1993 and 2004, Javier has always been fascinated by the gestures, facial expressions, movements, and actions of characters in film which invite audience scrutiny and interpretation: "Así que no es extraño que esta labor de 'traducción' de gestos, posturas o miradas [de una película] sea una de las actividades principales de los personajes de las novelas de Javier, ni que sus narradores interpreten constantemente lo que les rodea o les ha sucedido, que se planteen dudas e hipótesis alternativas sobre lo que va ocurriendo" ("Thus it is not strange that this 'translation' of gestures, postures, looks [from a film] is one of the main activities of the characters in Javier's novels, nor that his narrators constantly interpret what surrounds them and what has happened to them, that they propose doubts and alternative hypotheses about what is happening").[6] Marías himself has observed that all of his novels are layered with his memories of particular films – sometimes he mentions a specific movie while other times he appropriates a memorable scene. As he puts it, "También es raro que no haya en ellas [mis novelas] alguna escena o pasaje que, calladamente, no sea deudor de algo contemplado en la oscuridad de una sala y retenido en la memoria para siempre jamás" ("It is also rare that there does not appear in them [my novels] a scene or passage that, quietly, does not owe a debt to something that I contemplated in the darkness of a theater or retained in my memory forever and ever") ("Todos los días llegan," *Donde todo ha sucedido* 30). Even when the work of other authors forms the core of his work, as occurs with the connection between *Corazón tan blanco* and *Mañana en la batalla piensa en mí* and the plays of Shakespeare, Marías recalls more vividly, when writing

---

example, his collection of articles *Salvajes y sentimentales. Letras de fútbol* (Madrid: Aguilar, 2000); and "Ficciones bastardas," in *Mano de sombra*, pp. 17–20.

[5] For a detailed discussion of *Los dominios del lobo*, including a more general commentary on the impact of movies on Marías's writing, see chapter II.

[6] Miguel Marías, "El arte de recordar," in *Donde todo ha sucedido. Al salir del cine*, ed. Inés Blanca and Reyes Pinzás (Barcelona: Galaxia Gutenberg, 2005), p. 17.

his novels, the movies based on the plays rather than his original reading of them.[7]

In addition to the many associations between his writing and cinema, Marías often conveys in his columns the straightforward pleasure of watching movies. And the word "movies," with its hint of Hollywood, rather than "films," with the suggestion of pretentious art, accounts for Marías's full range of cinematic tastes. He recalls seeing at least two movies a week as a young boy at his local movie house, and he remembers his later excursions throughout Madrid to more distant neighborhoods to see movies that in many cases had already become treasured classics—Blake Edwards' *Breakfast at Tiffany's*, for example, or William Wilder's *Some Like it Hot* ("Todos los días llegan," *Donde todo ha sucedido* 27). Marías's passion for American movies is rooted in the cinema of the late 1930s and extends primarily over the following three decades, though many movies of the 1970s and 1980s also strike him as worthy of attention (such as *The Godfather, I* and *II*; *Annie Hall*; *Gandhi*).

In 1955, when the Royal Belgian Cinematheque released a list of the twenty most important films in the history of the cinema, Marías denounced their narrow devotion to the film culture of the 1960s, "aquella época en la que, para dignificar el cine, los pedantes de cine-club babeaban con las películas europeas más pretenciosas (Fellini, Antonioni y Bergman eran los ídolos) y desdeñaban en bloque el cine Americano, que ya entonces era – pero se ve más ahora – el cine por excelencia" ("that period in which, in order to elevate cinema, the pedants from the cine-club drooled over the most pretentious European films (Fellini, Antonioni, and Bergman were their idols) and they showed disdain for American cinema, which was already then – but which can be seen more clearly now – cinema par excellence") ("Caso crítico," *Donde todo ha sucedido* 213–14). For Marías, the golden era of Hollywood produced master films made by iconic directors: Alfred Hitchcock, George Cukor, Joseph Mankiewicz, John Houston, William Wilder, Orsen Welles, and above all, John Ford. Marías has often expressed his admiration for Ford's movies of the American West, especially those starring John Wayne (e.g., *The Searchers*; *The Man Who Shot Liberty Valance*) or Henry Fonda (e.g., *My Darling Clementine*; *Fort Apache*, also starring Wayne). Westerns such as these, along with other genre films (adventure and war movies, musicals, and thrillers) form the core of twentieth-century cinema, in Marías's view, and advance both technically and thematically what was still a

---

7   See "Todos los días llegan," pp. 31–33, for Marías's discussion of Orsen Welles's *Macbeth* as it relates to *Corazón tan blanco* and Laurence Olivier's *Richard III* as it informs *Mañana en la batalla piensa en mí*.

relatively new art form. As Marías has mentioned on more than one occasion, one of his favorite movies remains Mankiewicz's *The Ghost and Mrs. Muir*, not only because of the peculiar emotional hold that it has maintained over him for many years, and not only because it stars a ghost (one of Marías's preferred figures), but because it comes close to achieving what literature and film have only rarely dared to pursue: "la abolición del tiempo, la visión del futuro como pasado y del pasado como futuro, la reconciliación con los muertos y el deseo sereno e íntimo de ser por fin uno de ellos" ("the abolition of time, the vision of the future as past and of the past as future, the reconciliation with the dead and the serene and intimate desire to finally be one of them") ("El fantasma y la señora Muir," *Donde todo ha sucedido* 61).[8]

Marías also turns frequently in his columns to topics that are socially pertinent to his readers but largely innocuous on the scale of social conflict. For example, he often relates anecdotes about the poor telephone and postal service in Madrid, even writing a column in which he concludes that the telephone company has become superior to the post office – not in providing good service to the customers but in frustrating them.[9] Along with indignation, wit often accompanies his perspective on such matters. He points out, for example, that the postal service indeed merits ridicule, noting that Sherlock Holmes (one of Marías's favorite literary characters) "habría fracasado en todos sus célebres casos de haber vivido hoy entre nosotros" ("would have failed in all of his celebrated cases if he had lived among us today") ("Malos tragos," *Mano de sombra* 86), because he never would have received important information through the mail in a timely fashion.

Marías also regularly comments on the increasing difficulty of daily life in his beloved Madrid. For example, he writes an annual column in opposition to Holy Week processions which agitate and disrupt daily life (in one piece he compares them to the recent popular activity of *botellones* – the massive partying of young people in a designated space of the city for the purpose of consuming as much alcohol as possible in a short period of time and disturbing the peace).[10] He also condemns the disturbances associated with

---

[8] Perhaps not by coincidence, this particular article on Mrs. Muir and her ghost is also one of Marías's favorites. Several years later he notes concerning the article, "Hace años le dediqué un largo artículo ... que según mi indiferente criterio es el mejor que he escrito nunca" ("Years ago I devoted a long article to it ... which, according to my indifferent criteria, is the best that I have ever written") ("Si no han visto el río," *Donde todo ha sucedido* 38).

[9] "Noticias de mis favoritas," in *Seré amado cuando falte* (Madrid: Alfaguara, 1999), pp. 192–94.

[10] Marías links the Holy Week processions and the barbarity of the *botellones* in his

the construction of new buildings, the perpetual repair of streets and sidewalks, the constant noise (he reports that Spain has been classified, behind Japan, as the second loudest country in the world), and the ever-increasing problems with traffic (Marías often reminds readers that he does not drive). His tone generally varies from satirical to indignant, while the targets of his barbs (in particular, Spanish politicians) generally seem to shy from recognition in his writing.

In his political commentaries, Marías refuses to embrace the policies of one party or another, but his ideas can be cast as largely contrarian, with a tilt toward libertarianism – the fundamental belief that individual liberty should outweigh government impositions of authority. He notes in a 1996 column that he has never voted for any of the three main parties in the elections being contested that year and, further, that it would be a more accurate expression of voter sentiment if ballots were not cast in favor of a particular candidate but against all those whom voters would be unwilling to accept under any circumstances ("Una proposición muy razonable," *Mano de sombra* 208–10).[11] With intense cynicism (and acerbic humor) toward all politicians, he offers in a 1998 column thirty-one suggestions for political figures who seek success in public life, including the following:

> 2) Dedicar el tiempo y los esfuerzos verbales a minar al adversario, como si esa fuera la principal tarea y aquello por lo que cobran el erario. ... 8) Estar al servicio de [su] Partido hasta la abyección: trabajar para él, obrar por él, vivir por él y su beneficio, traicionarse y traicionar por él. ... 14) Saber tergiversar cualesquiera declaraciones de otros, por claras e inequívocas que sean. ... 20) Manipular la historia y tergiversar el pasado según sus deseos y su provecho. ... 27) Ser pomposos en su muy mala hablar, emplear sustantivos irreales como "posicionamiento" y adverbios infrarreales como "poblacionalmente."

> 2) Dedicate one's time and verbal efforts to undermining one's adversary, as if that were the principal task and that for which one receives public funds. ... 8) Be at the service of one's Party to the point of abjection: work

---

article "Botellón de encapuchados," in *Demasiada nieve alrededor* (Madrid: Alfaguara, 2007), pp. 192–94.

[11] It should also be pointed out that Marías harshly denounces the level (both in ideas and in language) of much of the political debate in Spain. In 2004, he was awarded the Miguel Delibes National Journalism Prize for two essays on this subject, "El oficio de oír llover" and "Locuacidades ensimismadas." See *El oficio de oír llover* (Madrid: lfaguara, 2005), pp. 113–15 and 116–18, respectively.

for it, act in its interest, live for it and for its benefit, betray oneself and betray on behalf of it. ... 14) Know how to twist the meaning of any statement made by others, no matter how clear or unequivocal it may be. ... 20) Manipulate history and twist the past based on one's desires and for one's personal advantage. ... 27) Be pompous in your very poor speaking ability, use unreal nouns such as "positionalment" and less than real adverbs such as "populationly." ("Qué hace falta," *Vida del fantasma* 276–79)

Marías generally has condemned in his columns the conservative initiatives of the *Partido Popular* ("Popular Party"), but also regularly dismisses attempts by the Left to intervene in the daily life and personal behavior of his fellow citizens. In a 2006 article entitled "La intromisión que no para," ("The Meddling that Never Stops") Marías makes his point without humor, and with a surfeit of unrestrained frustration:

La idea antigua de que sólo las dictaduras eran totalitarias resulta ingenua, porque el totalitarismo consiste, sobre todo, en la intromisión de los Gobiernos en *todas* las esferas de la sociedad, en el afán de regularlo, controlarlo e intervenir en *todo*, de condicionar la vida de los ciudadanos e influir en ella, en no dejarles apenas márgenes de libertad y decirles cómo han de comportarse u organizarse, no sólo en lo público y común, sino en lo personal y privado.

The old idea that only dictatorships were totalitarian turns out to be naïve, because totalitarianism above all consists of the meddling of governments into all spheres of society, of the desire to regulate, control, and intervene in *everything*, to affect and influence the life of its citizens, allowing hardly any room for freedom, and telling them how they should behave and organize themselves, not only in their public and common lives, but also in what is personal and private. (*Demasiada nieve alrededor* 144)

For example, government intervention in the "personal and private" stands firmly behind anti-smoking laws, which for Marías represent the despotic and oppressive targeting of an individual preference. Indeed, he refers to the restrictions on smoking as the "ley dictatorial antitabaco" ("the dictatorial anti-tobacco law") ("La intromisión que no para," *Demasiada nieve alrededor* 144), while noting that people die from pollution and automobile accidents each year without the government seeking to ban electricity or automobiles.

For Marías, the problem lies not only with the perverse overreaching of government into the daily life of Spanish society, but also with the passivity of individuals who refuse to forestall it. Indeed, not only have individuals shrunk from protecting their liberty, but they have implicitly invited government regulation by their unwillingness to bear responsibility for their own actions. As he writes in "Enemigos de la libertad,"

> La gente empieza a prohibir cosas y a pedir que se las prohíban. Como no puedo dejar de fumar, impídanme fumar. Como me entusiasman las películas porno de la televisión, censúrenlas. Como no me resisto a llamar a los teléfonos eróticos y me arruino con ellos, eliminen esos números. Estamos a un paso de la prohibición del chocolate, una vez que se ha descubierto que da placer – mucho placer – y es un poco adictivo.
>
> People begin to prohibit things and to ask that things be prohibited. Since I can't stop smoking, prevent me from smoking. Since porno films on television excite me, censor them. Since I can't resist calling erotic phone numbers and I'm ruining myself by doing so, eliminate those numbers. We're a step away from the prohibition of chocolate, once it is discovered that it gives pleasure – a lot of pleasure – and that it is a bit addictive.
> (*Mano de sombra* 303)

Marías further links government intrusion into individual lives to the practice of political correctness, which creeps into social thought as an insidious and pervasive form of oppression that fosters conformity while disallowing dissent. He has assailed in numerous columns what he views as the inanity of political correctness, with repeated emphasis on the use of language and the practice of stereotyping. On the one hand he opposes the social leveling of individuals into groups marked by certain traits as biased and unjust. As he does through much of his writing on social matters, he places the individual above the collective in relation to personal identity and the freedom to choose one's own behavior. But he grows nonplused when the practices of individual behavior within any group (racial, ethnic, religious) seem to fall outside the bounds of scrutiny and criticism simply because a group has suffered from discrimination. Marías insists that, because of political correctness, too many people become "predispuestas a saltar y a denunciar y a indignarse, a detectar actitudes o frases supuestamente machistas, sexistas, racistas, xenófobas, degradantes, inmorales, antinacionalistas, acosadoras, homófobas, misóginas o islamófobas, tanto da" ("predisposed to jump up and down and denounce and to become indignant, to detect attitudes or phrases that are supposedly machista, sexist, racist, xenophobic, degrading, immoral, antinationalist, harassing, homophobic, misogynistic, or Islamophobic, it's all the same") ("El viejo truco del grito en el cielo," *Demasiada nieve alrededor* 255).

For Marías, political correctness has grown even more pervasive in the way that many groups have sought to manipulate language to avoid offending others. This not only hints at reverse discrimination, in Marías's view, but also leads to mutations in the very structure and use of language. He mocks feminists in particular, who promote gender change in words while showing scant understanding either of the origin of language or of its historical transformations. Although he admits in a 2001 article that, "Me he ocupado del asunto demasiadas veces" ("I've spent too much time on the matter") ("Paridas o paridos," *Harán de mí un criminal* 60), he seems nonetheless unable to refrain from deriding the attempted degenderization of language that, in his view, consumes the time of *El Instituto de la Mujer* ("The Institute for Women") in Spain. Hence he refers to the Latin origin of words (neither sexist nor political in his view) and repeatedly notes, for example, that the masculine plural form of nouns contains the feminine within it not for reasons of discrimination but for grammatical and historical ones. It defies good sense, in Marías's view, to use phrases such as "los españoles y las españolas" ("male Spaniards and female Spaniards") when writing about males and females, because the latter is contained grammatically in the former. Furthermore, and following the logic of political correctness, it would be necessary to change all feminine words to masculine forms when referring to men—thus "persona" would become "persono" or "víctima" would become "víctimo" ("Paridas o paridos," *Harán de mí un criminal* 62). For Marías, those who advocate for gender modification of plural nouns or for the masculine/feminine distinction of words that already contain each within them, are best described as "unos cantamañanas y unos farsantes, unos cobistas, unos embaucadores y unos falsos (o, en el mejor de los casos, unos melindrosos y unos acomplejados)" ("a bunch of charlatans and shams, creeps, swindlers, and liars (or, in the best of cases, prudes and people burdened with complexes)").[12]

The many and diverse topics explored in Marías's articles should not be understood as merely the work of a writer compelled to meet a deadline with a specific number of words. The commitment to write once a week certainly accelerates the need to clarify one's thoughts and form an opinion—hence Marías's reluctance to take on the assignment to begin with in 1994. But it also instigates in Marías's writing something more profound: the development of an ethical posture through the accretion of discourses and the forging of a style. Writing a column within a template that defines length but not content allows Marías to ponder the daily perplexities of life (including at times its tangible banality), and to articulate a stance on politics and culture that might otherwise have remained closeted from public scrutiny. Marías

---

[12] Javier Marías, "Todas las farsantas son igualas," in *A veces un caballero* (Madrid: Alfaguara, 2001), p. 291.

thus creates a narrator, a voice—in short, a *persona* who becomes known to the public as Javier Marías, but who is not quite the Javier Marías of flesh and blood. As Maarten Steenmeijer has noted about Marías's columns, "deben persuadir al lector de que el mundo y las palabras del narrador son los del propio autor *aunque no lo sean*" ("they should persuade the reader that the world and words of the narrator are those of the writer himself, even though they are not").[13] It is easy, and even comfortable, however, for readers to assume that they know Marías somewhat intimately: the nature of his personality on the one hand and his set of core beliefs on the other. In Marías's case, as we have seen, readers have witnessed his indignation over the state of Spanish politics, his disapproval of political correctness, his hostility toward the hypocrisy of the Catholic Church, his antipathy toward anti-smoking laws, and the ability to modulate the tone of his writing between that of an irascible traditionalist and a witty satirist of Spanish customs.

Both the impetus and consequence of Marías's writing of his columns is the invention of a narrator in much the same fashion as a novelist creates a narrator in a work of fiction. Marías himself has suggested that he sets out to write his articles with literary intentions.[14] Although the line of difference between the literary and non-literary often cannot be clearly drawn, the distinction in both cases between narrator and author often turns more on the technique of narration than on the referential connection to history and biography. In other words, Marías unmoors his writing from strict categories of fiction and non-fiction, but nonetheless holds to these categories to sustain the fissile base of all storytelling rooted in the principle of "it was and it was not."[15] As a result, his columns most often have the feel of hybrid narrations that generally stem from the real and are bound to it to the extent that their internal coherence and verisimilitude depend on the reader's perception of Marías's success in representing an external referent. This of course stands opposed to fiction, whose verisimilitude turns upon its internal coherence and carries no ethical obligation at all to represent the external world. Hence

---

[13] Maarten Steenmeijer, "Javier Marías, columnista: el otro, el mismo," in *El columnismo de escritores españoles (1975–2005)*, ed. Alexis Grohmann and Maarten Steenmeijer (Madrid: Editorial Verbum, 2006), p. 86.

[14] Javier Marías, "Prólogo," in *Pasiones pasadas* (Madrid: Alfaguara, 1999), pp. 13–14.

[15] The commingling of what might traditionally be seen as "fiction" and "non-fiction" grows increasingly common in Marias's novel-writing beginning with *Todas las almas* (1989), and is especially prominent in his later work, such as *Negra espalda del tiempo* (1998) and the trilogy *Tu rostro mañana* (2002, 2004, 2007).

the double tension of all writing (between referring at once to itself and to the world) resonates with a particularly strong and unresolved presence for both author and narrator in Marías's columns. As Steenmeijer intelligently puts it, "La columna transmite las palabras de un autor que se viste de un narrador que es y no es él. ... Más que *ser* él mismo, el autor se *representa* a sí mismo" ("The column transmits the words of the author, who wears the clothes of a narrator who is and is not he. ... More than *being* himself, the author *is representing* himself") ("Javier Marías, columnista," *El columnismo de escritores españoles* 88). Seen in this way, it is possible to say that the discursive Marías stands as the origin of the *persona* created in his columns as well as its effect.

In general terms readers are able to distinguish between Marías's articles and what might be seen as his purely literary writing (such as his novels and short stories) – but not always and not without a measure of uncertainty. For example, in his prologue to the 1991 edition of *Pasiones pasadas* (a collection of articles written mainly between 1982 and 1990), he points to one of the ways in which the line between the two can easily be blurred. He includes an article written for *El País* in December of 1987 ("La venganza y el mayordomo") in which he recalls a conversation in New York City, while trapped in an elevator with the butler of a wealthy couple, about the butler's preparation for revenge should the couple ever mistreat him (which according to the butler would inevitably occur). Three years later Marías includes a short story ("Lo que dijo el mayordomo") in his collection of stories *Mientras ellas duermen* (1990), in which he refers to the earlier episode in New York, explains how he altered slightly some of the facts in his original article about it, and then writes a short story based on what had happened. In each case, as Marías makes clear, what had actually occurred and what he had imagined (not one or the other, but both) made the narrative possible. But his point is a larger one about how language gains meaning through the always varying process of contextualization. As he notes concerning the column and the story, "[L]as mismas palabras pueden ser ficticias o reales sin depender de ellas mismas (idénticas) sino de dónde se inscriben y con qué se envuelven o cuál es su tratamiento" ("[T]he same words can be fictitious or real without depending on the words themselves (which are identical), but rather on where they are inscribed and with what they are involved or how they are treated") ("Prólogo," *Pasiones pasadas* 14).

If there is a single tenet that defines nearly all of Marías's narrative, it is that the absolute distinction between the real and make-believe, between fact and fiction, enacts a false opposition that is unsustainable discursively as well as philosophically. In much of Marías's narrative the commingling of the two provides essential support for his perception of how writing and life are propped against one another, and for his belief that neither can stand alone. Life demands stories, and stories configure life—but not directly in either case and not without the incertitude inherent in the raw material of all storytelling: language. As Marías noted in 2008 in his induction speech to the Real Academia Española: "En el momento en que interviene la palabra, en el momento en que se aspira a que la palabra reproduzca lo acontecido, lo que se está haciendo es suplantar y falsear esto último. Sin querer se lo deforma, tergiversa, distorsiona y contamina" ("At the moment when the word intervenes, at the moment when you seek to have the word reproduce what has occurred, what you are doing is supplanting and falsifying. Without wanting to, you deform, twist, distort, and corrupt").[16]

The question of language, and of the closely related notions of storytelling, fiction, and reality, become recurrent themes in Marías's columns over many years and reveal foundational concepts for nearly all of his writing. Thus, in addition to the immensely varied focus of his articles, he returns with frequency to explore the very essence of what he does as an author and narrator within the discourses that he creates. He addresses not only the small and technical details of his own writing, but the historical practice of novel-writing in Spain, the influences of other writers on his fiction, and the highly pertinent role of translation in his literary formation.

Marías has not set out explicitly in his columns to fashion a literary theory, but he has written extensively on literature, and in particular on narrative fiction and the nature of telling stories. Above all, storytelling for Marías is a profoundly existential activity—it provides hermeneutical sustenance for exploring much of what is unknown about the world, and it stands as an epistemological tool for shaping the difficult and unending attempt to understand both the self and all that lies outside the self. In this sense, narration becomes for Marías central to living: it allows for reflection as well as for intervention ("la mayor intervención posible en las cosas del mundo") ("the greatest intervention possible in the things of the world"),[17] as he puts it, and it satisfies an unsated need of human beings to imagine and understand the world in which they live. Most importantly, narration both instigates and begets a special kind of cognition:

---

[16] Javier Marías, " 'Sobre la dificultad de contar': Javier Marías y el sillón R de la RAE (discurso íntegro)." http://blogs.periodistadigital.com/electroduende.php/2008/05/26/javiermarias-rae-sillon-88935, p. 1.

[17] Javier Marías, "Contar el misterio," in *Literatura y fantasma* (Madrid: Alfaguara, 2001), p. 122.

> Sé que al escribir o al contar historias e inventar personajes he sabido o reconocido o he pensado cosas que sólo en la escritura pueden saberse o reconocerse o pensarse. A veces sólo en la ficción, esto es, en la escritura de novelas y cuentos. A menudo recuerdo la existencia de algo que tiende a olvidarse y que antiguamente se llamó "pensamiento literario", diferente de cualquier otro, del científico y el filosófico y el lógico y el matemático y hasta el religioso o político. No se trata, claro está, de pensamiento sobre la literatura ni sobre lo literario; sino de un *pensar literariamente* sobre cualquier asunto, y es este un pensar privilegiado.
>
> I know that when I write or tell stories and invent characters, I have known or recognized or thought things that can be known, recognized or thought only in literature. Sometimes, only in fiction, that is to say, in the writing of novels and short stories. I often remember the existence of something that tends to be forgotten and that formerly was called "literary thought," different from all other forms of thought—scientific, philosophical, logical and mathematical, and even religious or political. It is not a matter, of course, of thinking about literature or about the literary; but rather a case of *thinking literarily* about any matter whatsoever, and this is a privileged type of thinking. ("Contar el misterio," *Literatura y fantasma* 122–23)

Writing is thus transcendent for Marías. He does not suggest that it stands above life as a divine endowment in a religious sense, but rather that it allows the writer to become more than a mere servant to existence: "El escritor cuenta y explica, y al hacerlo *se* cuenta y *se* explica lo que de otra forma no habría llegado a saber ni a entender jamás" ("The writer tells and explains, and when he does that, he tells to *himself* and explains to *himself* what he would never have managed to understand by other means") ("La huella del animal," *Literatura y fantasma* 170).

But what writers learn and reveal about themselves and the world stems not only from the product of their work (i.e., the finished story from which knowledge may be deduced or conferred) but also from the process of narrating, which entails seeing as well as writing. The nature of this process, and the multiple ways in which it is linked to literary invention, lie at the core of Marías's theoretical propositions. As Marías notes, to invent in literature does not mean to create from nothing but rather, as its Latin etymology (*invenire*) conveys, "no quiere decir otra cosa que 'encontrar,' o más bien, 'descubrir.'" ("it means nothing less than 'to find', or rather, 'to discover'") ("La huella del animal," *Literatura y fantasma* 171).

When writing about the novel (or about literature in general), Marías does not propose to develop a paradigmatic and totalizing set of norms and values with which all literary texts conform. Instead, he reveals in his essays a persistent effort to articulate his understanding of what he actually does when he writes as well as what lies beyond his grasp. While Marías ponders in his work nearly every aspect of novel writing (e.g., language, technique, character, referentiality), it is in the literary process itself—from creation of the text to its reception by the reader—where he defines the most compelling theoretical foundation for fictional narrative. Further, within the various aspects of the literary process, he gives saliency to two recurring problems: (1) the relationship between textual worlds constituted by narrative and the reality that lies outside of these textual worlds or, put more simply, the relationship between literature and life; (2) the critical role played by the reader in discerning this relationship and the broad existential connections among writer, text, and reader.

Marías's perspective on the relationship between life and literature is rooted to a large degree in his view of the history of the Spanish novel, for which he has affirmed on several occasions a profound disdain. Although he praises the literary value of writers such as Miguel de Cervantes (1547–1616), Leopoldo Alas (1852–1901), and Ramón del Valle-Inclán (1866–1936), and admires Juan Benet (1927–1993) as one of the most gifted novelists of the twentieth century, he dismisses the novel in Spain as a source of inspiration for his own work. As he puts it, "como todo el mundo sabe pero no todo el mundo está dispuesto a reconocer, la tradición novelística española es, además de escasa, pobre; además de pobre, más bien realista; y cuando no es realista, con frecuencia es costumbrista" ("as everyone knows, but not everyone is prepared to admit, novelistic tradition in Spain is, besides scant, poor; beside poor, rather realistic; and when not realistic, it frequently is *costumbrista* [a literature of manners]") ("Desde una novela no necesariamente castiza," *Literatura y fantasma* 55). Nonetheless, this rejection of the Spanish novel in general does not spur him to renounce the novel per se as an important genre in the history of modern literature. To the contrary, he recognizes the novel as the "forma narrativa dominante de este siglo [el siglo veinte]" ("the dominant narrative form of this century [the twentieth century]") ("Las bromas divinas," *Literatura y fantasma* 292).

Marías frequently points out that Spain boasts no writers such as Alexander Dumas, Jules Verne, Robert Louis Stevenson or Edgar Allan Poe to incite reading among Spanish youth. Further, he contends that between Cervantes' *Don Quijote* (1605 and 1615) and Alas's *La Regenta* (1884–1885), nothing emerges in Spanish fiction for young novelists to admire or emulate. From the beginning of their careers, Marías and many writers of his generation rejected what they viewed as the cynosure of Spanish fiction in the twentieth century—"España como tema" ("Spain as theme") ("Desde una novela no necesariamente castiza," *Literatura y fantasma* 56)—and also rebelled against what they saw as a leveling mediocrity in the whole of Spanish culture during the years of the Franco regime. Hence they opted, as Marías puts it, "dar la espalda a toda nuestra herencia literaria, ignorarla por completo" ("to turn our back on our entire literary heritage, ignore it completely") ("Desde una novela no necesariamente castiza," *Literatura y fantasma* 57). Above all, Marías rejects the Spanish novel because of its obsession with representing Spain, which in turn has led to a set of de facto principles that promotes an unequivocal coincidence between literature and life. In other words, a type of fiction founded upon the tenets of realism: the belief that objective reality exists and is translatable; the perceived coincidence between the word and its referent, and thus the utter transparency of language; the assertion that to narrate life is to re-present it in the whole of its authenticity; the notion that a literature committed to social action is able to transform the world into something other than it is. Furthermore, not only has the tradition of Spanish fiction grown from the desire to place life and literature on the same plain, it has cultivated that coincidence to such an extent that, with few exceptions, the novel in Spain no longer bears literary legitimacy. As Marías writes concerning the social realistic novel of the 1950s and 1960s, "lo juzgábamos enteramente desdeñable: ramplón, poco sutil, torpe, demasiado obvio, en último término extraliterario" ("we judged it to be wholly despicable: vulgar, scarcely subtle, clumsy, too obvious, and in the end, extra-literary") ("Desde una novela no necesariamente castiza," *Literatura y fantasma* 56).

The traditional desire of Spanish novelists to scrutinize reality and to incorporate it into the novel does not by itself undermine either its value or its efficacy as literature. Cervantes and Alas, for example, tell us much about the social life of their times without writing literature that is "clumsy" and "vulgar." Marías expresses concern that external reality in Spanish fiction has generally been perceived as its primary substance and, therefore, the degree to which it faithfully reflects that reality determines its success as a literary work. Such a position, in Marías's view, compels the novel to become "extra-literary" in the way that it is constituted by the small and often tedious matters of daily life. Marías is fully aware that a certain material reality exists outside of discourse and that this reality seeps into the fictional world created by the novelist. But the two worlds cannot be identical, in Marías's view, as many Spanish writers have insisted within the traditions of realism.

Much of Marías's writing serves to undermine fixed boundaries between fiction and reality within the context of narrative. In other words, fiction and reality cannot be wholly identical (as within certain precepts of realism) or wholly distinct (as with, for example, the general understanding of postmodernism). Marías's thinking on the matter evolves in a number of ways. First of all, it is clear that his probing of the literary process grows from one of his most important mentors, Juan Benet. Marías is drawn to Benet's writing not only because he admires him as a novelist (he asserts that Benet's 1967 novel, *Volverás a Región*, contains "[algunas de] las muestras de pensamiento literario más profund[a]s e inquietantes de nuestra lengua" ("[some] of the most profound and disquieting samples of literary thought in our language") ["Volveremos," *Literatura y fantasma* 237]), but also because he respects him as a serious theorist of literature.[18] Within Benet's views on writing that Marías embraces, ambiguity and uncertainty, coupled with the elements of language and style, move to the fore. Contradiction, mystery, and what Benet calls the "zona de sombra" ("zone of shadow") pervade the fictional world of his novels and provide the substance of much of his theoretical writing on the nature of narrative.[19] One has only to look at his essays in *La inspiración y el estilo* (1965), *El ángel del Señor abandona a Tobías* (1976), or *En ciernes* (1976) to confirm the point.

Benet forcefully opposed the canons of social realism that dominated the novel of his generation, commonly known as the Generation of 1950.[20] In *La inspiración y el estilo*, for example, he argues for the primacy of style over all other aspects of literature: "[L]a cosa literaria sólo puede tener interés por el estilo, nunca por el asunto" ("The literary object can only be of interest because of style, never because of its topic").[21] But Benet does not view style as an isolated, self-referring artifact that remains far removed from the world. To the contrary, he affirms that through language, and through the persistent development of a narrative style, the novelist sustains the possibility of

---

[18] As Marías writes in 1988, "No hay escritor español vivo que yo más admiro que Juan Benet" ("There is no other living Spanish writer whom I admire more than Juan Benet"), "Autobiografía y ficción," in *Literatura y fantasma*, p. 77.

[19] Juan Benet, "Incertidumbre, memoria, fatalidad y temor," in *En ciernes* (Madrid: Taurus, 1976), p. 50.

[20] By the mid-twentieth century in Spain, and more than a decade after the end of the Civil War, the novel had become part of the largely infertile terrain of Spanish culture. However, a new generation of novelists began to publish works in the early 1950s. Their intention was to revitalize fiction-writing through the representation of contemporary life in Spain in realistic fashion, with the secondary goal of bringing about social change. Included among this cohort of writers, most of whom published their first works under the influence of a social realistic aesthetic, are Jesús Fernández Santos, Luis Goytisolo, Juan Goytisolo, Carmen Martín Gaite, and Rafael Sánchez Ferlosio. The impact and influence of social realism in Spanish fiction during this period was short-lived, but it clearly dominated the thinking of this cohort of writers, whose work reflected the stark reality of both city and rural life in Spain during the first decades of the Franco regime.

[21] Juan Benet, *La inspiración y el estilo* (Barcelona: Seix Barral, 1973), p. 135.

exploring the world from without, and from a modernist perspective, also from above. As he puts it, "Ninguna barrera puede prevalecer contra el estilo siendo así que se trata del esfuerzo del escritor por romper un cerco mucho más estrecho, permanente y riguroso: aquel que le impone el dictado de la realidad" ("No barrier can prevail against style when it is a matter of the writer's efforts to breach a much narrower, permanent, and rigorous siege: the one which the dictates of reality impose on him") (*Inspiración y estilo* 179–180). Style enables Benet to explore the zone of shadow and what he has called the "imperio del oxymoron" ("domain of oxymoron"), which is a way for him to outwit reality without breaking from it.[22]

What is important here, however, and what Marías will draw upon as one of the overarching principles of his own writing, is that Benet neither embraces representation per se (understood as re-presentation of the real with linguistic transparency) nor formalism per se (discourse as a closed system of autonomous signs). When Benet writes that "el escritor se encara con el mundo que le rodea menos mediante una ciencia cognoscitiva que gracias a una estilística" ("the writer faces the surrounding world less with a cognitive science than thanks to style") (*Inspiración y estilo* 136), he does not propose to disconnect the word from the world but rather suggests that each gains sustenance from the other to draw out its ambiguous meanings.

For Marías, as for Benet, the postmodern rejection of metanarratives and emphasis on the dispersal of meanings through persistent links to other texts are insufficient foundations for the writing of novels. Much like Benet, Marías offers uncertainty as a narrative determinant and links it to the fundamental nature of both language and life. Speaking of Benet, Marías asserts the basic premise that ambiguity constitutes the foundational trait of all fiction writing: "[se trata en la novela de Benet] de no saber de manera cabal qué está pasando porque el pasar que interesa a Benet es el que más se asemeja al pasar de la vida, en la que nunca nadie tiene todos los datos o toda la memoria o toda la seguridad o toda la interpretación de cómo fueron o son las cosas, aun las que más nos atañen o más han condicionado nuestra existencia, teñidas todas de parcialidad e incertidumbre" ("[in Benet's novels it is a matter] of not knowing in a precise way what is happening because the happening that interests Benet is that which most closely resembles what goes on in life, where no one ever has all the facts or a complete memory or absolute certainty or a full interpretation of how things were or are, even those things that most concern or have most conditioned our existence, all of

---

[22] Benet elaborates on both the "zona de sombra" and the "imperio del oxymoron" in his essay cited in note 19, "Incertidumbre, memoria, fatalidad y temor."

which are tinged by partiality or uncertainty") ("Una invitación," *Literatura y fantasma* 244).

Marías's assertion that in Benet's fiction uncertainty relates intimately to "what goes on in life" helps to explain a fundamental part of Marías's own writing: it identifies the center of "not knowing" as a philosophical and practical problem rooted in both ontology and epistemology. The inability of narrative to convey certainty about reality does not represent a shortcoming of narrative, but rather it speaks to the nature of life itself, whose complexity and elusiveness remain beyond our ability to comprehend and define. In other words, Benet's novels are ambiguous because life is ambiguous, not because language or narrative technique or some other combination of formal components of the novel tells a story inadequately. In Benet's fiction as well as in his theoretical writings, language does not become narcissistic and self-referential and thus incapacitated in the face of narrative exigencies. Benet in fact always asserts the possibility of language to mean outside itself while admitting the momentary possibility of its failure to speak.

Marías lauds Benet's position on the centrality of language and style in literature, but he does not embrace it fully. Marías's novels are less complex stylistically than Benet's, and his articles on writing do not attain the depth of literary thought evident in Benet's much longer and more complicated theoretical discussions. Yet Marías's concern with how literature and life (or fiction and reality) are commingled occupies much of his writing about writing. Above all, he has sought to make the specific relationship between fiction and reality both a labyrinth and a puzzle. Similar to Benet, at least part of the impetus for his position lies in the belief that life itself is a labyrinth and a puzzle, and fiction (or at least fiction of high standing) inevitably embodies this idea through recurrent ambiguity and contradiction. The value of literature lies in its proposition that such a world exists, and that through writing we at once evoke its presence and reveal how it remains beyond our grasp. For Marías, that is precisely the challenge and the point: "Hay una enorme zona de sombra en la que sólo la literatura y las artes en general penetran; seguramente, como dijo mi maestro Juan Benet, no para iluminarla y esclarecerla, sino para percibir su inmensidad y su complejidad al encender una pobre cerilla que al menos nos permite ver que está ahí, esa zona, y no olvidarla" ("There is an enormous zone of shadow which only literature and the arts in general penetrate; surely, as my teacher Juan Benet said, not to illuminate and clarify it, but to perceive its immensity and its complexity by lighting a small match which at least allows us to see that it is there, that zone, and not forget it") ("Una pobre cerilla," *Literatura y fantasma* 414).

On occasion Marías seems to echo postmodern concerns about the inability of language to refer to any reality outside its own creation and context. In his speech to the Real Academia Española, for example, he suggests that the writer who seeks to relate anything at all about the world will inevitably fail: "Si bien se mira, la lengua misma no es más que un permanente tanteo, un esfuerzo más bien inútil ... es una especie de quiero y no puedo o un perpetuo amago condenado a no dar nunca en el blanco, o no de lleno" ("If one looks closely, language itself is nothing more than a permanent sizing up, a rather useless effort ... it is a type of I want to and I can't or a perpetual attempt condemned never to hit the target, or at least not completely") ("Sobre la dificultad de contar," *Real Academia Española* 2). In his novel *Negra espalda del tiempo* (1998), Marias's first-person narrator similarly hints at the collapse of all narrative creations into a vaguely framed ontological amorphousness: "En realidad la vieja aspiración de cualquier cronista o superviviente, relatar lo ocurrido, dar cuenta de lo acaecido, dejar constancia de los hechos y delitos y hazañas, es una mera ilusión o quimera, o mejor dicho, la propia frase, ese propio concepto, son ya metafóricos y forma parte de la ficción. 'Relatar lo ocurrido' es inconcebible y vano, o bien es sólo posible como invención"[23] ("The time-honored aspiration of any chronicler or survivor—to tell what happened, to give an account of what took place, to leave a record of events and crimes and exploits—is, in fact, a mere illusion or chimera, or, rather, the phrase and concept themselves are already metaphorical and partake of fiction. 'To tell what happened' is inconceivable and futile, or possible only as invention").[24] Hence any perceived confluence of the "inside" and the "outside" of the text, any intention to draw upon language to represent life as it really is, must be measured as a vain chimera spawned by the writer's desire to appropriate the world and give it meaning.

Marías indeed appears in this instance to embrace a postmodern view of the novel that allows scant hope for the writer to be able to speak authentically. He hints at the postmodern disenchantment with metanarratives as well as with the modernist possibility that they may synthesize and unify the heterogeneous. In other words, Marías seems to deny to the writer and to writing any form of transcendent authority to engage the world and reveal something about it. In line with postmodern thinking, he positions language outside of the real and suggests that its meaning lies beyond all that which it mediates and effects. Such a view also squares with Marías's broader posture on the pre-eminence of style over content in the writing of novels, a position closely associated, as we have seen, with Juan Benet.

---

[23] Javier Marías, *Negra espalda del tiempo* (Madrid: Alfaguara, 1998), p. 10.
[24] Javier Marías, *Dark Back of Time*, trans. Esther Allen (New York: New Directions), p. 8.

While Marías explores certain ideas associated with postmodernism (in particular, the idea that language distorts rather than reproduces the real, that narration configures the world rather than imitates it, and the idea that writing is largely recombinant—i.e., a dialogue sustained with other texts and constantly nurtured by them), in the end the weight of his work points to an understanding of literature more closely aligned with high modernist writers such as Benet or Faulkner. Indeed, to label Marías's ideas on literature as postmodern accounts for only a small part of his thinking. This can be seen in two important ways: first, through his recognition of a privileged position for the writer in relation to truth; second, in the way that the pre-eminence of style over content in his thinking stands not as a rejection of the mimetic capacity of a literary text but as recognition of its inventiveness.

Marías attributes to the act of writing a special epistemological entailment. As he puts it, "A diferencia del científico o el filosófico, el pensamiento literario se caracteriza por dos privilegios que son sólo suyos: no está sujeto a argumento ni a demostración ... no depende de un hilo conductor razonado ni necesita mostrar cada uno de sus pasos; por consiguiente, le está permitida la contradicción" ("Literary thought, as opposed to scientific or philosophical thought, is characterized by two unique privileges: it is not subject to argumentation or proof ... it does not depend on a line of reasoning nor does it need to demonstrate each one of its steps; therefore, it is allowed contradiction") ("Volveremos," *Literatura y fantasma* 236). The truth of fictive narrative for Marías lies not in its ability to reproduce reality within a linguistic system that is identical to this reality. Instead truth is explored and imposed within language which is able to discover and invent the world. It is this dual task of the novelist, rooted in perception and imagination, that gives to writers their transcendent authority and authenticity. As Marias puts it, "También lo real ha de ser imaginado" ("The real also has to be imagined") ("Los malditos detalles," *Mano de sombra* 325).[25] What is important to remember here, however, is that imagination does not act as an abstract or amorphous muse, disembodied and therefore unknowable. To the contrary, it is embodied always by and within language. And while Marías consistently proposes that word and object are not two entities which co-exist in the same system and therefore do not have the same ontological standing, they cannot remain

---

[25] The necessary process of imagining the real forms the foundation of much of Marias's writing. In particular it serves as the principal point of departure for *Negra espalda del tiempo*, where the narrator affirms, "para relater lo ocurrido hay que haberlo imaginado antes" (196) ("to tell what has happened you have to have imagined it as well" [*Dark Back of Time* 161]).

forever disconnected. As he affirms, the nature of this connection determines the ultimate standing of truth and reality as each relates to the novel.

Marías does not offer a lapidary statement concerning the power and authority of language and style in the same manner as Benet. Nonetheless, he allows us to infer from his writing the unique place that language occupies at the center of the writer's consciousness. Above all, in Marías's view, the writer perceives and understands the world with words: "Pues bien, la verdadera anomalía, una anomalía que no sólo se ha de dar y expresar forzosamente en la escritura, sino posiblemente también en la verbalidad, esto es, en la manera de relacionarse con el mundo y con los semejantes, es, para los escritores, que sus cabezas estén llenas de palabras" ("Really, the true anomaly, an anomaly that must not only be given and expressed forcefully in writing but possibly also verbally, that is, in the way of relating to the world and its beings, is for writers, that their heads are full of words") ("Cabezas llenas," *Literatura y fantasma* 427). These words serve as agent and substance within the narrative, but should never be confused with the substance external to the narrative. As Marías puts it, the writer "nunca intenta pasar la huella del animal por el animal mismo" ("never sets out to have the footprint of the animal pass for the animal itself") ("La huella del animal," *Literatura y fantasma* 168).

The "footprint" and the "animal" are at once absent and present in the narrative, and it is ultimately this duality which links Marias more closely to the modernist transcendence of presence suggested by Benet than to the despair of absence conceived within the postmodern aesthetic. Style dictates invention and exploration in the novel, and style finally gives to the novel its figurative essence: "Pues al fin y al cabo, lo que es *contable* en una novela es sólo lo que se puede decir también en unas pocas e intercambiables palabras. Las novelas, sin embargo, suelen tener muchas palabras, y esas, justamente, nunca son intercambiables" ("In the end, what is *tellable* in a novel is only what one can say in a few and interchangeable words. Novels, however, usually have many words, and those, precisely, are never interchangeable") ("Errar con brújula," *Literatura y fantasma* 110). In other words, what is "tellable" in a novel (or what can be paraphrased) has little to do with what makes it literary. While Marías would agree that, in response to a comment such as, "I have just read a good novel," a person might ask, "What's it about?" he (like Benet before him) cannot embrace the immediacy of that "aboutness" as the matrix of its literary value.

To emphasize this point Marías refers to the work of his friend, Cuban author Guillermo Cabrera Infante (1929–2005), and to the English writer Laurence Sterne. Marías attributes to Cabrera Infante "el mejor relato largo ["Amazona"] escrito en castellano en la segunda mitad del siglo [veinte]" ("the best long story ["Amazon"] written in Spanish in the second half of the [twentieth] century") ("Cuéntale el cuento," *Literatura y fantasma* 269), and sees the Cuban as "el más aventajado discípulo de Laurence Sterne" ("the most outstanding disciple of Laurence Sterne") ("Cuéntale el cuento," *Literatura y fantasma* 269). The legacy comes not through imitation per se, nor through theme or referential focus but through the narrative accretions in Cabrera Infante's style which Marías finds originally in the work of Sterne (and also, of course, in Juan Benet)—the ability to construct one sentence upon another, one paragraph upon another with tergiversations, ambiguities, and contradictions which lead the reader away from the specificity of plot and into the more slippery terrain of the content of the form of a work: style. In other words, while a plot may move in one direction or another, with varying degrees of complexity, it remains always "tellable." In contrast, Marías celebrates in Sterne (and in Cabrera Infante and Benet) what he calls "una de las más fértiles fórmulas narrativas: *You progress as you digress*" ("one of the most fertile narrative formulas: *You progress as you digress*") ("Cuéntale el cuento," *Literatura y fantasma* 269).

This emphasis on digression—that is to say, on the useful accumulation of words—has led Marías to write frequently about his work as a translator and its link to his own novel writing. Marías has taught the theory of translation at universities in Spain, England, and the United States, but more importantly, he is well known for having translated many pre-eminent authors from Europe, Great Britain, and the United States into Spanish.[26] The complicated and highly creative nature of translation allows Marías to address in his columns a number of issues related to language. For example, in several articles he has expressed his indignation at translators who misunderstand

---

[26] Marías has translated works by Thomas Hardy, Frank O'Hara, Vladimir Nabokov, William Faulkner, Edith B. Holden, Robert Louis Stevenson, Joseph Conrad, Isak Dinesen, William Butler Yeats, John Ashbery, Thomas Browne, Anthony Burgess, W. H. Auden, J. D. Salinger, and Wallace Stevens. His best known translation, for which he won the national translation prize in 1979, is of Laurence Sterne's *La vida y las opiniones del caballero Tristram Shandy*. Marías has also admitted, with some degree of chagrin, that one of the first translations for which he was paid was a collaboration with his friend Gustavo Pérez de Ayala: "corregir y pulir la traducción argentina de aquel libro tan malo que gozó de enorme éxito, *Love Story*. Me temo que él y yo fuimos los responsables de la formulación española de la muy ridícula frase convertida en lema de enamorados durante una temporada: 'Amar significa no tener que decir nunca lo siento'" ("to correct and polish the translation of the awful book which enjoyed great success, *Love Story*. I'm afraid that he and I were responsible for the formulation in Spanish of that ridiculous phrase that became a motto for lovers during a period of time: 'Love means never having to say you're sorry'") ("Los antiguos amigos," *Demasiada nieve alrededor* 265).

words in one language or misuse them in another; he rails against the general lack of cultural and linguistic sophistication among many translators that distorts their work and makes it unreadable; and he has expressed dismay at how most readers are unaware that they often read bad translations.[27] He has criticized Jorge Luis Borges for rendering a poor translation of Faulkner's *The Wild Palms*, and he has further accused Borges and Adolfo Bioy Casares of tampering with an original text: Marías claims that in their translation of chapter five of Sir Thomas Browne's *Urn-Burial* (a text which Marías himself translated into Spanish in 1986), the two translators added a segment not found in the original.[28]

While Marías devotes several articles to the linguistic dissonance of specific translations and has frequently offered examples of what he views as alarming distortions of original texts, his broader comments more commonly address the translation as a highly imaginative act linked to the writing of his own fiction. For example, in his article "Mi libro favorito" (*Literatura y fantasma* 398–401), Marías outlines his admiration for Laurence Sterne's *Tristram Shandy*. For most readers, of course, preferred books stem from the pleasures (intellectual, aesthetic, emotional, etc.) derived from the act of reading. But for Marías, as he notes, his preference for Sterne's novel responds to a different pleasure: "además de leerlo, también lo he escrito" ("In addition to reading it, I have also written it") (*Literatura y fantasma* 399). Marías's assertion that he has written the novel is of course a curious one, but it points to an understanding of translation, language, and meaning that clearly allows the practice of translation to transcend the mere exchange of one language for another, with the coincident understanding that the translated text stands identical to the original but merely with a different set of words. Marías perceives translation as a process of creation rooted in epistemology, hermeneutics, empathy, and not unimportantly, arduous and complicated work. As he notes, he easily could have declared that Cervantes' *Don Quijote*, Flaubert's *Madame Bovary*, Conrad's *Heart of Darkness*, or even Constant's *Adolphe* headed his list of preferred books.

---

[27] See respectively the following articles by Marías: in *Harán de mí un criminal*, "¿Es usted el santo fantasma?" 139–41; in *Demasiada nieve alrededor*, "¿Mande?" 114–16; "Productos podridos," 27–29; and "El camino de nuestra lengua," 300–02.

[28] Marías reports that when he spoke to Borges about the segment, the Argentine denied that he had made such an addition, though he suggested that Bioy Casares may indeed have taken liberty with the original text by Browne. See Marías's discussion of this in "Falsificaciones literarias," *Pasiones pasadas* 185–90.

Pero con ninguno de esos textos pasé casi dos años de mi vida; en ninguno, por cuidadosamente que los haya leído ... me sumergí como en *Tristram Shandy*; ninguno me obligó a escribir o redactar o componer alrededor de un millar de folios, cada folio hecho y rehecho numerosas veces ... ninguno, por último, se apoderó de mi prosa, me hizo ponerme literalmente en la piel del autor, del otro, pensar como él, hablar como él, decir lo que él como lo dijo él.

But with none of those texts did I spend almost two years of my life. In none, no matter how closely I may have read them ... did I submerge myself as I did in *Tristram Shandy*; none compelled me to write or redact or compose approximately a thousand pages, each page done and redone many names ... none, finally, took over my prose, made me put myself literally in the skin of the author, of the other, think like him, speak like him, say what he said as he said it. ("Mi libro favorito," *Literatura y fantasma* 399–400)

It is the working through of his translations that allows Marías to understand what defines his own writing and to clarify what occurs during the creative process. For indeed, writing fiction is not merely the practice of suturing words together with the aim of reproducing in a text a world that exists external to it. As we have seen, the coalescence of the word and world embraced by authors of social realism is anathema to the very core of the novel as Marías conceives it. Thus when Marías claims that he "has written" *Tristram Shandy*, he understands that his work as a translator and his work as a novelist are not tasks of imitation but of invention: he discovers in both activities how language is used to speak of itself and of the world at the same time. This tension—the split-referencing inherent in all literary narrative—moves acutely to the fore in translation, whose first-order referent, as Marías has pointed out, is not specifically the original text but rather the translator's memory of it ("Ausencia y memoria en la traducción poética," *Literatura y fantasma* 378), and whose second-order referent can be deduced from the social and linguistic context of that text. Both of these referents are then re-inserted into a new context, and in a new language, where meaning and interpretation are connected to the real world, offer more than perfunctory glimpses into it, and ultimately re-signify it.

Much like creative writing in one's own language, translation begins with an absence which the writer converts into a presence through the act of narration. As Marías affirms, "El traductor, al encararse con su tarea, siente el texto original como una ausencia ... de ese texto en su lengua, en la llamada lengua receptora, y por ende en el sistema de pensamiento de dicha lengua. El traductor no reproduce, no copia, no calca ..." ("The translator, upon facing his task, feels the original text as an absence ... of that text in his language, in the so-called receiving language, and therefore in the system of thought of that language. The translator does not reproduce, does not copy, does not trace ...") ("Ausencia y memoria en la traducción poética," *Literatura y fantasma* 378). The passing of time opens texts to new interpretations and, analogously, it demands of a text new translations. In turn, each translation creates a new work and thus explores a new reality, and in this way offers a different understanding of both.

For Marías, translation relates to how texts come into being and to how texts and contexts nurture one another through hermeneutic reciprocity under the arch of language. But it is also clear that the meanings attached to texts are not generated in an abstract or passive fashion but by the active participation of the reader. Of course, there is nothing particularly new in the idea that readers make meaning. Indeed, much of the literary theory of the past three decades has underscored the creative role of reading and the diversity of meanings linked to the experience and knowledge of multiple readers. In Marías's thinking, however, the polisemic nature of the novel, which is shaped by reading but incited by writing, is at once affirmed and denied in ways parallel to his view of how the novel itself operates as both a creative and a mimetic enterprise. In other words, Marías affirms in his writings how the reader is trapped between the desire to reconcile the make-believe and the real and the need to recognize and affirm their difference.

On the one hand, Marías proposes a link between our perceptions of what we read and how we live: "En realidad podría decirse que [el lector] admite ver y saber de manera no muy distinta de cómo ve y sabe en su propia vida, en su propia experiencia" ("In reality it could be said that the reader goes about seeing and knowing in a way not very different from how he sees and knows in his own life, in his own experience") ("La huella del animal," *Literatura y fantasma* 168–69). From this perspective, the structure of literary perception for the reader correlates with the structure of ontological perception. In each case the perceiver must sort through reliable and unreliable information, facts and fictions, certainty and ambiguity, in order to justify the creation of one meaning or another. In these instances, whether or not the referent is believed to be real or fictive is less important than the multi-tiered process through which readers attend to their task: "el lector asiste a una historia, la escruta y la espía; pero además asiste a la narración de esa historia, es decir, a la actividad relatora del autor; por último, asiste asimismo a su propia actividad lectora" ("the reader accompanies a story, scrutinizes it and spies on it; but in addition he accompanies the narration of that story, that is to say, the narrating activity of the author; finally, he accompanies himself in his own reading activity") ("La huella del animal," *Literatura y fantasma* 168).

In this sense, reading becomes for Marías not a way of viewing reality but a reality in its own right. The world of the novel (of narration) is constituted by rules and codes, which readers gradually absorb and process as they read. Hence for Marías, each reader becomes a spy "por partida triple: espía lo que se le cuenta y lo que no se le cuenta, y también se espía a sí mismo mientras espía ambas cosas" ("in a three-part game: he spies on what is told and what is not told, and he also spies on himself while he is spying on both things") ("La huella del animal," *Literatura y fantasma* 168). Thus not only are readers made aware of what they understand by reading a text and how they understand it, but also they recognize the basis for their understanding to be the relationship between the self and text through the interpretive act. Reading here is thus perceived as a phenomenological act linked to epistemology and to hermeneutics. Hence referentiality forms a component of the interpretive strategy but remains secondary to the more urgent matter for the reader of arranging what has been observed into sense-making patterns. In this way the reader deciphers texts through the use of internal mechanisms (the formal and configurative elements of a work) which order and create meaning in relation to the work's structural composition.

On the other hand, Marías remains fully aware that readers inevitably make connections between text and context. He thus addresses the ontological contentiousness of the novel as it relates both to truth and to referentiality. As Marías sees it, most readers begin to read novels hoping to specify determinant referents for what they are reading. To do this, they often isolate parts of the text that seem to be anchored in real life as they know it. For example, many readers of Marías's novel *Todas las almas* not only sought to establish correspondences between people and places in the novel and the town of Oxford (the spatial referent of the work), but also related the first-person narrator of the novel directly to the life of the author. As Marías writes in *Negra espalda del tiempo*, "De todas mis novelas hay una [*Todas las almas*] ... que invitó a sospechar que cuanto se contaba en ella tuviera su correspondencia en mi propia vida. ... En todo caso, esa novela ... se prestó también a la casi absoluta identificación entre su narrador sin nombre y autor con nombre, Javier Marías" (16) ("Among my novels there is one [*All Souls*] ... that invited readers to suspect that whatever was recounted in it had its counterpart in my life. ... In any case, this novel ... lent itself to the almost absolute identification of its nameless narrator with its named author, Javier Marías" [*Dark Back of Time* 13]).

While there exists a referential tie between what a novel represents and what lies outside it (otherwise the words of the text would bear no meaning), the most important aspect of reading lies in the various meanings invented through the active participation of the reader in the creative process. Above all, the reader must develop a corresponding consciousness, related to but not identical with that of the narrator of the text. Such self-consciousness is affirmed through the act of reading as long as the foundation for the understanding of narrative is recognized as mutual and reciprocal between the text and the reader—though the perspective of each may be distinct and even contradictory. In other words, the reader not only sees elements of the world represented in the text, but ultimately understands those elements passed through the filter of an ephemeral experience (the act of reading) that reifies the self. As Marías puts it, reading is "la cristalización de una experiencia que ignoraremos siempre fuera de su cristalización y en la que sin embargo podemos reconocernos" ("the crystallization of an experience that we will always ignore outside its crystallization and yet in which we are able to recognize ourselves") ("La huella del animal," *Literatura y fantasma* 168). Marías thus proposes the comprehensive integration of writer/text/reader based on the creative conjoining of all three. The text creates the illusion of an authentic world that is similar to external reality, and within this illusion, as Marías observes, "el lector sabe que ... hay inevitablemente atisbos de verdad" ("the reader knows that ... inevitably there are traces of truth") ("La huella del animal," *Literatura y fantasma* 168).

But reading ultimately has less to do with truth in relation to the world, or with what is important within the text itself, than with what each reader knows through individual experience. And while Marías has expressed concern over "incorrect" readings of his novels, and has affirmed the need for the reader to embrace the hermeneutic consciousness implicit in a literary text, he also understands that meaning is uncertain, changeable, and always elusive. Hence reading which seeks absolute authority offends against the multiple meanings always inherent in texts, whether intended by authors or imposed by readers.

Throughout his various columns on literature, Marías has consistently sought to define the bi-modal functioning of the literary text, and specifically of the novel. On the one hand, a literary work refers back to itself and reveals its transcendent authority through words that are not interchangeable. On the other hand, however, the novel can never be only about itself or its authority; it also exists in relation to reality outside of its linguistic make-up. For this reason, the reading and rereading of novels articulates a kind of hermeneutic superstructure through which meanings are constantly proposed and displaced. As Marías notes in *Negra espalda del tiempo*, "cada lectura altera [el libro], y en cambio no lo reescribe ninguna" (22) ("each reading changes it [the book], though none rewrites it" [*Dark Back of Time* 18]). Marías perceives the novel as an unstable site, but instability is regarded as a virtue which enables the complex confluence of the writer's creation and the reader's response. This confluence affirms the existential nature of both writing and reading, and ultimately gives to the literary text its unique standing.

II

Two Early Novels:
Los dominios del lobo and *Travesía del horizonte*

When asked in 2006 about the relationship between his second novel, *Travesía del horizonte* (1972) (*Voyage Along the Horizon*, 2006), and the general tendencies in Spanish fiction at the time of its publication, Marías promptly linked it to his first novel, *Los dominios del lobo* (1971) (*The Dominions of the Wolf*), and then located both outside the narrative mainstream in Spain. Indeed, he placed his first two works in a context of difference from important works of Spanish fiction of the 1960s and early 1970s that were lauded for their combination of stylistic experimentation and political antagonism toward Francoism. As Marías put it about his two novels: "(a) they were not at all autobiographical; (b) they were not 'experimental,' as was the trend with novels in those days; (c) they were not 'antinarratives,' another trend back then; (d) they were not set in Spain; (e) they were not set in the same era in which they were written; and (f) they had no particular 'message,' neither ideological nor political nor any other kind."[1] To a large degree, Marías confirms here what most critics and literary historians have perceived about his early writing: it bears little resemblance to other Spanish fiction and is vested largely with the traditions of foreign literatures. In both *Dominios* and *Travesía* Marías imbues his narrative with a large dose of English and American discourses (fiction and cinema). Hence his first two works embody what might fruitfully be termed "derivative innovation" within the history of the contemporary novel in Spain, an oxymoronic description that points to deep roots in other texts and that is highly pertinent, as we shall see, to Marías's early approach to his craft.

---

[1] "Eight Questions for Javier Marías," in Javier Marías, *Voyage Along the Horizon*, trans. Kristina Cordero (San Francisco: Believer Books, 2006), p. 182.

Los dominios del lobo (1971)

At first glance, *Los dominios del lobo* appears to be a loosely constructed novel, pieced together with multiple stories that remain largely disconnected from one another. The novel seems, in fact, constantly to be shifting gears, changing places, and moving unsteadily through time. *Dominios* follows seven main story lines extended spatially throughout the United States and temporally from 1861 to 1962.[2] The American Civil War, the Great Depression, and the gangster era of prohibition in the 1920s and 1930s gain prominence in the novel, while tenuous connections among characters and locations from different stories are marked by a thin sense of unity. This unity in fact seems in many ways to turn upon a fortuitous (and sometimes gratuitous) linking of characters who cross paths in a particular location (for example, the singer Terence Barr from one story and the drifter Osgood Perkins from another end up in the same prison in Alabama) or who have mutual acquaintances (for example, Susan Bedford in the Arthur Taeger segment had once been the young lover of Coleman Elwood from the Terence Barr story). Furthermore, characters and social contexts remain largely undeveloped in *Dominios*: there is scant psychological exploration of motives or consequences of characters' decisions to pursue one course of action or another, and little background is provided to anchor the work in complex historical circumstances. Indeed, the novel offers a myriad of fast-moving actions involving love, lust, violence, crime, and death that require the reader only to follow plots that never defy credibility, but often slip closer to melodrama than to the mimetic practices of realism.

However, at the heart of *Dominios* lies not what Dorrit Cohn has called the "mimesis of other minds"[3] commonly found in novelistic fiction—that is to say, the idea that characters think, feel, and perceive with the aid of a narrator

---

[2] The main story lines, developed in the ten principal segments into which the novel is divided, focus on the dissolution of the Taeger family in the 1920s; the travails of Osgood Perkins through many years of his life; the crimes of Patrick Rambeau (also known as San Patrick el Rural), a former slave, during the 1860s; the acting career of Arthur Taeger; the criminal career of Milt Taeger; the petty blackmail and swindling of Terence Barr; the duplicity of ex-convict Wes McMullan; the hard-boiled detective Andy Michen and his relation with Laura Lee, a singer kept by the criminal Milt Taeger. All of the stories are sutured together by coincidence, legacy, or space, though each can also stand by itself as a mini-representation of recurrent thematic concerns related to violence, treachery, criminal activity, and the general notion of social pathologies.

[3] Dorrit Cohn, *Transparent Minds: Narrative Modes for Presenting Consciousness in Fiction* (Princeton: Princeton University Press, 1978), p. 7.

who makes their private lives public. Instead, what shapes the work might felicitously be termed the "mimesis of other media," or the "mimesis of other genres." Indeed, the mimetic practices of *Dominios* can be directly linked to film, and more concretely to Hollywood cinema of the 1940s and 1950s. Put most succinctly, *Dominios* is a novel made of movies. Yet the impetus for writing *Dominios*, as well as the material used to construct it, entails more than the whimsical imitation of film or the playful rendering of character types from movies. As Marías himself has noted, both historical and biographical factors weigh prominently on the origin of the novel and insinuate themselves deeply into its execution.

Dominios in large part grew from Marías's youthful desire to infuse his writing with difference and newness. It indeed stood in 1969 as a radical departure from the immediate literary context of the late 1960s, from the larger traditions of novel writing in Spain, and from the dominant referential material of the Spanish novel of the time—Spain itself.[4] As Marías notes in the prologue to the 1987 edition of his work, "yo no deseaba escribir *necesariamente* sobre España ni *necesariamente* como un novelista español" ("I did not want to write *necessarily* about Spain nor *necessarily* as a Spanish novelist").[5] In other words, he sought unequivocally to distance himself (and thus to free himself) from "lo español." But for Marías, the idea of Spanishness was referentially complex. On the one hand, he set out to separate his writing from the generic traits of the Spanish novel of social realism, which had dominated fiction writing in Spain during the 1940s and 1950s but which had clearly begun to wane by the middle of the 1960s. At the same time, he chose to differentiate his work from the incipient stages of experimental fiction that by the late 1960s had taken hold in Spain (e.g., novels such as Juan Goytisolo's *Señas de identidad*, 1966, or Juan Benet's *Volverás*

---

[4] In his essay "Contar el misterio" published in 1996 (reprinted in *Literatura y fantasma*, Madrid: Alfaguara, 2001), Marías writes that *Dominios* appeared in May of 1971 rather than in March of that year because of strong disagreement between two directors of the publishing house (Edhasa) about the quality of the work. As Marías tells it, Rosa Regás expressed great enthusiasm for the work, while Félix Grande strongly opposed it. Marías cites a letter written by Grande in which the director defends an author with a realist approach to writing and denounces Marías: "En una sola página de este escritor hay más literatura de la que escribirá Javier Marías en toda la vida" ("On a single page of this writer there is more literature than Javier Marías will write in his entire life") (118). Marías recalls that when the novel was published, the publicity poster for his work described him as "El autor novel más polémico del año" ("The most polemical author of the year") (118).

[5] Javier Marías, *Los dominios del lobo* (Madrid: Alfaguara, 1999), p. 15.

a Región, 1967) with an emphasis on narrative fragmentation, the contingencies of memory, and the often labyrinthine uses of language. On the other hand, however, Spain as the foundational material for both realistic and experimental fiction informed the negative point of reference for Marías ("yo no deseaba escribir *necesariamente* sobre España"). Hence not only does Marías set the plot of *Dominios* spatially outside of Spain, he populates the novel with non-Hispanic characters who would have no apparent reason even to know Spanish as a language. In brief, Marías proposes to unmoor *Dominios* from all that might be perceived as traditionally Spanish, as well as from all that might be understood referentially within the political and historical context of Francoist Spain.

As readers we of course do not permit authors to restrict our perceptions of their writing, in particular as we work through the process of sense-making. What authors have declared (or even hinted at) about their work extrinsically may become pertinent within a particular strategy of reading, but it may not become determinant. Indeed, "the intentional fallacy," formulated in 1946 by Wimsatt and Beardsley and viewed now as one of the cornerstones of modern criticism, argues persuasively against using authorial interventions to define textual meanings.[6] Nonetheless, the biographical component at the point of origin of a work cannot be discarded out of hand, especially in those instances (as occurs with *Dominios*) where external intention is authenticated through textual achievement.

For example, to confirm that Marías eschews a Spanish focus in *Dominios* (as he proclaims in his prologue) we need simply read the novel, perceive the characters, and understand the plot. Quite clearly, he creates a novelistic world set in America and populated with Americans. What draws attention to the representation of America in particular, however, stems from character types largely familiar but only vaguely present in American society itself. And it is here where the external impetus of the novel converges with the construction of the text, for we are able to link the narrative lines of the work to prototypical Hollywood movies of the 1940s and 1950s, especially the detective and gangster films associated with *noir* cinema of this period.[7] In

---

[6] See W.K. Wimsatt, Jr and Monroe C. Beardsley, "The Intentional Fallacy," in Walter Sutton and Richard Foster, eds, *Modern Criticism: Theory and Practice* (New York: Odyssey Press, 1963), pp. 248–57.

[7] Numerous books have been written on *noir*, gangster, and detective cinema (with much overlap among the three). See, for example, Martin Rubin, *Thrillers* (Cambridge: Cambridge University Press, 1999); Jack Shadoian, *Dreams and Dead Ends: The American Gangster Film* (Oxford: Oxford University Press, 2003); and Ian Cameron, ed., *The Book of Film Noir* (New York: Continuum, 1993).

fact, Marías himself has disclosed that the composition of the entire novel (its conception, its plots, its characters, and the adequacy of its representations) turns upon his visit to Paris in the summer of 1969, where he wrote much of *Dominios* at the same time that he viewed eighty-five movies over a six-week period at the Cinémathèque Henri Langlois.[8] As Marías sees the novel, "fue una mezcla de homenaje y parodia del cine americano de los años cuarenta y cincuenta, y decidí que para escribirla debía estar en permanente y exhaustivo contacto con el material elegido como fuente de inspiración" ("it was a mixture of homage and parody of American film of the 1940s and 1950s, and I decided that, in order to write it, I ought to be in permanent and exhaustive contact with the material I had chosen as the source of inspiration").[9] The critical question, however, is not what scene here or character there in the novel is derived from a particular movie—in fact, while several movies play a key role in the novel, the characters are generally composite figures recognizable as types (such as the *femme fatale*, the detective, the ex-convict, the gangster). Rather, it is important to determine how the novel accumulates meaning in the context of its cinematic foundation and within the broader social paradigms (for example, those related to morality, violence, crime, disintegration of the family) that it addresses.

The intense awareness of the contingencies of storytelling, which lies at the heart of all of Marías's fiction, shapes both the narrative and social foundation of *Dominios*. To some extent, *Dominios* may be viewed as a metafictional novel:[10] it reveals various degrees of awareness of its own creation and of the filmic tradition on which it is constructed, which in turn allows it to slip in and out of self-consciousness and establish intertextual associations. Marías even absorbs into his narrative the playful ambiguity of traditional metafiction through which the reader at first is led to believe that a particular narrative segment forms part of the "reality" forged by the text,

---

[8] For details about Marías's trip to Paris in 1969 to view movies and work on the manuscript of *Dominios*, see the prologue to the 1987 edition of *Dominios*, also included in the 1999 edition used here.

[9] Javier Marías, "Todos los días llegan," in *Donde todo ha sucedido. Al salir del cine* (Barcelona: Círculo de Lectores, 2005), p. 29. In this same essay Marías names several movies and sources for his novel, including the following films (some of which are from the 1960s): *The Hustler, Sweet Bird of Youth, From the Terrace, Gone With the Wind, North by Northwest, Ruby Gentry, Splendor in the Grass,* and *Kaleidoscope*.

[10] For a study of metafiction in the postwar Spanish novel, see Robert Spires's *Beyond the Metafictional Mode* (Lexington, KY: University Press of Kentucky, 1984). For a look at more recent metafictional and self-conscious writing in Spain, see Samuel Amago, *True Lies* (Lewisburg, PA: Bucknell University Press, 2006).

only to discover that the segment represents a literary commingling of life and film. Such is the case, for example, in the segments on the actors Arthur Taeger and Glenda Greeves. During the course of their story, their marriage and subsequent marital strife bleeds into the film they are making, *Muerte en el bosque*, which portrays the marriage of an older man (Lem Wainscott) to a young and beautiful woman (Virginia). In the movie, an ex-convict, Wes McMullan, insinuates himself into the arms of Virginia and manipulates her husband into murdering a suspected lover of Virginia. Not only does the line between reality and fiction blur in this instance (as readers, we are not informed that the Wes/Virginia story is in fact a movie until the very end of the segment), but the entire story forms an extrinsic parallel with Hollywood genre films of the 1940s such as *Double Indemnity* (1944) and *The Postman Always Rings Twice* (1946) and their portrayal of the archetypical *femme fatale*.[11] The reality/fiction/film connection is brought to the fore in this instance through the artifice of storytelling, but its efficacy demands an intertextual component that assumes certain reader competencies in the traditions of cinema (most importantly, familiarity with American movies, generic characters, and plots). The result here, as elsewhere in the novel, entails parody within homage as well as the blending of fiction and reality to show how each can be used to represent and give meaning to the other.

The biographical link between storytelling and movies that occupied a large part of Marías's youth also remains pertinent to the writing of *Dominios*. Not only did Marías learn and refine the art of storytelling by watching movies, but he actually performed storytelling as a result of the movies that he saw. His brother Miguel points out that when Javier was young he practiced "el perdido hábito de contar las películas vistas a los amigos" ("The lost habit of telling about the movies that one has seen to friends") ("El arte de recorder," *Donde todo ha sucedido* 19), while Javier himself attests to the critical significance of performing films through the art of "retelling" them: "Yo veía por lo menos dos películas a la semana durante la infancia, y sin duda uno de mis primeros ejercicios narrativos era contar a mis amigos del colegio, los lunes, las historias que habían pasado ante mis ojos el domingo o el sábado: 'Y entonces va el malo y le dice al bueno que se largue, porque si no ...'. Los relatos eran desde luego pedestres, pero no dejaban de exigir una cierta ordenación mental, necesaria, siempre para contar" ("I saw

---

11 For an overview of the tradition of the *femme fatal* see E. Ann Kaplan, ed., *Women in Film Noir. New Edition* (London: British Film Institute, 1998). For a broader exploration of women in *noir* films, see Helen Hanson, *Hollywood Heroines: Women in Film Noir and the Female Gothic Film* (London: I.B. Tauris, 2007).

at least two movies per week when I was young, and without doubt one of my first narrative exercises was to tell my friends at school, on Mondays, the stories that had passed before my eyes on Sunday or Saturday: 'Then the bad guy goes and tells the good guy to get out, because if he doesn't …'. The stories were of course pedestrian, but they did demand a certain mental ordering, which is always necessary in storytelling") ("Todos los días llegan," *Donde todo ha sucedido* 27–28).

The explicit awareness of stories and their telling resonates throughout *Dominios*. Above all, the novel relies on a large number of small stories to give it a loose structure and broad coherence, and in doing so places emphasis on "happening" rather than on character development. It is not simply that *Dominios* consists of an assemblage of stories, however, but also that characters often relate to one another and perceive the world through the stories they tell. In the segment on Osgood Perkins and Owen MacPherson, for example, the older MacPherson "le contó [a Osgood] otras muchas historias" ("told [Osgood] many other stories") (*Dominios* 56) in order to pass the time and to teach his young friend about life. Osgood is pleased to listen to his mentor ("[las historias] le encantaban y gozaba con ellas como con pocas cosas") ("[the stories] delighted Osgood and he enjoyed them like few other things") (*Dominios* 57), but he is reticent to embrace their truth value: "le parecían demasiado fantasiosas" ("they seemed too fanciful to him") (*Dominios* 57). Still, Osgood (as well as the reader of *Dominios*) understands that, while the stories may muddle the edges of the real, they effectively stand in for life and offer useful lessons about the truths of storytelling and the pleasures of listening.

In other segments of the novel "telling" also plays a central role. For example, the manipulative *femme fatale* Susan Bedford seeks to break up the marriage of film stars Arthur Traeger and Glenda Greeves, luring Arthur into her confidence by urging him to narrate his concerns: "Ven, siéntate aquí, a mi lado, y cuéntame tus problemas" ("Come, sit here by my side, and tell me your problems") (*Dominios* 179). In another segment the young and beautiful wife of Lem Wainscott flirts with farmhand Wes McMullan and appeals to him, "Cuénteme algo de usted" ("Tell me something about yourself") (*Dominios* 200); while in the Osgood Perkins segment an old prisoner, on his deathbed, "les contó [a Osgood y a MacPherson] con dificultad, una historia interesante" ("told them [Osgood and MacPherson], with much difficulty, an interesting story") (*Dominios* 51). While the novel thus persistently reveals an awareness of narration as a way of shaping the world for a variety of uses (and while, as we have seen, it is composed of the accumulation of separate stories which occasionally—and loosely—connect to one another), it further brings storytelling to the fore by alluding to how stories might be understood.

As the narrator notes concerning Owen MacPherson, "Todas esas historias constituían la pasión favorita del Viejo, que aseguraba una y otra vez que eran verídicas, pero al mismo tiempo, se reía de una forma que indicaba que no lo eran" ("All of those stories constituted the favorite passion of the old man, who repeatedly asserted that they were truthful, but at the same time, he laughed in a way that indicated they were not") (*Dominios* 57).

Such a position underpins the whole of *Dominios*, of course (implied in the oxymoronic paradigm of all storytelling of "it was and it was not"), but more narrowly underscores the complex and convoluted referential base of the novel through which film gives clear intertextual substance to the narrative and implicit intertextual direction to the reader. What is more, these films are derived primarily from hard-boiled detective fiction of the 1920s and 1930s, with its well-known cast of characters and generic forms of behavior.[12] Hence Marías's novel moves through amorphous and concrete layers of representation linked to other films and other novels which project stylized characters from literary and filmic history as well as socially recognizable ones. *Dominios* thus becomes in synthetic form (synthesis here in its double meaning of artifice and hybrid) a story woven of stories. Importantly, however, it is neither fully an exercise in parody nor an outright deconstruction of realistic paradigms of novel-writing. As a result, *Dominios* can be perceived through receding degrees of reality and fiction that "delight the reader" (as with the stories that Owen MacPherson tells Osgood Perkins) and also represent broad social themes prevalent in the United States over a period of one hundred years as seen and heard in Hollywood movies.

The social tableau that Marías constructs in *Dominios* depends upon two closely related aspects of the films on which the novel rests: (1) the reception of these films by the public and the meanings and iconography that have already gained social recognition; (2) the specific elements of social behavior that are represented. First of all, there exists in *Dominios* an implied text-reader whose ability to give meaning to the narrative correlates closely with knowledge of movies. Indeed, without the knowledge of an informed reader, the richness of meanings in the novel can only be diminished. Hence the social circulation of *noir* and gangster films in Spain (and beyond) is critical not only to Marías's explicit intention to make a novel out of movies, but

---

12 For an overview of hard-boiled detective novels of this period, as well as their relationship to movies, see Leonard Cassuto, *Hard-boiled Sentimentality: the Secret History of American Crime Stories* (New York: Columbia University Press, 2009); also see John T. Irwin, *Unless the Threat of Death is Behind Them: Hard-boiled Fiction and Film Noir* (Baltimore: Johns Hopkins University Press, 2006).

also to the insinuation of these films into social and intellectual practices of Marías's generation. In other words, Marías assumes in *Dominios* that his readers will be familiar with the artistic media and narrative forms that are embedded in its core. In this respect it might be said that the Hollywood movies of the 1940s and 1950s are to Marías's real and implied readers what the *novela rosa* (romance novel) was to young women in Spain during the 1930s and 1940s.

As Spanish novelist Carmen Martín Gaite (1925–2000) has pointed out, romance novels were among the most popular works of fiction during her youth and served both as a form of escape for teen-age girls as well as an artifice from which codes of social behavior were derived and promulgated. In her metafictional novel *El cuarto de atrás* (*The Back Room*, 1978), when the main character Carmen sets out to write a fantastic novel guided by Tzvetan Todorov's theoretical book *The Fantastic: A Structural Approach to a Literary Genre*, her reflections on writing are broadly framed by the romance novel. *El cuarto* itself turns upon standard romance formulas (including the generic ambience of "it was a dark and stormy night" and the arrival of a mysterious gentleman), but it is the actual inscription of the romance into social mores and perceptions of her generation that Carmen emphasizes: "Aquel verano releí también muchas novelas rosa, es muy importante el papel que jugaron las novelas rosa en la formación de las chicas de los años cuarenta" ("That summer I also reread several romance novels, the role that romance novels played in the development of girls during the forties is very important").[13]

In similar fashion, as we have seen, Marías has frequently commented on the importance of movies to his generation as a way of perceiving the world and, in the case of Marías himself in *Dominios*, as a way of writing a novel. As he notes in "Todos los días llegan," "Los nacidos en los años cuarenta y cincuenta ... sabíamos que narrativamente hablando debíamos tanto a la literatura como al cine, aunque nos valiéramos de las palabras en nuestra tarea" ("Those of us born in the forties and fifties ... knew that, from a narrative perspective, we owed as much to literature as to film, even though we drew upon words in our work") (*Donde todo ha sucedido* 27). Marías's emphasis here on his debt to film, with implications for the style and technique of his narrative, clearly links writing to the artistic terrain of filmmaking. In the prologue to the novel, however, Marías broadens the cinematic influence to underscore the absence of Spanishness and to include the

---

[13] Carmen Martín Gaite, *El cuarto de atrás* (Barcelona: Destino, 1981), p. 138.

role of his own experiences in the writing of *Dominios*: "[Otros críticos y escritores] me reprocharon que no me ocupara de la cruda realidad española y que no me basara en mi mundo y en mis experiencias personales, sino en un mundo ficticio y ajeno al nuestro. La verdad es que a mis diecisiete o dieciocho años casi no tenía más experiencias que las adquiridas en la butaca de un cine o leyendo en un sillón" (["Other writers and critics] reproached me for not concerning myself with the harsh reality of Spain and for not basing my writing on my world and my personal experiences, but rather on a fictitious world that was alien to our own. The truth is that at the age of seventeen or eighteen I barely had experiences other than those acquired in the seat of a movie theater or reading in an armchair") ("Prólogo," *Dominios* 14).

If *Dominios* thus represents Marías's "experience" (though clearly his real-life experience at the age of eighteen extended far beyond watching movies), it also portrays certain social issues filtered, quite literally, through a lens. Indeed, the novel engages social problems as a re-presentation of Hollywood, whose directors during the 1930s through the 1940s often sought to portray and challenge the array of myths that constitute the great American dream—above all, the foundational myths of advancement and success in America through which anything could be achieved with honesty and individual effort. *Dominios* begins with one of the prominent themes of American films of the 1940s, the disintegration of the family as the cornerstone of society. The Taeger family saga occupies the first segment of the novel, and in it we witness the physical and moral dissolution of a prominent family in Pittsburgh through scandal, suicide, and murder. As occurs throughout the novel, this first segment is clotted with plots and characters and rarely stops to explore the destructive social and individual forces that tear the family apart. *Dominios* never aspires to social inquiry, but it does lay out a social grid that represents Hollywood's view of a young America already corrupt and incontinent by the 1930s and overlaid with immorality.

This vision of America is prominently displayed in each of the stories, with the concurrent impingement of violence onto the very soul of American life. In nearly every case Marías portrays the pessimism and alienation of Hollywood movies, with the overarching sense of moral ambiguity that gnaws at traditional myths of hope built upon an open horizon of expectations. Indeed, *Dominios* most often portrays the obverse of the American dream, revealing a rampant corruption of ideals that diminish Horace Greeley's well known admonition for success in America (with its literal spatial implications and metaphorical call to action) of "Go West, young man." In fact, to a large degree in *Dominios*, the idea of self-advancement not only betrays the American values of hard work, persistence, and honesty, but explicitly reveals them as a fraud.

This is exemplified in all of the stories (which of course are rooted in movie plots), from the young song writer Terence Barr, who extorts money from nearly everyone he works with and eventually ends up in prison for murder, to the ex-convict Wes McMullan, who works at a farm in Minnesota where he contrives a plot that leads to deception and murder. Milt Taeger becomes a famous and feared gangster; Osgood Perkins works as a pool hustler and minor thief before killing his boss; San Patrick el Rural murders and plunders during the Civil War before he himself is killed; Arthur Taeger helps his brother Ed escape charges of beating his wife to death. In these and other stories of the novel a quest for advancement and for the fulfillment of desire reveals a destructive mendacity that begets a dispassionate sense of bleakness. An America that is obsessed with striking gold (literally for San Patrick el Rural in the nineteenth century and for Osgood Perkins in the twentieth—hence the plot connection between the two) instead becomes in *Dominios* an America where the incitement of individual triumph creates moral strains, duplicity, and crime. Marías's representation of American films suggests his own sense of how the movies work and come to bear meaning—they are fast-moving stories that persistently reveal the underside of the success myth. As Jack Shadoian has noted, Hollywood movies of this period portray "the urge for [success], the fear of it, and the consequences both having it and not having it entail" (*Dreams and Dead Ends* 6). In Marías's view, it seems clear, the consequences are not only troubling but dark and destructive.

Much of the darkness grows not only from the moral ambiguity or the unambiguous immorality that pervades the stories of *Dominios*, but also from the pervasive violence that serves as a synecdoche for what troubles American society. There are two broad inducements to violence in the novel: (1) the machinations of the *femme fatale*, who appears in several stories of *Dominios*; (2) the need for self-advancement that is generally portrayed as a virulent rather than progressive compulsion in individual characters. The *femme fatale*, of course, stands as one of the most recognizable figures in the Hollywood films whose story Marías retells in *Dominios*. Endowed with erotic power to draw the male protagonist toward self-destruction, and able to lure him into desiring, possessing and pleasing her, this female character is portrayed as typically disingenuous and deceitful in *Dominios*. In the Wes McMullan story, for example, the young wife of Lem Wainscott cultivates the jealousy of her older husband while seducing a young farmhand, only to kill the young man when he threatens to blackmail her. When Wes, who has been recently released from prison, arrives to work at the farm, he soon understands the plot of his story and concocts a new plot that will lead both to the death of another family member, the conviction of Virginia's husband for the murder, and his own ascension into the arms of the soon to be available Virginia.

Likewise, in the final segment of the novel, Laura Lee's beauty and apparent innocence are revealed as a deceit: she is closely kept by the gangster Milt Taeger but her seduction of detective Andy Michen leads to the violent killing of Michen and several others. In another of the stories, Owen MacPherson most succinctly spells out the danger of women: "Siempre te quitan todo, lo consiguen todo de ti, te retienen en contra de tu voluntad, y todo ¿por qué? Sólo porque tienen pechos" ("They always take everything, they get everything from you, they hold on to you against your will. And why? Only because they have breasts") (*Dominios* 49). In brief, the women of Hollywood in the 1930s and 1940s and the women of *Dominios* share a highly sexualized power often linked to a disingenuous toughness that is at once seductive and dangerous.

Marías captures the behavior of the *femme fatale* throughout *Dominios* and ties it closely to the persistence of violence in his novel. What is most striking about Marías's portrayal of violence, however, is not the sheer quantity of it (there are numerous beatings and murders in nearly every story), but rather the narrator's insouciant representation of it as merely a natural part of the story itself, as if violence were embedded in the life of the characters and thus the stories about them as they inevitably need to be told. For this reason, Marías closely associates the fracturing of the American dream with the moral dislocation that runs throughout *Dominios*. Characters do not stop to internalize or contemplate what they have done, while the narrator offers scant reflection on their actions. Rather, violence appears as a primitive but direct means of communication in a society where dishonesty and deceit have become normal, even expected. Milt Taeger murders his competitor in the crime business and mutilates his body; Osgood Perkins kills his boss and flees his job at a pool hall; Ted Taeger murders his wife; San Patrick shoots young women and others without hesitation or remorse. None of the murders are justified nor are any condemned in the novel through moral discussion or philosophical debate—they serve rather as a symptom of a culture where the goal of pulling oneself up is paramount and where the achievement of status and power often trumps restrictions placed on the means to gain them.

The Hollywood movies of the 1930s and 1940s sensed the peril in the myths of American culture, and Marías captures this peril faithfully and repeatedly throughout his novel. Indeed, the movie violence that becomes the novel violence of *Dominios* represents Marías's retelling of his way of seeing and interpreting his "experience" of the movies. While this second-order emplotment from movie to novel has little to do with the social circumstances of Spain, it does provide a paradigm through which fiction becomes the mediating structure that, as Paul Ricoeur has written about narrative in general, "adds something to the world which was not previously there."[14]

Travesía del horizonte (1972)

The construction of *Dominios* largely from Hollywood films makes it unique among Marías's novels, though the presence and importance of movies remains visible in much of his later writing as well. However, the more general concern in *Dominios* with drawing other genres and plots into its narrative, and with the concurrent impositions on the reader to make intertextual associations and explore the processes of storytelling, resonates deeply in *Travesía del horizonte*. Indeed, Marías offers in his second novel a familiar storytelling paradigm: a small group of characters (three in this instance) gather to listen to the reading of a novel written by Edward Ellis, a friend of one of the characters. The story that unfolds in the novel then becomes the main part of the work that we are reading. In this way, Marías creates in *Travesía* two distinct but closely related narratives: (1) an inner novel with its own narrator and set of characters; (2) an outer or frame novel with characters and a narrator whose function is primarily (though not exclusively) to listen and react to the inner novel—to comment on its plot, wonder aloud about its truth, and speculate on its unresolved ambiguities. The inner novel, not yet published, happens to bear the title *La travesía del horizonte*, and the characters who inhabit this novel are based on many figures who exist in the world of the outer novel (*Travesía del horizonte*).[15] This blending of spheres of fictionality, of characters who cross from one fictional plain to another, coupled with the intense interest in storytelling as a way of understanding the world, constitute the metafictional base of Marías's novel and provide as well the hermeneutic tools for exploring its meanings.

Marías is not content in *Travesía* simply to commingle fictional worlds intrinsically, so that the potential meaning of each is shaped by its contextualization within the other. In this instance, *Travesía* as a whole (and *La travesía* in particular) is further bracketed by the broad generic profile of both the adventure and detective novel.[16] Indeed, Marías creates in *Travesía*

---

[14] Paul Ricoeur, *Time and Narrative*, trans. Kathleen Blamey and David Pellauer, Vol II (Chicago: University of Chicago Press, 1985), p. 20.

[15] The only difference between the title of Marías's novel and the inner novel written by the fictional character, Edward Ellis, is the article "La." The English translation does not account for this difference.

[16] In an interview that accompanies the English translation, Marías discusses a range of works that he had been reading and how they influenced the writing of *Travesía*. He

an implicit reader in largely explicit fashion: the inner novel of adventure and mystery requires the readers (listeners) from the outer novel (and thus the real reader as well) to make intertextual associations that shape expectations about how the novel will develop—e.g., the adventurer will complete his journey or be thwarted in his attempts; the mystery will be solved and loose ends tied together in the traditional movement of detective fiction toward closure. In this sense *Travesía* calls forth the same intertextual strategies used in *Los dominios del lobo*, which to a large degree demands reader knowledge of other texts (Hollywood movies, as we have seen) in order to comprehend fully the multiple materials used to construct the narrative and give it meaning beyond its immediate social and historical context of twentieth-century Spain.

The plot of *Travesía* is filled with a large number of small stories. Put simply, the novel relates the following: an unnamed narrator joins with a literary scholar known only as Miss Bunnage to meet at the home of Holden Branshaw, who is in possession of the manuscript of a novel (*La travesía del horizonte*) written by his deceased friend, Edward Ellis. The novel tells the story of a well known author named Victor Arledge, who abruptly abandoned his writing in 1904 following a voyage on the ship *Tallahassee* with a group of other writers and scientists who planned to journey to the South Pole. Branshaw reads the manuscript aloud over the course of two days, though Miss Bunnage unexpectedly dies after the first day and only the narrator is present to hear the complete reading of the novel.

The inner novel follows the "happenings" (as Patricia Spacks calls the multiple actions of adventure stories)[17] of the passengers and crew aboard the *Tallahassee*. The two principal characters, Victor Arledge and Joseph Dunhill Kerrigan (adventurer and leader of the expedition), become the focal point of the narrative through a series of plot machinations that echo narrative paradigms of nineteenth-century adventure and detective fiction. Arledge is obsessed with finding out more about the mysterious kidnapping several

---

specifically mentions Joseph Conrad, Henry James, and Arthur Conan Doyle. See Javier Marías, *Voyage Along the Horizon* (San Francisco: Believer Books, 2006), pp. 175–76. Alexis Grohmann also discusses the influence of Marías's reading of other authors in his writing of *Travesía*, and places special emphasis on the relationship of the novel with Henry James's *The Turn of the Screw* and *The Aspern Papers*. See Grohmann, *Coming Into One's Own: The Novelistic Development of Javier Marías* (Amsterdam and New York: Rodopi, 2002), pp. 36–49.

17 Patricia Meyer Spacks, *Novel Beginnings: Experiments in Eighteenth-Century English Fiction* (New Haven and London: Yale University Press, 2006). See specifically her chapter on the adventure novel, pp. 28-58.

months earlier of Hugh Everett Bayham, who is now one of the passengers aboard the ship. Arledge had learned of Bayham's kidnapping in a letter from a British friend and fellow writer, Esmond Handle. Bayham himself had related the curious story of his kidnapping to Handle, explaining how he was taken to Scotland one night following a musical performance in London. After being sequestered for four days in a house, where he was treated gruffly by his kidnappers (though he was not harmed) and seduced by a young woman, he was set free and managed to return to London. There remain many gaps in Bayham's story, and Arledge anticipates that during the voyage he will have the opportunity to query Bayham about the kidnapping and thus satisfy his own curiosity about the whole of his fellow passenger's experience.

For his part, Kerrigan had set out to organize the expedition for "hombres y mujeres de letras"[18] ("men and women of letters" [*Voyage* 18]) as well as for a group of scientists who would conduct research in Antarctica.[19] Through a series of stories Kerrigan's life of adventure prior to the expedition comes to light—primarily his stealing, smuggling, and murderous conduct throughout the world, his gradual movement toward a law-abiding life after he marries the wife of one of his victims, and finally the death of his wife and his preparation for the present journey on the *Tallahassee*. On board the ship, however, he has again resorted to his violent behavior of the past. He is charged with throwing a passenger overboard, stabbing the captain of the ship, and killing the boatswain. He manages to escape from the ship, but not before telling Arledge about much of his life as a way of justifying his violent behavior. The expedition ends long before it completes its intended journey, thus frustrating the original quest of the passengers to experience their planned adventure. Kerrigan disappears from the narrative in flight from the law, while the mystery of Bayham's kidnapping remains unresolved. Arledge decides to live the remaining years of his life in seclusion with a distant relative, never to write again.

Storytelling often overwhelms the narrative of *Travesía*. At its simplest, it is the point of convergence for various plots and numerous happenings as characters tell and listen to stories. In the inner novel, the story of Kerrigan's expedition and Arledge's quest to uncover the mystery surrounding Bayham are recounted through multiple narrations, while the entire impetus for the outer novel stems from Edward Ellis's desire to investigate and narrate what

---

[18] Javier Marías, *Travesía del horizonte* (Madrid: Punta de Lectura, 2001), p. 29.

[19] In some instances, where the translation of *Travesía* by Kristina Cordero takes flight from the original text, I will use my own translation and so indicate in the text.

led Arledge to a life of isolation. Storytelling is the way in which many of the passengers on the ship earn their living (i.e., they are professional writers); it serves at various points as a means to clarify mysteries as well as to further obfuscate them; it is used to justify actions in the past; it serves as a source of pleasure and delight for tellers as well as for listeners; it allows for a prescriptive reflection in the novel on how narrative ought to be composed and used as an instrument for social and ethical behavior. In other words, while at various points along the way *Travesía* may be perceived as being about many things (adventure, crime, violence, honor, and love, to name only a few), these are always circumscribed by the explicit or implicit awareness within the novel of how they are shaped by narration and storytelling. This narrative framing obtains not only intrinsically, through the use and scrutiny of stories, but also extrinsically through the appropriation of other narrative traditions and the expectation that readers will know and understand these traditions as they make their own journey through the novel.

At the heart of *Travesía*, then, lies a mystery built around an adventure—stories derived from two literary genres of the nineteenth century that fascinated Marías when he was writing his work.[20] The mystery explored in *Travesía* is twofold, but it turns primarily on a single character: first, Victor Arledge's persistent tracking of Bayham in order to draw from him the untold story of his kidnapping; second, the subsequent tracking of Victor Arledge by Edward Ellis in order to learn how he lived the final years of his life. Both of these mysteries are embedded components of the inner and outer novels of *Travesía*, and both advance the structure and plot of the work. More importantly, both become critical components of the purposeful unsettledness that characterizes every aspect of *Travesía*, in which omission of information and irresolution of plot subvert the traditions of mystery in narrative fiction and Hollywood cinema that have long captivated Marías's imagination.

Coupled with the mysteries of *Travesía*, the adventure segment of the novel clearly moves to the fore early in chapter two, with the reading of *La travesía* by Holden Branshaw. In addition to the paradigmatic structure of the journey, *Travesía* as a whole is built on the concept of narrative speed. It contains many characters and stories set in a wide range of spaces (e.g., London, Scotland, Marseille, Alexandria, Tangier), and it rarely lingers for detailed description or psychological exploration. Hence it does not aspire to

---

[20] It should be pointed out that Marías has always been open to discussing the influences on his work, especially those from English literature. Concerning the influence of the mystery novel and Conan Doyle, Marías has noted that for *Travesía* he sees the presence of Sherlock Holmes by way of William Wilder's movie, *The Private Life of Sherlock Holmes* (1970). See "Eight Questions" in *Voyage Along the Horizon*, p. 175.

realism through traditional forms of mimetic adequacy, nor does it engage the fantastic or the exotic as a challenge to the real. Instead, as Patricia Spacks notes about the adventure novel in general, Marías's stories in *Travesía* "gesture at events without inviting readers to believe in them" (*Novel Beginnings* 34). *Travesía* achieves this less through the intricacy of its plot or characters than through the sheer abundance of examples and the constant association with other stories and other texts.

Importantly, however, *Travesía* also gestures at the generic paradigms of both the adventure and detective novel rather than attempt to reproduce them—hence the split-referencing in the novel between the world of other texts and the world of its own text. While *Travesía* depends upon the reader's familiarity with these generic paradigms, and therefore on the reader's expectations concerning the development and resolution of problems posed by these paradigms, it withdraws from embracing them fully. For example, in the principal adventure story of the novel in which Joseph Kerrigan organizes and leads the expedition to Antarctica, Marías clearly grasps that much can happen to a single individual. He thus builds a story with many sub-plots around Kerrigan's life as an intrepid adventurer, but he also shows in Kerrigan's story that sequencing matters more than causality. Furthermore, and in contrast to what the reader of adventure fiction has come to anticipate, the implicit quest myth of the adventure itself in *Travesía* does not proceed toward an end but simply loses steam and stops. This is true both for the quest itself and for the narrative that has moved it forward—i.e., Kerrigan disappears and the *Tallahassee* never completes its voyage. But the story of Kerrigan's journey has as much to do with storytelling as it does with which stories are actually told, and it sets out to remind the reader of how stories may be used to persuade, to instruct, and to delight—the most traditional functions of narration. As the narrator notes concerning Arledge's appreciation for Kerrigan and his narrative skills:

> Poco sabía [Arledge] de él [Kerrigan], pero su conversación, y más aún los relatos con que le obsequiaba, expuestos siempre de la manera más abstracta que pueda concebirse y sin localizar nunca ni en el tiempo ni en el espacio, representaban para Arledge un libro interminable de aventuras y peligros que hacía revivir con toda intensidad las emociones suscitadas por sus lecturas de infancia; y la imaginación de Arledge, a falta de datos concretos que le permitieran situar sus andanzas en algún punto determinado del globo, le presentaba la audaz figura de Kerrigan en los más variados escenarios o atuendos. (*Travesía* 36)

> He really didn't know very much about Kerrigan, but his conversation, not to mention the little tales he occasionally told, always in the most abstract

form imaginable, unidentifiable in time and space, were for Arledge an endless book of adventure and peril that allowed him to relive the same intense emotions that he had felt while reading his very first books as a child. Often lacking the precise facts that would have allowed him to situate Kerrigan's stories in some specific place in the world, Arledge actually preferred to envision the captain in the most wildly varied situations and uniforms. (*Voyage* 23)

Kerrigan later narrates the story of his life to Arledge (who will then re-narrate it to some of the passengers), but it is a story that defers an end in the same way that the principal story related to Arledge and Bayham also refuses closure, which in turn reflects the open-ended story of *Travesía* as a whole.

It is in the mystery narrative of *Travesía*, however, where Marías most fully limns the principles and parameters of his own sense of storytelling. On the one hand, he is fully aware of the traditional resolution generally demanded by the detective story, especially, as he has pointed out, in the stories of Conan Doyle. When Sherlock Holmes is confronted with a crime to be solved (often times a murder) he draws upon the recently developed tools of forensic science to scrutinize at close range the clues already available, discovers new clues along the way, and deduces a conclusion that satisfies the reader's expectation of closure as well as society's demand for justice.[21] On the other hand, however, Marías is more pointedly directed by indecisiveness in his own mystery stories and would no doubt embrace Anthony Trollope's quote about Wilkie Collins's early detective novel, *The Woman in White*: "The author seems always to be warning me to remember that a woman disappeared from the road just fifteen yards beyond the fourth milestone. One is constrained by mysteries and hemmed in by difficulties, knowing, however, that the mysteries will be made clear, and the difficulties overcome at the end of the third volume. Such work gives me no pleasure."[22]

Marías's disaffection with resolution and his embrace of uncertainty in *Travesía* grows to a large degree from his reading of Henry James. He notes, for example, that "I was influenced by James stylistically but also by the atmosphere of his novels" ("Eight Questions," *Voyage* 175). Further in line with James, Marías offers a perspective on literature in *Travesía* that unmoors storytelling from the teleological traditions of realism, where full representa-

---

[21] For an excellent overview of the detective story in Victorian fiction (including Conan Doyle), see Ronald R. Thomas, "Detection in the Victorian Novel," in Deirdre David, ed., *The Cambridge Companion to the Victorian Novel* (Cambridge: Cambridge University Press, 2001), pp. 169–91.

[22] Cited in Ronald Thomas, "Detection in the Victorian Novel," p. 180.

tion of the external world is possible and conclusions about it desirable. In contrast, he offers throughout his novel an overriding sense of unsettledness and ambiguity that guides our understanding both of the world and of storytelling. Of course, ambiguity can appear in fiction in many forms and for many reasons, and it may emerge from the formal elements of narrative technique as well as from a broad philosophical base of epistemological skepticism.[23] It may be located primarily in the reader and be seen as a temporary response to a mysterious occurrence, as with Todorov's definition of the fantastic,[24] or it may be a product of the challenges faced when authors attempt to understand and write about the world outside of the text, as in Juan Benet's evocation of the "zone of shadows." As Benet (one of the writers whom Marías most admires, and who helped Marías get his first novel published in Spain) puts it: "[E]n un momento determinado, una combinación casi fortuita de palabras o ideas le llev[a] [al escritor] a una zona de sombra, no sólo donde el conocimiento no ha entrado todavía, sino ante el cual se detiene y suspende toda actividad. Eso es el misterio. Entonces es posible que elija su campo, para dirigirse en lo sucesivo … en la dirección opuesta a la del saber" ("At a particular point, an almost fortuitous combination of words or ideas takes [the writer] into a zone of shadow, not only where knowledge has not yet entered, but in the face of which he stops and suspends all activity. That is mystery. It is then possible for him to choose his terrain and make his way from then on. … in the direction opposite of knowing") (50).[25] What is clear in *Travesía*, however, is that the "zone of shadow" does not emerge from postmodern disillusion or deconstructive angst over our capacity to know the world. Rather, the matter of uncertainty and irresolution in the novel might be conceived most fruitfully within a Jamesian perspective and posed in the form of a question. Is it possible, following James's well known metaphor, to see the "figure in the carpet" in *Travesía* and, if so, what does it look like and how do we identify it?[26]

---

[23] For an overview of ambiguity in literature, see William Empson's classic study of ambiguity, *Seven Types of Ambiguity* (London: Chatto & Windus, 1947).

[24] Tzvetan Todorov, *The Fantastic: A Structural Approach to a Literary Genre*, trans. Richard Howard (Ithaca, NY: Cornell University Press, 1975). Todorov argues that the fantastic is a period of irresolution within the text when the reader vacillates, trying to determine if a particular occurrence transgresses against the norms of reality established by the text. For Todorov, the fantastic is always resolved either in the form of the uncanny or the marvelous. Marías would of course disagree, and generates unresolved ambiguity throughout *Travesía*.

[25] Juan Benet, *En ciernes* (Madrid: Taurus, 1976), p. 50.

[26] James develops this image in his famous story from 1896, "The Figure in the Carpet."

The image of a complex but perceivable "figure" has often been used synecdochically by critics to refer to the essence of a writer's story. Although James's assertion begs the question of production and ownership of the metaphorical figure (do authors consciously weave it into their fiction or do readers construct it?), it seems to imply that if readers can discern the figure they will have tamed the story's natural resistance to their interpretive efforts. To a large degree, however, James's metaphor convolutes more than clarifies, and thus becomes strongly pertinent to Marías's fascination with James's writing as a whole. While the Jamesian figure may indeed suggest an aesthetic (and sometimes epistemological) reductivism by hinting that specific solutions are always embedded in the text and available to the reader, for Marías in *Travesía* the idea of a narrative figure lays the ground for asserting precisely the opposite. First, in the interview that accompanies the English translation of the novel, Marías calls attention to the intended diffidence of the plot and, in retrospect, the larger role of this diffidence in the development of his fiction as a whole: "[*Travesía*] ... may be the first novel in which I turned the question of doubt and indecision into part of the narrative method and the story itself" ("Eight Questions," *Voyage* 181). Furthermore, he implicitly locates his narrative in a larger European tradition of novel-writing, where represented and constructed realities resist totalizing assertions aimed at conveying whole and complete worlds. As he puts it, "European novelists tend not to be so concerned about [the desire to encompass everything], and perhaps they are more conscious that the shadow zones of the world are limitless in scope, and that the only thing a novel can do is illuminate them a bit, not to see anything in them, but rather just to admire the darkness with more clarity, the apparent contradiction notwithstanding" ("Eight Questions," *Voyage* 178).

While Marías's comments about *Travesía* disclose his intentions in the work, the text itself espouses and embodies the narrative principles that he asserts. And once again, Marías turns to the practices of storytelling to make the critical point. To begin with, the mystery of Hugh Bayham explored by Victor Arledge opens as an enigma story that, according to tradition and thus to reader expectations, will progress toward resolution. As occurs in much of Marías's fiction, the author draws on the technique of indirect narrators who assume the narrative voice and thus tell the story for someone else.[27] In this

---

[27] This is one of the most common narrative techniques found in Marías's fiction, and it allows him to filter and change stories without concern for consistency and reliability of the narrative voice. As he remarks in "Eight Questions" in *Voyage* when asked who is narrating the book, "[W]hen I wrote it I wasn't very concerned about who was narrating

instance, the narrator allows Bayham to tell his story to Arledge's friend, Esmond Handle, who in turn re-narrates the story in a long letter to Arledge. Handle comments on the pleasing nature of the story before he tells it ("... estoy seguro de que el relato que voy a ofrecerte será de tu agrado; ello permite que por adelantado goce de tu agradecimiento" [42]) ("... I am certain that you will find the story I am about to tell you most satisfying and intriguing; I am so convinced of this ... that I am permitting myself to savor your appreciation even before you yourself can express it" [26–27]), and also notes its remarkable events ("las inauditas jornadas de Hugh Everett Bayham" [42–43]) ("the truly startling story of Hugh Everett Bayham" [43]). He then sets out to re-present the story that Bayham had told to him and to a group of friends.

But as typically occurs in Marías, the original narrator (Bayham) first comments on the nature of his story and the events within it, thus preparing readers for what follows and assuring them of his intention to get the story right. He admits, for example, that the task of accuracy is a daunting one: "No es sencillo hacer una exposición clara y completa de lo sucedido durante estos cuatro días puesto que ni yo mismo lo sé con certeza; sin embargo, con las oportunas reservas ... lo intentaré" (45–46) ("Now, bear in mind that it will not be easy for me to give you a clear and complete account of everything that has happened over these past four days, given that I myself am not entirely certain of it all. Nevertheless, with certain reservations ... I will attempt [to do so]" [29]). Importantly for Bayham, if he does not narrate all that has happened it is because he cannot recall events rather than because storytelling itself is insufficient. He promises that "lo que relato fue real y no producto de mis fantasías" (59) ("what I am telling you is true and not a product of my fantasy" [*my translation*]), but acknowledges near the end of his story that his listeners "pueden creerme o no, sé que mi historia es harto inverosímil" (59) ("Perhaps you believe what I say, perhaps not; I am fully aware that my story sounds terribly implausible" [38]). Above all, however, he wishes to tell the story following his own narrative principles: "Déjame seguir como yo lo juzgue conveniente" (45) ("Please allow me to continue as I see fit" [29]).

The question that comes to mind, of course, grows from Bayham's own sense of verisimilitude as channeled through Arledge, who assumes the role

---

the story in the first place. That element, in fact, may be one of the few distinguishable characteristics of my later novels; they are all narrators who are nobody, in reality, just voices, interpreters, people who lend their voices to others or who simply transmit what they have received," p. 176.

of proxy reader within the text for the real reader outside the text. It is Arledge who then asks the questions that may uncover the figure in Bayham's carpet. For example, who is the man who kidnapped Bayham and why did he do it; who is the young girl who seduced Bayham; where is the house in which Bayham was imprisoned; what was the reason for setting him free? But as the narrative progresses, the only answers that result from Bayham's story generate additional critical questions. First, why the persistent deferral in the laying out of answers to the mystery? (In Jamesian terms, why does the figure in the carpet not become progressively more visible as the narrative develops?) And further, will the reader perceive the story as unbelievable because of gaps in its content and because expectations concerning detail and outcome have not been met? This in turn generates the fundamental question, is there in fact a figure in the carpet at all? Although Marías does not set out to provide concrete answers, the questions return us to the core of his storytelling whereby he avoids certainty in favor of ambiguity. Miss Bunnage, the professional reader who has written on the work of Alredge, makes the critical point. When the narrator of the outer novel asks her if she believes that the expedition described in the inner novel really took place and if the characters in it actually existed, her response, though brief, speaks to the content of the form of *Travesía* as a whole: "Hay que saber prolonger la incertidumbre" (115) ("One must know how to prolong uncertainty" [*my translation*].

Miss Bunnage's evocation of uncertainty could be understood in a variety of ways in *Travesía*. For example, it might be seen as an efficacious narrative strategy for sustaining the interest of readers—after all, mystery stories often turn upon keeping certainty at bay. It might reflect an epistemological posture that suggests certitude can only result from philosophical arrogance; it might imply that the world itself is complex—a "zone of shadow" as Marías calls it in his interview about *Travesía*. In this sense, the uncertainty in his novel would actually represent the world as it really is. While each of these possibilities resonates in the structure and meaning of *Travesía*, as well as in Marías's general approach to writing, in this instance uncertainty inheres principally in the process of reading and how readers ascribe meanings to texts. Once again, the figure in the carpet moves to the fore.

The unnamed narrator of James's story "The Figure in the Carpet" feverishly seeks to find the figure of the work of a renowned novelist named Hugh Vereker. He eventually grows frustrated and concedes his failure, but the task is then taken on by another young and brilliant critic, George Corvick, who later claims to have discovered the figure but dies after revealing it only to his wife. She in turn decides to maintain silence about what her husband has told her, and the story ends with the enigma intact. From the outset of the tale, the reader is asked (implicitly by the text) to identify with those within the narrative who are seeking to solve the mystery. This identification in fact creates the compulsion for resolution inherent in mystery narratives, whose paradigmatic structure enables the outcome to be clear and the essence (figure) to be knowable. As Vittoria Intonti has pointed out, however, what really interests James in his story is the "psychology of obsession" that drives readers to want to uncover the hidden essence of Verker's novel.[28] In *Travesía*, Victor Arledge assumes the role of obsessive reader and spends nearly all of his time on the expedition seeking to complete the story of Bayham's kidnapping, fully convinced that there is a mystery to be solved and an essence to be discerned. He queries Bayham about the incident at every opportunity, even after Bayham angrily proclaims that he does not want to talk about it. Arledge grows depressed as they leave Alexandria for Antarctica, believing that Bayham's story, "El coche, los secuestradores, la música, la casa junto al mar, el encierro y los celos y rencores de las tres hermanas no tendrían ya explicación" (95) ("The carriage, the kidnappers, the music, the house by the sea, the captivity, and the jealousy and rancor of the three sisters would never be explained to him" [62]). Furthermore, as the cruise continues, Arledge's mood grows darker, and he begins to see Bayham as "un ser odioso que se complacía en torturarle con su tenaz silencio" (136) ("a hateful man who derived pleasure from torturing him with his obstinate silence" [86]).

What is important to bear in mind here, and what gives principal substance to the narrative paradigm of *Travesía* as a whole, is that the open spaces in Bayham's story, which Arledge seeks to close, cannot in fact be filled in—the narrative does not permit it. While on the one hand the story encourages an alliance between Arledge's perspective and that of the real reader, as both search for the secret, on the other the entire novel frustrates that search. What Marías proposes, in other words, is that the essence of Bayham's story (and as a principle of fiction, of any story) is the uselessness of pursuing an essence, of seeking out a single meaning that reassures the reader with its clarity and decisiveness. The acts of obsession that compel such a search can only accrete to frustration and failure, and in severe cases like Arledge's, to seclusion and despair. As the narrator tell us:

> Victor Arledge [tomó] la inusitada decisión de dejar de lado temores, cortesía, prevenciones y cautelas para poner en juego su reputación en el

---

[28] Vittoria Intonti, " 'The Figure in the Carpet' as an Allegory of Reading," in David Garrett Izzo and Daniel T. O'Hara, eds, *Henry James Against the Aesthetic Movement* (Jefferson, NC and London: McFarland, 2006), p. 162.

empeño—su importancia inicial ya rebasada y ya entonces desmedida—de averiguar por qué Hugh Everett Bayham había sido secuestrado y llevado a Escocia y cuál era la identidad de la joven que le habia otorgado sus encantos[.] Nunca logró saberse; y mucho importaría saberlo cuando tal decisión trajo como consecuencia la desaparición del gran escritor; su reclusión, su abandono, su renuncia y finalmente su muerte en circunstancias quizá no del todo desdichadas pero que probablemente ningún creador, es decir, ninguna persona que aspire a la inmortalidad, habría deseado. (105)

Victor Arledge [made] the unusual decision to set aside fear, tact, prudence and caution and put his reputation—its initial importance already exaggerated and by then excessive—at risk in order to find out why Hugh Everett Bayham had been kidnapped and taken to Scotland and what was the identity of the young woman who had bestowed her charms on him. Nobody ever knew for certain; and as time passed it would become important to know because the decision resulted in the disappearance of the great writer; his reclusion, apathy, surrender and finally his death under circumstances perhaps not completely terrible but under which no creator, that is to say, no person who aspired to immortality, would have wanted. (*my translation*)

The obsession with finding the essence and of resolving the mystery does not end with Arledge's withdrawal to the countryside of Scotland. The narrator of the outer novel (the unnamed reader/listener of the inner novel) cannot resist his own growing curiosity about Arledge—a curiosity inspired but left unsated by Edward Ellis, author of the inner novel. Although the outer narrator notes at first that he is an "Enemigo de las indigaciones" (118) ("Enemy of investigations" [*my translation*]), the novel arouses in him the teleological desire inspired by the tradition of mystery fiction, and at the end of Branshaw's reading he sets out to learn as much about Arledge as he can: "El libro, en verdad, me había entusiasmado y, más que la obra de Edward Ellis en sí, lo que había acabado de despertar mi curiosidad había sido la historia y la personalidad de Victor Arledge. ... Por ello ... me encontraba en un inusitado estado de excitación, tan impaciente estaba por saber detalles ... acerca del asunto que entonces ya me obsesionaba" (274–75) ("The book, if truth be told, made me very excited and, more than Edward Ellis's work itself, what had ended up awakening my curiosity had been the story and personality of Victor Arledge. ... For that reason I found myself in a strange state of excitement, impatient to know details ... about the matter that by then I was obsessed with" [*my translation*]).

His obsession of course closely resembles the obsession of Arledge to complete the story of Bayham, and then that of Ellis to complete the story of

Arledge. In this way Marías establishes the thematic parallel within the two novels of *Travesía* between resolution and certainty as a readerly expectation and the principle of ambiguity and irresolution as a narrative determinant. In other words, both the inner and outer works of the novel point to the reader's desire to tighten the looseness of the narrative, which then works consistently against the reader to frustrate those desires. For the narrator of the outer novel, this frustration begins with the death of Miss Bunnage, who might have been able to clarify information about Arledge, and it continues to the very end of the novel, when the narrator finally obtains Miss Bunnage's notes, which are themselves incomplete. At this point the stories of *Travesía* finally do divulge their essence, which is not an affirming closure with a compact and discernible meaning, but rather a disconcerting end that forestalls disclosure of the sought after figure in the carpet.

When asked about the ending of *Travesía*, Marías implied in his answer that the question itself is beside the point, for he argued that endings of stories are largely inconsequential ("Eight Questions," *Voyage* 182). Indeed, for Marías's fiction in general, and specifically for *Travesía*, the solution is not a teleological one but a narrative one. Readers will never learn what happened to Kerrigan after his escape from the *Tallahassee*, why Arledge chose seclusion following the expedition, or what really occurred during Bayham's kidnapping because for Marías, as the narrator of the inner novel concludes about the Bayham episode, "no merecía ser contado" (257) ("it is not a story really worth repeating" [157]). In other words, for Marías the sense of an ending is not determined epistemologically but discursively. And the significance of the narrative turns not on how it ends but on how it is composed: "What counts the most—and what we remember the most—is the atmosphere, the style, the path, the journey, and the world in which we have immersed ourselves for a few hours or a few days while reading a novel or watching a movie. What matters, then, is the journey along the horizon—in other words, the journey that never ends" ("Eight Questions," *Voyage* 182). There is no pleasure to be derived from one outcome or another for any of the stories narrated in *Travesía*. Rather, the pleasure of the text is to be inferred from the title, which points us to the uncertain content of traditional forms, whose reassuring closure in generic tradition has yielded in *Travesía* to enriching openness and indecision. It is the narrative journey that compels Marías to write, and the reader must find joy as well as solace in joining Marías on that journey rather than in reaching a comfortable destination.

III

Two Transitional Novels: *El siglo* and *El hombre sentimental*

El siglo

El siglo (1983) is an unabashedly stylized novel. Its narrative technique (alternating chapters told in the first and third persons), its complicated sentence structure (largely baroque-like), and the slow pacing of its plot stand in marked contrast to Marías's earlier novels, *Los dominios del lobo* and *Travesía del horizonte*.[1] In the latter two works, as we have seen, Marías moves deftly but swiftly through multiple stories with sometimes tenuous connections. He rarely slows to allow for the development of complex characters, and he shapes the perspective of each novel largely through third-person narrators who may not possess sufficient information to tell the entire story or bring it to a sound conclusion. While these early works by no means stand apart from what will become the core of his fiction (they reveal, for example, his central concern with storytelling, the influence of movies on his literary formation, and important connections to non-Spanish literature), they nonetheless reflect the sometimes inchoate narrative practices of a young writer who has only begun to understand the more intricate malleability of language and the deliberate construction of characters.

In *El siglo*, however, Marías retreats deeply into the narrative discourse itself and allows it to dilate and grow through the ever more dense accretion of words, which in turn leads to the embodiment of one of the essential principles (as he himself has pointed out) of the whole of his narrative produc-

---

[1] The style of *El siglo* is unlike any other of Marías's novels, not in its general fluidity or even in the recurrent complexity of its sentences and paragraphs, but in the intensity of both. It is also his novel that is most similar to the writing of his mentor, Juan Benet. For a detailed study of many of the stylistic intricacies of *El siglo*, see Alexis Grohmann, "*El siglo*: A Question of Style," in *Coming Into One's Own: The Novelistic Development of Javier Marías* (Amsterdam and New York: Rodopi, 2002), pp. 55–88.

tion: "You progress as you digress."² The digression/progression paradigm functions throughout *El siglo*, not only in the style of the novel, but also in the portrayal of time and space, and thus moves Marías closer to the language and technique that will come to define much of his later fiction. The connection to his more mature writing can be seen, for example, in his use of a first-person narrator in *El siglo*, which anticipates the first-person narration of all of his subsequent novels. The progression/digression paradigm is also visible in the sheer accumulation of words in lengthy and complex paragraphs, in particular those offered by the first-person narrator, Casaldáliga. His labyrinthine style in fact becomes the content of the form of much of the novel as well as a substantive tool for exploring the social and historical world represented by the text. In addition, Marías shows in *El siglo* his recurrent interest in how the telling of stories requires the teller of the tale to imagine the real within the inherent contingencies of storytelling itself. This allows him at once to affirm the necessity of narration in the social construction of reality while undermining any certainty that it is able to represent life as it really is. Further, certainty grows even more tenuous as stories are parsed, re-imagined, and inserted into other stories, never settling into a final and stable destination. In brief, while *El siglo* engages the external world and probes specific existential and historical dilemmas, it also anticipates the central lines of Marías's later writing as a whole: a concern for the speculative nature of truth as well as its incitement to instability within language; the always conditional representation of the real gained through storytelling; protracted authority over stories which can never be held by a single narrator bent on controlling their meaning or restricting their circulation in society.

El siglo tells the story of a man known only as Casaldáliga, whose life spans many decades of the twentieth century.³ Although the novel makes no explicit references to Spain, it is clear that Casaldáliga's life is deeply immersed in Spanish geography and modern Spanish history, thus making *El siglo* Marías's first novel to be set in his native country.⁴ The four chapters

---

[2] For a discussion of how this idea relates to Marías's view of style and technique on a more theoretical level, see chapter I. Marías references this quote in relation to Laurence Sterne. See his "Cuéntale el cuento," in *Literatura y fantasma* (Madrid: Alfaguara, 2001), p. 269.

[3] Casaldáliga had already appeared as a character in Marías's experimental/hybrid novel, *El monarca del tiempo* (1978). Many of Marías's characters return for sometimes small and sometimes prominent roles in various of his novels, especially in his fiction beginning with *Todas las almas* (1989).

[4] Marías has written about various aspects of *El siglo*, including specific literary influences, historical circumstances, and geographical location for the novel. Concerning

narrated in the third person relate various elements of Casaldáliga's life from his birth in 1900 to the end of the Spanish Civil War in 1939: what Casaldáliga thought was the death of his mother when he was very young but which turns out to be her planned abandonment of him and his father; his father's peculiar life of work and solitude, and especially his father's repeated insistence that his son forge a clear destiny for himself; Casaldáliga's marriage to Constanza Bacio when he believed that she was ill and close to death; his flight to Lisbon to escape involvement in the Civil War; his work following the war as a judge and informer for the government.[5]

The five chapters narrated by Casaldáliga in the first person take place in an unspecified present time. Now an old man, Casaldáliga awaits death in his house near a large lake and reflects on the events of his life and the people who have played an important role in it. More introspective than the third-person narrator, Casaldáliga ponders many facets of his past and of what he perceives as his impending death: his intense desire from a very young age to define a personal destiny; the writing of his will and how those around him will be affected by his legacy;[6] his relationship with Colonel

---

its setting in Spain, he notes, "Bien, un jurado no podría probar que *El siglo* transcurre en España, pero de hecho es allí donde trascurre. ... El lector perspicaz o enterado podrá incluso reconocer Barcelona, Madrid, las alusiones a Sevilla, el paisaje de marismas de la provincia de Huelva que a veces se asemeja a un paisaje lacustre" ("Well, a jury could not prove that *El siglo* takes place in Spain, but in fact it does take place there. ... The perspicacious or informed reader will even be able to recognize Barcelona, Madrid, the allusions to Seville, the salt marshes from the province of Huelva that sometimes seem like a lake"), "Desde una novela no necesariamente castiza," in *Literatura y fantasma*, p. 66.

  5 Carmen Moreno-Nuño sees *El siglo* primarily as an exploration of why "un sujeto decide involucrarse voluntariamente en una acción tan vil como la delación a favor de un régimen político totalitario" ("an individual decides willingly to involve himself in such a vile activity as being an informant for a totalitarian regime"), *Las huellas de la guerra civil. Mito y trauma en la narrativa de la España democrática* (Madrid: Ediciones Libertarias, 2006), p. 139. The novel indeed addresses the issue of informing for a totalitarian government, though in my view only indirectly and not as the central focus of the narrative. But as Moreno-Nuño importantly points out, *El siglo* can be linked to historiographic metafiction in the way that it draws historical memory to the fore, and it serves, as well, as a meditation "sobre los mecanismos de la delación, la traición, el ejercicio fascista del poder y el funcionamiento corrupto de la justicia, siendo por eso respuesta para algunos de los interrogantes que todavía plantean la memoria traumática de la Guerra Civil y la dictadura franquista" ("on the mechanisms of informing, treason, the fascist exercise of power, and the corrupt functioning of justice, thus serving as an answer to some of the questions still posed by the traumatic memory of the Civil War and the Francoist regime") (p. 182).

  6 Among those who are awaiting Casaldáliga's death (and thus his inheritance) is el

Berua, who recruited him to become an informer for the regime following the war;[7] the ways in which he has shaped the lives of others; his amorphous sense of identity coupled with reflections on the purpose that his life has served and what his death will mean. What Casaldáliga relates about his life, together with the information provided about other characters narrated in the third person, coalesce to produce a complex but also contradictory novelistic world. Both narrations offer personal and historical information that fills in many gaps of Casaldáliga's story, but these same narrations serve to undermine the information they provide with irony and ambiguity. The resultant tension—between knowing and doubting, between self-understanding and self-deception—creates a somewhat perplexing portrayal of character in *El siglo*, but one that supersedes the emphasis on plot-bound characters who dominate Marías's first two novels.

The principal impetus for Casaldáliga to have done anything at all in his life, and subsequently for him to reflect upon his past as he nears death, begins with admonitions from his father when he is a young boy. Above all, his father tells him during their Sunday walks in the park, he must not only shape his own destiny but must make this destiny unlike that of anyone else. As his father puts it, "Sé original, hijo mío, sé original. ... Sé único" ("Be original, my son, be original. ... Be unique").[8] In this sense, Casaldáliga's father issues a call to action, which serves as well as a call for his son to consider that the meaning of his life cannot be passively received but rather must be vigorously pursued. Casaldáliga thus concludes early on not only that the horizon of expectation in his life stands open before him, but that his existential duty requires him to fill in its contours. Furthermore, he believes that it is wholly possible to do so. As the narrator observes, Casaldáliga "había poseído desde muy pronto la rara facultad de considerar la existencia como ... algo moldeable y que se hallaba a la entera disposición del usuario" ("had

---

León de Nápoles, an unacknowledged son who has become a well-known opera singer. El León de Nápoles will become the central character in Marías's next novel, *El hombre sentimental* (1986). He may also be the unnamed character in Marías's 1978 hybrid text *El monarca del tiempo*, where we can infer (though not affirm) that he appears in the segment entitled "Portento, Maldición."

[7] Marías's interest in the role of the informer has clear biographical roots: his father, well-known philosopher Julián Marías, was briefly imprisoned following the Civil War and banned from teaching because an informant (and colleague of Marías) had given information to the government that pointed to the philosopher's former and on-going Republican sympathies. Javier Marías will later return to this episode in his father's life and explore it in greater detail in his trilogy, *Tu rostro mañana*.

[8] Javier Marías, *El siglo* (Barcelona: Seix Barral, 1983), p. 29.

possessed at a very young age the rare ability to consider existence as ... something moldable, and which was fully at the disposition of the user") (*Siglo* 27).

In nearly all of his fiction Marías conveys a foundational belief that the seeking and being of existential fulfillment can be conceptually rigorous and ardently acted out (what Paul Ricoeur refers to as "a hermeneutic of action").[9] But action alone is never sufficient. To be defined and affirmed, fulfillment must be represented. In other words, it must be part of a story. As Casaldáliga's father tells his son, "Así que escucha lo que te digo; ponte manos a la obra sin más dilación, lábrate un destino, hazte con un nítido e inconfundible, que merezca contarse y se pueda contar, que sea sólo tuyo y desde un principio reconocible como tal" ("So listen to what I am telling you; get to work without further delay; forge a destiny for yourself, make yourself one that is clear and unmistakable, that deserves to be told and that can be told, that is yours alone, and from the very beginning recognizable as such") (*Siglo* 28). For Marías, of course, creating one's destiny and telling the story of that destiny entail a strained alliance. As he has frequently pointed out (see chapter I), representing the real through storytelling never occurs without an epistemological rupture; it never proceeds simply and wholly without uncertainty. Not only do stories misrepresent the world, despite the teller's intention to re-present it objectively and accurately, they actively configure the real and thus shape both the way we are able to know it and the meanings that we attribute to it.

In *El siglo*, this shaping moves both forward and backward in time; it is able to influence the past as well as the future. Referring to a specific process of storytelling that seems to have taken hold among the people in the area where he now awaits his death, Casaldáliga makes the critical point: "Y en consecuencia esta historia ... pues no sólo se desarrolla y crece hacia adelante—como es costumbre—, sino también hacia atrás" ("And thus this story ... not only develops and grows forward—as is usually the case—but also backward") (*Siglo* 74).[10] Casaldáliga's perspective in this instance suggests not only that stories have the capacity to define the past as well as the future, but that they become part of the very substance of that past and future. They are not only epistemological instruments but ontological ones as

---

[9] Paul Ricoeur, *Memory, History, Forgetting*, trans. Kathleen Blamey and David Pellauer (Chicago and London: University of Chicago Press, 2004), p. 217.

[10] The idea that stories move forward as well as backward in time, and that they have an influence on the past as well as the future, is first articulated in *El siglo*. It will become the cornerstone of Marías's masterpiece, the trilogy *Tu rostro mañana* (2002, 2004, 2007).

well—they exist and circulate in society and thus bear upon all that they convey as well as upon those who are touched by them. In *El siglo*, Marías explores how being and telling necessarily converge, but not without contingency and not without irony that at once reinforces and undermines the central role of narration in the novel.

In chapter five of *El siglo*, Casaldáliga offers two pivotal observations on his life that redound sharply to the understanding of destiny and storytelling in the novel. First, when reflecting on his relationship with Colonel Berua, who had offered him the position as informer following the war, Casaldáliga affirms that he has always managed to impose his will on the sometimes complex plot of his life. As he puts it, "Soy dueño absoluto de cuanto me ha acontecido" ("I am the absolute owner of all that has happened to me") (*Siglo* 154). In other words, Casaldáliga has embraced the advice of his father, has sought to create his own destiny and, as he sees it, has imposed his will upon the form that it has taken. As much of the novel serves to show, however, Casaldáliga's observation represents jarring blindness, which he conveys in his narration as unequivocal insight.

While it is certainly the case that much has happened to Casaldáliga in his life, the irony of his perspective begins with its phrasing, "all that has happened to me." That is to say, rather than configure his life through desire, rather than zealously pursue one thing or another as his father had insisted, Casaldáliga has grown old while standing still, curious about his destiny but unable and unfit to determine its shape. A brief survey of critical events in his life confirms the point. The first revolves around his marriage to Constanza Bacio not long after he makes her acquaintance at a dinner party. Casaldáliga knows nothing of her before the event, but after speaking with another guest named Donato Dato (whom Casaldáliga has never met before)[11] and learning something about Constanza (she is ill, Dato tells him, and does not have long to live), Casaldáliga drifts into marriage with her. As the narrator remarks, "Casaldáliga se encontró ya casado y en un nuevo hogar sin haberle dedicado al asunto excesiva meditación" ("Casaldáliga found himself already married and in a new home without having devoted much thought to the matter") (*Siglo* 106). Casaldáliga endures years of dullness with Constanza, which he

---

[11] Marías refers to Donato somewhat randomly as Dato or Dado, reminiscent of the way that Juan Benet invests his character Rumbal with other names (e.g., Robal) in his novel *Volverás a Región* (1969). Although it remains unclear if Marías is mimicking his mentor, the ambiguity associated with Donato's last name in *El siglo* creates fitting uncertainty, in the context of an ironic narrative, concerning the reliability of the story about him.

had sensed would be the case from the outset ("el sesgo sedentario y romo que tomaría su vida matrimonial") ("the sedentary and dull slant that his married life would take") (*Siglo* 106), but he is willing to do so because he believes that his destiny turns upon her death and his status as a widower at a young age. In this way, as Casaldáliga sees it, "podría cumplirse el destino asignado" ("he could fulfill the destiny assigned to him") (*Siglo* 122). When Casaldáliga later learns that his wife has never been ill and thus he will not be left as a widower any time soon, he grows sullen and depressed. He understands that his destiny with her has nothing to do with the assertion of his own will, but rather with something else that will happen to him. Indeed, he concludes that his destiny must lie elsewhere.

The second key event in Casaldáliga's life likewise grows from his inertia. When the Civil War breaks out in Spain, Casaldáliga remains uncommitted to one side or the other. Within a few days, however, his wife decides that they should flee to Lisbon and remain there until the conflict in Spain ends and they can safely return to their home. Casaldáliga accedes to the wishes of his wife, who now has delineated for him the contours of a possible destiny without his consent. As the narrator notes,

> Y tan rápido y contundente había obrado el espanto en la cabeza de Constanza Bacio que cuando ésta llegó al domicilio conyugal dispuesta a rebatir y esgrimir tantos argumentos como fuera necesario para persuadir y urgir al marido, no creyó sino ver confirmado lo justo de sus disposiciones y su pavor al comprobar que en Casaldáliga no había más que asentimiento y docilidad: prácticamente sólo tuvo que anunciarle la inmediata partida e instarle a que se encargara de los preparativos más técnicos.
>
> And just as quickly and forcefully as fear had worked its way into Constanza Bacio's thoughts, upon returning home she was prepared to refute and set forth as many arguments as necessary to persuade and urge her husband; but she saw only the soundness of her inclinations and her fear confirmed when she verified that in Casaldáliga there was nothing but agreement and meekness: she merely needed to announce to him their immediate departure and get him to take charge of the technical arrangements. (*Siglo* 173)

Casaldáliga remains in Lisbon for three years, walking aimlessly through the streets and wondering what destiny awaits him. He spends much time visiting an old church (Sao Vicente de Fora), exploring the streets of the neighborhood where the church stands, scrutinizing its appearance, and seeking to comprehend his deep attraction to the structure and how it relates to the meaning of his life. One day, in a moment of epiphany that temporarily shakes him from his lethargy, he appears to understand: "Se había distraído de la única meta de su existencia entera, se había dejado vencer por un fracaso aislado. Había que intentarlo otra vez, ese era el mensaje que a él, diminuto e insignificante a su lado, le transmitía aquella blanca e inmensa basílica lisboeta abandonada en su desgarbada plaza como un viejo crucero" ("He had been distracted from the only goal of his entire existence, he had allowed himself to be vanquished by an isolated failure. It was necessary to try again, that was the message that the immense, white, Lisbon basilica, abandoned in its ungainly plaza like an old ship, had communicated to him, as he stood small and insignificant beside it") (*Siglo* 190). Yet this paroxysm of understanding fails to incite action. Casaldáliga concludes that he must return home and fight in the war, but his abulic casuistry affirms nothing but his continuing indecision.

> Quería ir al frente, pero le faltaban imaginación y temple para planear de veras la puesta en práctica de sus deseos. ¿Qué frente? ¿Qué filas? ¿Qué bando? ¿Cómo ofrecerse? ¿Dónde presentarse? ¿Y a quién? Aquellas eran cuestiones insolubles, preguntas sin posible contestación. Seguía sin tener opinión ... se sentía incapaz de tomar la iniciativa, de dar un paso en ninguna dirección. ...
>
> He wanted to go to the front, but he lacked the imagination and temperament to truly plan putting his desires into practice. Which front? Which branch? Which side? How to present himself? Where to go? Present himself to whom? Those were insoluble questions, questions with no possible answer. He continued not to have an opinion ... he felt incapable of taking the initiative, to make a move in any direction. ... (*Siglo* 193)

Hence Casaldáliga remains in Lisbon, allowing the war to continue in Spain without his involvement and deferring a destiny that he could have forged for himself.

    The final event that shapes Casaldáliga's life further reveals the dull edge of his passion and his willingness to accede to the propositions of others. Following the war he leaves Lisbon and returns to his hometown with his wife (though shortly she will abandon him and return to Lisbon). He unexpectedly comes across Donato Dato, the man who had proposed his marriage to Constanza and who now appears to have a close association with the new regime. When Casaldáliga meets him, he expresses anger over Dato's role in urging his marriage to Constanza, but Dato disarmingly notes that he is now in a position to introduce Casaldáliga to certain persons and thus help him gain favor with the government. As Dato explains, Casaldáliga needs simply to become an informer. With a clear and concise offer before him, the appeal for Casaldáliga to confirm his destiny is strong, most importantly because it seems to match the requirements laid out by his father many years before by which Casaldáliga should embrace a concise destiny uniquely his own: "A diferencia de los [destinos] que había vislumbrado en otras ocasiones, éste no era brillante, ni enorgullecedor, ni heroico, ni digno de compasión, pero sí mucho más nítido e inconfundible que los anteriores. Era, sobre todo, mucho más concreto: lo podía casi palpar; en verdad lo sentía al alcance de su mano. Ahora sólo tenía que dar él un paso y asirlo" ("Unlike those [destinies] that he had glimpsed on other occasions, this one was not lustrous, nor did it fill him with pride, nor was it heroic or worthy of compassion, but it was much clearer and not to be confused with the previous ones. It was, above all, much more concrete: he could almost touch it; to be truthful he could feel it within his grasp. Now he just had to take the step and grab onto it") (*Siglo* 251). Casaldáliga vacillates once again, however, and rather than insert himself into a role that will indeed come to define the remainder of his life, he becomes mired, "simplemente y una vez más, en su inveterada falta de resolución" ("simply and once again, in his inveterate lack of resolution") (*Siglo* 254). In the end, however, Casaldáliga assumes the role (and thus his destiny) of informer and judge. As he correctly perceives in his old age, "mi destino consistía en determinar los [destinos] de mis semejantes" ("my destiny consisted of determining the [destinies] of my peers") (*Siglo* 154).

What becomes clear by the end of *El siglo*, however, is that Casaldáliga has succeeded in his profession but that he has failed in his life. This is so for a number of biographical reasons—for example, the psychological scars of his childhood, the abandonment by his mother. But quite unexpectedly, it has to do with something more abstract: his perception of time—his beingness in time and his conception of progressing through time. Unlike many novels of the twentieth century, where time betrays individuals who seek to explore the crosscurrents of their lives through recollection and narration, in *El siglo* time per se stands indifferent to Casaldáliga's plight. Both the third-person narrator and Casaldáliga himself seem unperturbed by the ambiguity of temporal representation or the perplexities of memory, even as the novel serves to assess the whole of Casaldáliga's life from the time he was a young boy at the turn of the twentieth century through his old age many decades later. Hence it is not the process of remembering or of evoking the shards and fragments of the past that diminishes Casaldáliga, even though nostalgia occasionally overdraws the longing for his youth, "un período opaco y árido que ahora se le representaba como un paraíso difunto" ("an opaque and arid period that now seemed to him like a defunct paradise") (*Siglo* 171). Rather, it is the way in which time (and therefore destiny) stands for him not as a dynamic process of becoming but as a static paradigm for being that begins and ends in inertia.

The central motivation for all that Casaldáliga has done in his life turns upon the pursuit of his destiny (or upon desire for knowing his destiny), which suggests both movement (psychological and physical) and, therefore, change. Hence on the face of it, the business of living for Casaldáliga is embedded in the quest myth, which implies a dynamic becoming that is vital and procreative. Questing impels the self toward enrichment and suggests process over outcome; it implies consent to incompleteness over the safe resting offered by end or result. It also compels activation of the human will when positioning the self on the scale of possibilities. In short, it directs characters to act, and it always implies purpose.

Yet as the entire novel reveals (and despite his reflections on the pursuit of his destiny), Casaldáliga remains passive before life. He allows others consistently to impose their will on what he does, but more importantly, he embraces states of being over processes of becoming. Put another way, he endorses the stasis of need over the dynamism of desire. While desire is able to stir the self to action and thus to the realm of freedom, to eros or becoming, when that desire seeks only to arrive at an end (i.e., when the individual desires the ending of desiring), need moves to the fore and vitiates the quest by imposing being over becoming.[12] Such is the case with Casaldáliga, who scrutinizes the future to secure an outcome rather than to engage in a process. In his marriage to Constanza, in his flight to Lisbon during the war, and as an informer for the government following the conflict, Casaldáliga remains detached from authenticity so that, as the narrator puts it, "podría cumplirse el destino asignado" ("he could fulfill his assigned destiny") (*Siglo* 122). The idea of "fulfilling" and "assigned" is critical here, for it emphasizes outcome over process and reception over pursuit. In this way authenticity (of decision, of intimacy, of desire) is held at bay. However, the destiny that he accepts, the need to be rather than the desire to become, creates a life for Casaldáliga bereft of meaning—a destiny in which nothing has happened and in which nothing is bound to happen.

As Casaldáliga reflects on his past the inertia of beingness resonates deeply in his narrative, and he envisions it as reified by the waters of the lake outside his balcony. From the outset of the novel, Casaldáliga understands his need for beingness by projecting his thoughts onto the lake, as if it both

---

[12] For a succinct overview of need and desire in character portrayal, see Thomas Docherty, *Reading (Absent) Character* (Oxford: Oxford University Press, 1983), pp. 228–38.

understood and reflected his plight. As he puts it, "Esas aguas están acabadas y mientras yo viva seguirán estancadas, presas de sí mismas, sumidas en el abismo y ausencia de su soliloquio errátil" ("Those waters are spent and as long as I am alive they will remain stagnant, prisoners of themselves, submerged in the abyss and absence of their inconstant soliloquy") (*Siglo* 16). While the lake contains within it all that has occurred during Casaldáliga's life, it has no memory or form able to reveal markers of time and identity.

There is no indication of temporal differentiation or continuity in the waters of the lake, no sense of movement from the past to the present or from the present to the future. Casaldáliga imagines in them his anxieties as well as his failure to forge meaning in his life, though he is unable to pin down the cause or impetus: "Quién sabe si cumplen una condena que dioses ya depuestos hace tiempo les impusieron y olvidaron levantarles en su lento languidecer amnésico o en una precipitada huida. ... Sea como fuere, yo ya desespero de ver satisfechos sus deseos de metamorfosis" ("Who knows if they are carrying out a sentence imposed on them long ago by gods now deposed and who forgot to raise them [the waters] up in their slow, amnesic languishing or in their precipitate flight. ... Be that as it may, I have lost hope that I will ever see their desire for metamorphosis satisfied") (*Siglo* 13). In the end, therefore, Casaldáliga envisions his life as an extended moment of paralysis, void of "movement toward," bereft of process, and mired in a liquefying amorphousness. As he puts it, "Yo he sido muchos, pero en esencia no fui nunca nadie, lo que equivale a decir que fui siempre el mismo, el esqueleto, desde el principio" ("I have been many people, but in essence I was never anyone, which is the same as saying that I was always the same person, the empty shell, from the beginning") (*Siglo* 156). In this way Casaldáliga collapses life, beingness, and death into a single concept tied closely to a destiny of "estancamiento y letargo" ("stagnation and lethargy") (*Siglo* 156).

The second critical assertion of chapter five, linked closely to the first (i.e., "Soy dueño absoluto de cuanto me ha acontecido") ("I am the absolute owner of all that has happened to me"), draws attention to the nature of storytelling as well as to its formative influence on the lives of individuals and groups. For Casaldáliga, as we have seen, destiny does not presuppose an existential paradigm within which individuals accede to traditional forms of identity or select from among given structures of meaning. To the contrary, destiny must be constructed from a unique and original object of desire, as Casaldáliga's father forcefully reiterated to his son even as he allowed his life to devolve into nostalgia for the object of desire absent from his own life, Casaldáliga's mother.

The uniqueness and originality of one's destiny, however, stand meaningless if they remain merely preclusive. Hence their embodiment within narration becomes critical, though it is never easy to nail things down within the structures of a single story. First, as Casaldáliga's father insists, a destiny must deserve to be narrated. While Casaldáliga doubts that his father's destiny reaches the threshold of uniqueness that merits narrative attention ("La sola duda de Casaldáliga ... se cifraba en si aquella era una historia que mereciera contarse") ("Casaldáliga's sole doubt ... lay in whether that story deserved to be told") (*Siglo* 35), he is more concerned about how storytelling relates to his own destiny. Hence similar to protagonists in much of Marías's fiction, Casaldáliga reflects on both the impetus and the contingencies of storytelling. Yet in an ironic parallel to his assertion that he has controlled his own destiny, he avers as well that he has shaped how that destiny has been narrated, especially those elements that may have threatened to controvert his authority or social standing. As he notes, if he was unable to dictate the outcome of an incident, he positioned himself to configure the story told about it:

> [H]e esperado hasta que quien me los [los momentos ingratos] acarreó hubiese muerto, o hubiese quedado enmudecida su lengua por el confinamiento o el desprestigio; y entonces yo, único testigo y relator posible del incidente, sin nadie con quien carearme, lo he contado a mi manera y le he dado la vuelta si se terciaba. Las cosas no son como ocurren, sino como se zanjan, se juzgan, se archivan y se sepultan.
>
> [I] have waited until those who caused them [unpleasant moments] had died, or whose ability to speak had become muted by confinement or loss of reputation; then I, the sole witness and only possible person who could tell about the incident, without anyone to confront me, told the story in my own way and changed it if the opportunity presented itself. Things are not as they occur, but rather as they are settled, judged to be, archived and buried. (*Siglo* 133–34)

However, much like the irony that enshrouds Casaldáliga's claim of control over his destiny, the undermining of his narrative voice resonates throughout *El siglo*. This occurs in two important ways. First, Marías does not permit Casaldáliga to shape his own story, just as he does not allow him to secure his own destiny. The very existence of the alternating chapters narrated in the first and third persons belies Casaldáliga's assertion of authority. The two narratives in fact stand largely counterpoised to one another, with one inflating and the other deflating the character of a man whose life stands at the center of both. In general terms, of course, the plot of a novel is rooted in some form of narrative coherence (even when shaped by multiple voices), which in turn arises from the intention to explain events and articulate their meaning. But rather than expand a coherent single plot with complementary events that build one upon the other, the two narratives of *El siglo* invite readers to question the soundness of Casaldáliga's self-scrutiny and thus to challenge the truth value of his entire narrative.

In addition to the two perspectives in the telling of a single story, with the subsequent calling into question of Casaldáliga's reliability as a narrator, Marías also focuses on Casaldáliga's view of storytelling per se. In other words, he uses Casaldáliga's stories to assert the problems of storytelling within a context packed with stories. This is most fully seen in the importance ascribed to the basic act of narration in the town where Casaldáliga now resides in his old age. Casaldáliga himself makes the critical point in a lengthy commentary on the truth, verisimilitude, and social circulation of stories that form the cultural foundation of the area:

> [C]ualquier nuevo personaje, dato, observación o anécdota, aunque hayan sido a lo mejor forjados esta misma mañana por la imaginación de algún labriego haragán o desocupado, pasará de inmediato a engrosar el riquísimo, inabarcable e imprevisible acervo del pasado y de lo pasado sin que para ello se le exijan más verificación o refrendo que su propia relación. A partir de tal momento, esa anécdota, esa personalidad, esa noticia, ese elemento podrán ser citados y aludidos, y referidos y vueltos a referir mil veces sin que nadie ponga en duda su veracidad, y podrá recurrirse a ellos en cuantas ocasiones se apetezca o se tercie.
>
> Any new person, fact, observation or anecdote, even though it may have been made up just this morning by the imagination of some lazy or idle worker, will immediately come to augment the hugely rich, overly large and unforeseeable patrimony of the past and of what has previously happened, with no demand for more verification or approval than the fact of its own telling. After such a moment, that anecdote, that personality, that news, that element can all be cited and alluded to, referred to and referred to again a thousand times without anyone questioning their veracity, and all of those things can be called forth as often as one feels like doing so or as the situation arises. (*Siglo* 74)

Casaldáliga's observation here of course underscores the centrality of storytelling to the daily living of his neighbors, and it affirms as well the centrality of imagination in the representation of the real. Above all, however, Casaldáliga proposes that stories do not grow from a specific origin and do not move toward a discernible conclusion. Indeed, beginnings and endings are always sutured to other stories, which in turn are inscribed in the world of readers and in the plots of still other stories, and remain open to the sequence of reinscriptions that submit all stories to the relentless process of revision. Thus when Casaldáliga claims that he controls his destiny as well as the stories about it, he creates the double irony of the novel through which he embraces a reality that is shown to be a deceit. He reveals this irony as he reflects on the pragmatic outcome of storytelling:

> Mi presencia continua a la orilla del lago les brinda oportunidad no sólo de convertirme en un elemento más de su descomunal y rebosante historia, sino además de tejer e hilvanar cuantos lances, pormenores y anécdotas referentes a mi insigne persona y a las de mis allegados se les crucen por la cabeza. Nadie jamás los pondría en entredicho, y no sólo eso: si yo, por ejemplo, incurriera en tal desafío o atrevimiento, no conseguiría con ello sino que mi actitud contradictoria y rebelde pasara a ser a su vez nuevo objeto de toda clase de conjeturas e infundios que tampoco nadie osaría poner en tela de juicio; y así sucesiva e indefinidamente.

> My continuing presence on the shore of the lake gives them the opportunity not only to convert me into one more fantastic and overflowing element of their history, but also to weave and put together as many incidents, details, and anecdotes concerning my renowned person and my followers as might pass through their minds. No one would every question them, and not only that: if I, for example, dared to challenge them, the only thing I would achieve would be that my contradictory and rebellious attitude would become, in turn, a new focus of all kinds of conjectures and tales that no one would dare place in doubt; and so forth and so on indefinitely.
>
> (*Siglo* 76)

What Casaldáliga lays before the reader in this instance of both blindness and insight affirms the foundational contradiction that Marías establishes in the novel about storytelling: while on the one hand Casaldáliga has argued that he holds authority over experience and narration, on the other the text itself works to belie those assertions. Even Casaldáliga seems to grasp that texts and experiences are formed without what Bakhtin calls "permanent resident rights,"[13] as they spin beyond the individual's control and become implicated in the texts and experiences of others. While the referential authority of stories remains slippery, rooted always, as Marías has noted, in the teller's ability to imagine the real, the meanings of these stories insinuate themselves

---

[13] Mikhail Bakhtin, *Problems of Dostoevsky's Poetics*, trans. Caryl Emerson (Minneapolis: University of Minnesota Press, 1984), p. 88.

into the social order. Hence they have the power to influence social behavior, even though, as Casaldáliga fully understands, "todos los destinos del teatro y la novela universal quedaron ... invalidados por definición y relegados, según su entender, a una esfera parcial, resumida, empobrecida y falaz de la vida, de inferior categoría y distinto signo que la realidad" ("all the destinies of the universal theater and novel ... were invalidated by definition and relegated, according to his understanding, to a partial sphere, a summarized, impoverished, and fallacious sphere that was not even whole, inferior in standing and different from reality") (*Siglo* 36). In this way, the stories speak to effects that extend far beyond their initial telling without the ability to constrain the boundaries (hermeneutical, epistemological, and ontological) of their subsequent telling.

This idea is further enhanced in the novel not only in the way that Casaldáliga's life and story may be appropriated and recast in other stories and other contexts, but in the way that Casaldáliga himself has drawn on the writing of others to frame his own storytelling. While intertextual allusions abound in *El siglo*, from the *Elegies* of Propertius to Robert Browne's *Hydriotaphia* and *Religio Medici*,[14] and offer strong assertions of Marías's reliance upon other texts to enrich the meaning of his own, two sonnets by John Milton bring clearly to the fore the ironic recontextualizing of meaning that runs throughout *El siglo*. The first and most important comes from the final line of "To His Deceased Wife": "I waked, she fled, and day brought back my night" (*Siglo* 126). Here Milton links his sadness to absence, but he experiences momentary hope as he dreams (at night) of reuniting with his wife in the hereafter. His dream is cut short, however, by the waking of the world to the light of day. In the context of *El siglo* and of Casaldáliga awaiting the death of his wife, the reference to Milton's profound bereavement turns utterly farcical. Casaldáliga feels no passion or intimacy with his wife while she lives, and he theatrically awaits her anticipated death, which of course turns out to be a grand deception. In this way, the story of Milton's desire to have a blissful reunion with his wife is wholly subverted by Marías's relocation of it in Casaldáliga's story. Milton's original wish to join his wife, who in fact has passed away, is now co-opted by Casaldáliga in his story, where his wish is that his wife will die quickly so that he can fulfill his perceived destiny to become a widower.

The second example, from "On his Blindness," contains one of the best

---

14 For an excellent discussion of the many intertextual allusions in *El siglo*, see Gareth J. Wood, "Literary Allusion in Javier Marías's *El siglo*," *Bulletin of Hispanic Studies* 84 (2007): 589–607.

known lines from Milton's sonnets, "They also serve who only stand and wait" (*Siglo* 202). In Milton, of course, the line is linked to patience, to the strong feeling of self-esteem, and to the belief that there are various ways to serve God and humankind. In the context of Casaldáliga's story, however, the line refers to fighting in the Civil War and to Casaldáliga's inaction in the face of his expressed desire to enter the conflict. While he rambles endlessly through the streets of Lisbon, seeking the resolve to enter the fray, Milton's words echo in his mind. They do not describe the nobility of his desire, however, but rather underscore the cowardice of his inertia. Again here, the recontextualization is critical. As Gareth Wood points out, Milton's poetry "proves a source of mockery" ("Literary Allusion" 604), not of nobility as Milton had originally intended.

Marías notes in his preface to the 1995 edition of *El siglo* that, in part, he wrote the novel to try to understand "de qué modo personas valiosas o meritorias, de las que en principio era difícil esperar vilezas, podían llegar a cometer la mayor de todas sin verse aparentemente conminadas ni forzadas a ello" ("in what way esteemed and meritorious people, from whom it would be difficult to expect vile acts, could come to commit the greatest of all without apparently being threatened or forced to do so").[15] Yet the novel offers less an exploration of why Casaldáliga became an informer than a peripatetic negation of his capacity to become anything at all. If character is destiny, as Heraclitus proposed, Marías pries open the character of Casaldáliga to reveal it as an absence, thus affirming the only assertion that Casaldáliga makes about himself not subverted by irony: "en esencia, no fui nunca nadie" ("in essence, I was never anyone") (*Siglo* 156). Casaldáliga sets out to position himself, as both he and the third-person narrator observe, "en dueño absoluto de su propio destino" ("as the absolute owner of his own destiny") (*Siglo* 22). Such a proposition of course not only defies the social and historical forces that constitute the complexity of living, but also conflicts sharply with the nature of storytelling, which serves as the principal instrument for representing and defining one's destiny. Memory and imagination give substance to Casaldáliga's assertion, but his conception of both disallows their inherent contingency and richness. In the end, therefore, the novel offers a loathsome vision of the character that it has created, not simply because he is a government informer but because he rids life of its discreet enchantments (incompleteness, process, intimacy) without even realizing it. His horizon of expectations is never enriched by uncertainty and possibility, but instead is

---

[15] Javier Marías, *El siglo* (Barcelona: Anagrama, 1995), p. 9.

tainted by his need for completeness—both in how he lives and in how he narrates. Thus when he decides, as he puts it, "que debía desterrar de su vida lo contingente" ("that he ought to rid his life of the contingent") (*Siglo* 22), he misses the entire point. As the novel convincingly argues, living and narrating are inevitably filled with aporias, even if we seek to disallow or supersede them.

El hombre sentimental

At first glance, there seems to be little that is compellingly new in the story that Marías tells in *El hombre sentimental* (1986) (*The Man of Feeling*, 2003). It is loosely grafted onto the form of the classic love triangle, and as Juan Benet observed in his 1987 epilogue to the novel, "no añade nada nuevo al asunto, apenas aporta algo inédito a un argumento no por muy extenso en sus escasas variables" ("it adds nothing new to the matter, it scarcely brings anything unusual to a plot that is not very broad in its few variables").[16] In Marías's version of the love triangle, a Spanish opera singer known only as "el León de Nápoles" recounts parts of his four-year affair with a wealthy but lonely married woman named Natalia Manur. León recalls how they met, the role played by her escort, Dato (hired by her husband to accompany her both in her activities at home and during her travels), in facilitating León's acquaintance with Natalia, and various aspects of León's life and career as a professional singer. Natalia eventually leaves her husband (the third member of the triangle, a Belgian banker named Manur), who later dies from complications of a suicide attempt following his discovery that Natalia has abandoned him. After four years of living and traveling with León, Natalia suddenly leaves him without explanation or even letting him know with certainty that she is leaving, much in the same way that she had abandoned her husband. Here, the novel comes to an end.[17]

The relative simplicity of the plot of *El hombre sentimental*, however, belies certain areas of complexity and tension that refashion the generic

---

[16] Juan Benet, "Ningún terreno clausurado," in Javier Marías, *El hombre sentimental* (Mexico: Alfaguara Mexico, 2000), p. 169.

[17] It is important to point out that several characters who form the main focus of *El hombre sentimental* appeared previously in Marías's novel *El siglo* (1983). In particular, Donato Dato plays a critical role in the plot of *El siglo*, while León plays a less substantial role but one that carries over into the plot of *El hombre sentimental*. Dato maintains a somewhat mysterious, almost amorphous role in both novels; León is presented in *El siglo* as the hovering godson awaiting the death of Casaldáliga in order to receive his inheritance from the now wealthy old man.

structure that Juan Benet finds commonplace and mundane in the novel. First of all, in the broad context of Marías's own writing, *Hombre* offers specific connections to several concerns that are threaded through much of his fiction: the efficacy of narration as a means of representing the real, the entanglements of intertextuality, the forging of individual identity, the contingencies of memory, and the uses of storytelling. Furthermore, and perhaps most curiously, *Hombre* does not simply stand as the remembering and recounting of a four-year love affair between Natalia Manur and León de Nápoles, but is rather the chronicling of a dream about that affair, which León happened to have had the very morning of the present time of the novel and which forms the basis for the telling of his story. In other words, his first-person narrative re-presents a dream about certain incidents from his relationship with Natalia—a dream which he claims on more than one occasion conveys with unfailing accuracy events that occurred in real life.[18]

We might logically ask, of course, why does Marías choose to structure his novel around a dream? What purpose does it serve? If, as León claims, his dream offers a complete and precise representation of what actually happened to him in reality, why not simply exclude the dream and proceed directly to the representation? Furthermore, within what would appear to be receding levels of distance from the real—León's memory of the dream, his narration of it, the dream itself, the reality about which he dreams—we discern scant apprehension in the novel about the capacity of narrative to represent either the fullness of the dream or León's role within it. For example, the text posits no deconstructive negation of language through which words gain meaning only in relation to other words, as many contemporary novels propose. Nor does Marías appear to doubt the ability to make the dream fully present to the reader; there is no hesitation in using it to help define León's sense of self. Further, the text never posits through any structural or technical device that all that happens to León exists only tenuously as a result of imagining and constructing the story itself. Although León is clearly aware that he is telling/writing a story, the novel does not bear the markings of a metafictional

---

[18] This is the case early in the novel, for example, with León's description of Natalia, Manur, and Dato when all four share a train compartment on their way to Madrid. León's precise description of each, based on what he is able to see of their faces, is conveyed in the dream with great detail. The scene from the train establishes the accuracy of the dream: León could have provided more detail based on his subsequent contact with them, but his dream evokes the scene at the time that it took place, when León had not met the other three. Hence he narrates precisely what he was able to perceive at that time as it was accurately re-presented in the dream.

work—the text turns outward to León's dream and beyond, rather than inward to its own organization.[19] And rather than undermine the ability of León to recall fully his dream, or question the mimetic adequacy of his writing, as occurs in much fiction of the past several decades, the novel develops as if stories, dreams, and life co-existed on the same ontological plane. In this sense, then, *Hombre* seems to grow from a signifying scheme that is steadfastly unvexed by the contingencies of memory and the potential ambiguity of words. In brief, it embraces the real even as it immerses itself in a dream.

Yet as we know from his theoretical writing on the nature of narrative, from his novels prior to *El hombre sentimental*, and from what will grow more intensely clear in his later fiction, storytelling for Marías is never a matter of simply narrating what happened in a given space and at a particular moment to an individual or a group of people, even when such basic elements of storytelling appear straightforward. In *Hombre*, Marías certainly is interested in the telling of his story, but the core of the novel lies in the admixture of other elements: what he conveys about the nature of dreams (a single dream, we must remember, constitutes nearly the whole of León's story); how the task of narrating the dream characterizes León himself; why León's dream compels the reader to infer that León perceives love largely disengaged from feeling (hence the misdirection and irony of the novel's title); how the intertextual connections to León's musical roles serve to define his behavior and his identity.

León begins the story of his dream by expressing his ambivalence about actually telling it: "No sé si contaros mis sueños"[20] ("I don't know whether I should tell you my dreams").[21] In other words, León is fully aware of narration and reception, of narrators and readers (here, a first-person narrator and a plural "you" of readers), and implicitly, of the process through which representations of life come into existence and gain meaning. Although his interest in storytelling moves to the fore at various points throughout the work, he

---

[19] Metafiction is generally defined as fiction that turns inward to explore the nature of its own creation, with emphasis on the interplay between reality and fiction. Often times the protagonist of a metafictional work is a novelist writing a novel, which turns out to be the work that we are reading. To a large degree, works of metafiction place emphasis on the process of creation, the contingencies of representation, and in many instances, the creative role of the reader in the construction of meaning.

[20] Javier Marías, *El hombre sentimental* (Mexico: Alfaguara Mexico, 2000), p. 13. All references to the novel in Spanish are to this edition.

[21] Javier Marías, *The Man of Feeling*, trans. Margaret Jull Costa (New York: New Directions, 2003), p. 1. All references to the novel in English are to this edition.

offers no further commentary on the process at this early juncture of the novel (thus eschewing metafictional digressions). Instead, he turns to explore the foundational component that shapes what he is about to relate: the nature of dreams and, in particular, the nature and content of his own dream that very morning. Such a discussion creates a certain amount of risk for the writer seeking to control the story, for it would seem to send the reader scurrying to essays of Freud or Lacan on the meaning of dreams, with the anticipation of uncovering complex emotions and experiences that León has suppressed in order to protect himself from unfathomable harm. In other words, when the narrator of a novel begins his story with a mini-disquisition on dreams, and the narration itself largely consists of a dream, readers are implicitly steered toward a tradition of interpretation and revelation broadly rooted in hermeneutics, on occasion in science, and always in speculation.

Yet the initial activation of dreams, with its implicit demand for exegesis, is somewhat of a deceit. For rather than reflect on what his dreams might come to mean, or urge his readers to probe more deeply into his psyche (it must be remembered that from the outset León speaks directly to the implied readers of the narrative, "vosotros"), León quickly grows more concerned with the practical matter of narration. Hence in some ways the first sentences narrated by León contain the interpretive scheme of the novel ambiguously layered within them, but they do not offer enough information to reveal it.

First of all, León's dreams are at once "historiados y a la vez precisos" (13) ("elaborate and precise" [1]); they are dreams which "acaban cansando un poco, porque quien los sueña despierta siempre antes de su desenlace, como si el impulse onírico quedara agotado en la representación de los pormenores y se desentendiese del resultado, como si la actividad de soñar fuese la única aún ideal y sin objetivo" (13) ("become somewhat tedious after a while because the person dreaming them always wakes before the end, as if the dream impulse had worn itself out in the representation of all those details and lost interest in the final result, as if dreaming were the only truly ideal and aimless activity left" [1]). León confesses uncertainty about how his dreams end, and thus, as he puts it, "puede ser desconsiderado relatarlos sin estar en condiciones de ofrecer una conclusión ni una enseñanza") ("it might be inconsiderate of me to tell you about them, knowing that I can offer neither conclusion nor lesson" [1]). Such an understanding of course brings much to bear on how León narrates. He awakens from his dreams before they are finished—not necessarily finished in a physical or psychological sense, but before they seem complete discursively, before they have a sense of an ending. That morning León wakes up in his room and conveys no confusion about being "there," in a certain place at a certain time. He understands that dreams spawn a vertigo of images that disperse, re-form, become lost, and are replaced with other images. Most importantly, all of the images fall outside a particular narrative shape that appears to be demanded by his post-dream memory of them. He perhaps expects them to burst forth in the form of a story in which they are naturally embedded, and though he is puzzled by what and how they mean, he hopes to lean upon them for comforting stability.

However, something curious has happened to León that morning that his narrative will reveal: "lo que soñé esta mañana, cuando ya era de día, es algo que sucedió realmente y que me sucedió a mí cuando era un poco más joven" (13) ("what I dreamed this morning, when it was already light, is something that really happened and that happened to me when I was slightly younger" [2]). And thus León's story begins. But in the same breath, León adds a descriptive statement about himself, giving it weight from the outset as one of the main framing devices of the novel and as the primary source of his self-identity: "soy cantante" (13) ("I am a professional singer" [2]). As his story develops, this identity serves as the critical hermeneutic reference point for how he sees and understands the world. However, while affirming what he embraces as the measure of his identity (his singing), and while assuring us of the importance of his dream, much of the narrative serves to diminish any special status that might be attributed to either.

From the outset, León unmoors dreams from the unconscious and anchors them instead in memory—a disconnect that fails to hold firm, of course, since he also recognizes the involuntary nature of memory, which may conjure a world of things that are doubtful rather than certain, possible rather than actual, and unknown rather than known. At various points in his narrative León reflects on his dream about Natalia, how it has come to him in that particular form, and why it has come on that particular morning. He of course eschews divine revelation or even reasoned epiphany as a component of his ability to understand, and instead views his dream as a space of experience that clings to a fragment of time, the meaning of which can be perceived and communicated through narration. This meaning may be hidden from everyday awareness but not embedded in the psyche beyond scrutiny. As he notes, "No sé por qué la memoria selectiva de los sueños es tan distinta de la de nuestros sentidos despiertos, pues no puedo creer en esas explicaciones justicieras según las cuales aflora en los primeros, bajo disfraces diversos, lo que los segundos suprimen. Hay en esa creencia un elemento que me parece religioso en exceso ..." (42) ("I don't know why the selective memory of dreams is so different from that of our conscious senses, but I cannot believe in those vengeful explanations according to which the things that the latter suppresses resurface, in various guises, in the former. Such a belief, I feel, contains an excessively religious element ..." [29]).

León affirms that in dreams the juxtaposition of images can create new perceptions and ways of understanding not evoked by conscious reflection, thus giving life to what otherwise might become immense patches of oblivion. But this does not mean, in León's view, that dreams rake the deep unconscious, pulling forth bits and pieces of the psyche that otherwise would remain inscrutable. As he puts it, "veo en los sueños intuiciones y explicaciones que no están reñidas con la conciencia alerta, comentarios explícitos—por metafóricos que sean: no hay contradicción en ello—acerca del mundo, del mismo y único mundo que alberga al día, por muy ajena que nos parezca por la mañana la esfera nocturna" (41) ("I see in dreams intuitions and explanations that are not in the least at odds with our alert consciousness, but which are, in fact, explicit comments about the world—however metaphorical: there is no contradiction in that—about the same and only world that accommodates the daylight world, regardless of how alien the nocturnal realm may seem to us in the morning" [31]). However, his view that dreams are effects of memory also ties them to the contingencies of narration. He admits, for example, that even though his dream of what happened four years ago is propped wholly against reality, the external cultivation of his dream turns upon his rhetorical skills, which is a way, of course, of saying that it depends on his talent as a storyteller.

León's awareness of his role as narrator is made clear from the outset. He confesses, for example, that "soñé lo ocurrido en otro orden, con otro tiempo, y con otros cortes o divisiones del tiempo, concentradamente, selectivamente" (41) ("I dreamed about what happened in another order, in another tempo, and with time apportioned and divided differently in a concentrated, selective manner" [31]). In other words, he performs narration as any narrator must, connecting certain pauses and disruptions in time in his dream to what he sees as "convencionales respiros de carácter dramático o narrativo o rítmico, como el fin de un capítulo" (40) ("[the] conventional breathing space of a dramatic or narrative or rhythmic nature, like the end of a chapter" [30]). León recognizes here that plot organizes time which would otherwise be dispersed and perhaps never made whole. His dilemma, however, is not whether such imposiciones diminish the authenticity of what is conveyed (as postmodern thinking would have it), but rather how they give shape to it. Most importantly, he understands that writers never simply extract from events a story that they believe is already embedded within those events (despite what historians, biographers, and many nineteenth-century realist novelists might proclaim), but rather create the story through choice and tradition. "Lo extraño," as León observes about his narration, "es que en mi sueño hubiera sucesión cuando en mi cabeza ya había síntesis" (42) ("The strange thing is that, while in my mind there was synthesis, in my dream there was progression" [32]). In this way, León points to narration as selecting, organizing, and interpreting. Most importantly, in doing so, he sees the material of his narrative—dreams, memories, and stories—as all complementary parts of the same epistemological terrain.

The second matter that shapes León's sense of self, and thus his sense of his love affair with Natalia, grows from his work as a professional singer. For the most part he conveys a perception of his identity awash in irony—he diminishes, and even vitiates his profession, yet consistently turns to it to understand and explain both his thoughts and his actions. His many reflections on his career as an opera singer do not constitute part of his dream per se, but rather help align the frame within which he presents himself. For example, during a long fragment of his narrative early in the novel, he compares his life as an itinerant singer with the life of a traveling salesman (though he recognizes that the singer enjoys greater financial means and public acclaim). It is clearly not a happy comparison. As León comments on his life before meeting Natalia, he describes his persistent loneliness and isolation, his time spent in rehearsals and hotel rooms, the difficulty of meeting people in the cities where he performs, and fleeting sexual encounters with prostitutes. Although León imagines himself as different from other professional singers (for example, in the way that he is curious about the cities he visits and how he enjoys learning about their uniqueness), he reluctantly accepts that the cheerless and often despairing life of the salesman parallels the dreary personal existence of a singer. For the singer, however, the illusion of transcendence often distorts reality: "nunca está tan seguro como el viajante de que esa vida suya sea efectivamente solitaria y triste. Por culpa del maquillaje tiene menos clarividencia" (29) ("he is never quite as convinced as the traveling salesman that this life of his is, in fact, sad and solitary. The greasepaint makes him less clear-sighted" [17]). The make-up worn by the singer is metaphorically critical as well as ironic—it allows him to become someone other than he is, to play a role created by someone else and then imagined as his own, if only for a while. This professional role-playing not only shapes León's perception of himself and defines his relationship with Natalia Manur, but also circumscribes both characters as they emerge within León's narrative.

With full awareness of the loneliness of his existence, and at the stage of his career where he has won critical acclaim for secondary roles in well-known operas, León first observes Natalia, her husband, and Dato seated in his train compartment, though he does not speak with them at the time. A few days later in the bar of his hotel in Madrid, León meets Natalia (with Dato as her companion), whom León will come to perceive as "la salvación y el milagro" (60) ("the salvation and miracle" [52]) that give rise to a transformational moment in his life: "Por primera vez en mi carrera operística no me sentí solitario y triste en una gran ciudad. ... El yo que existía antes de conocer a Dato y a los Manur ha estado ausente o amortiguado durante tanto tiempo, y aun habría dicho que había muerto de no ser porque esta mañana que avanza a la vez que yo escribo me parece estarlo reconociendo" (59) ("For the first time in my operatic career I did not feel sad and solitary in the big city. ... The 'I' that existed before meeting Dato and the Manurs has been absent or damped down during all that time, and I would go so far as to say that it had died, were it not for the fact that this morning, which is advancing as I write, I seem to recognize that 'I'" [50–51]). León's full understanding of his encounter and subsequent four-year relationship with Natalia is revealed not in his dream, of course, but after he awakens and begins to write about it. Only then is he able to grasp its significance and gain insight into the nature of his life before and after he had met Natalia.

As León acknowledges, he had long lived a solitary existence as a singer. He had abandoned the space of his youth (Madrid and its environs) as well as those with whom he was associated, most notably his rigid and demanding godfather, Casaldáliga (though he correctly suspects that Casaldáliga is really his father). While he expresses a desire to know and understand the multiple places where he performs, he has no sense of home. Even his visits to Madrid are without interest or hope of pleasure: "Madrid es rústico y dicharachero y no encierra misterio, y nada hay tan triste ni tan solitario como una ciudad sin enigma aparente o apariencia de enigma, nada tan disuasorio, nada tan opresivo para el visitante" (26) ("Madrid is rustic and talkative and lacks all mystery, and there is nothing so sad or so solitary as a city with no apparent enigma or even the appearance of an enigma, there is nothing so dissuasive, nothing so oppressive to a visitor" [13]). Indeed, as León points out, his visits to Madrid serve only to exacerbate his dislocation and detachment. León's life as a singer has allowed him to free himself from the debilitating numbness of his youth and to pursue professional advancement far removed from the familiar space and time of Madrid. Yet, on the whole, there is little that is extraordinary about the larger plot of León's past: put succinctly, a young man leaves home to construct a life for himself and has the good fortune to gain professional success. Nor is there compelling novelty in León's story when, during the course of his professional ascent, he discovers the personal desolation of an existence that consists unyieldingly of work and travel. Indeed, he finds himself largely disconnected from life outside of his profession.[22] In other words, before Natalia entered his life, León lived a

---

[22] This had been especially the case four years earlier, before his more highly

largely despondent existence whose tediousness was alleviated only by his immersion in the imaginary roles that he played.

It is precisely this immersion, however, and the bleeding of fictional roles into his real life, that serves as impetus for León's passion—and also as the source of its gnawing inauthenticity. For despite the importance that León ascribes to his affair with Natalia, despite his desire to eliminate Natalia's husband as his main rival for her attention and affection, and despite the dream of his love affair with Natalia that constitutes nearly all of what León writes in the present, he manages to recognize and affirm himself only through music. Indeed, he remains emotionally impotent when seeking to attach feelings to anything outside of it.

León meets Natalia for the first time in the bar of his hotel following a lengthy conversation with her companion, Dato. León had shown interest in Natalia during the conversation and, when asked by Dato if he was married, León had quickly responded that he was not. León's answer is deceitful but not untrue: he admits to the reader (but not to Dato) that he has been living with a woman named Berta for the past four years. What is striking about León's denial is not that it opens for him the possibility of pursuing a relationship with Natalia, but that it brings fully to the fore his crippled capacity for intimacy in real life and his inability to escape the profession that defines him. For example, while León learns about Natalia's life from Dato, he processes the story through opera: "era como si también él [Dato] recitara, una lamentación, la introducción a un aria" (50) ("It was as if he [Dato] too were reciting something—a lamentation, the introduction to an aria" [40]). More importantly, his purposeful renunciation of Berta in his conversation with Dato was actually drawn up several months earlier, during his performance of Puccini's *Turandot*. Even though he admits that "Berta, en realidad, es perfecta" (95) ("Berta is actually perfect" [95]), his realization that he does not love her (in real life) correlates with the paroxysm of emotion that overwhelms him in relation to Liu, the impassioned lover of Puccini's opera:[23]

> Allí [en Barcelona] vivo con Berta, a la que quizá no amo, a la que sin duda no amo, como supe hace unos meses durante una representación de

---

acclaimed operatic roles of the present, which have won him widespread fame. Earlier in his career, when he had obtained only modest success, he was compelled to play secondary parts, such as Spoletta (the police agent in Puccini's *Tosca*); Trabuco (the muleteer and peddler in Verdi's *La forza del destino*); Dancairo (a smuggler in Bizet's *Carmen*); and Monostatos (a servant in Mozart's *The Magic Flute*).

[23] Liu is the loyal slave girl in *Turandot* who refuses to reveal the name of the Prince to Princess Turandot, despite being tortured. Her passion is so strong that, rather than betray the Prince, she commits suicide.

> *Turandot* en Cleveland, cuando Liu me emocionó de tal manera con sus célebres arias premortuorias que me descubrí sintiendo un amor invencible sin que el objeto de ese amor fuera Berta en modo alguno, aunque tampoco fuera ninguna otra persona en particular, desde luego no la cantante que hacía de la esclava enamorada y sacrificada. (94–95)

> There [in Barcelona] I live with Berta, whom I may not love, whom I doubtless do not love, as I realized a few months ago during a performance of *Turandot* when Liu's famous pre-funeral arias moved me so much that I was filled by a sense of invincible love whose object was definitely not Berta, although neither was it anyone else, certainly not the singer playing the part of the enamoured, selfless slave. (94)

It is not the external world of León's existence (Berta, with whom he lives, or the actual singer who plays the part of Liu) where he finds his desire, but rather he derives it from the text of the opera. In this way, desire becomes for him as he imagines it ought to be. Indeed, it is as if León has peered into the real world of emotion, grappled with its deficiencies, and stepped back into the artifice created by the imagination of others. He thus cannot attain, as Proust posits, the equilibrium between desire fashioned by imagination and passion grounded in reality that allows authenticity to exist and to flourish. As Proust has written, "For a desire seems to us more beautiful, we repose on it with more confidence, when we know that outside ourselves there is a reality which conforms to it, even if, for us, it is not to be realized."[24] If reality conforms to León's desire he may be able to feel and believe in it, but his affect remains sharply restricted by his filiation with his music. In short, he does not (and effectively cannot) love Berta, for she stands outside of any textual object with which his desire is fused.

It is not by chance in the novel that when León meets Natalia in Madrid he is rehearsing the role of Cassio in *Othello*.[25] Marías not only loosely folds the plot of *El hombre sentimental* into the plot of Verdi's opera (and by implication, Shakespeare's play), thus establishing both the musical and literary intertexts for his work, but also continues to draw on the roles that León plays to show how the singer's desire is shaped by texts that impair his capacity to love in real life. It is important to point out, however, that unlike characters

---

[24] Cited in Georges Poulet, *Studies in Human Time*, trans. Elliott Coleman (Baltimore and London: Johns Hopkins University Press, 1956), p. 300.

[25] For an excellent discussion of the various ways in which Verdi's *Othello* forms important intertextual connections with *El hombre sentimental*, see Isabel Cuñado, "Realidad y ficción en *El hombre sentimental*," in *Foro Hispánico* 20 (2001): 95–103.

such as Don Quijote or Emma Bovary, León does not come to believe that the referents of the operas or the characters represented within them exist in reality. Further, he never mistakes the actor (singer) for the character, nor does he suffer from madness or loss of reason so as to confuse the internal story conveyed by the text with life outside the text. Indeed, he constructs in his narrative a textured self-awareness founded upon thoughtful reflection on both the word and the world. Nonetheless, the roles that he plays seem to impair him personally, even as they increasingly suit him professionally.

First of all, it is clear that the love triangle involving Manur, Natalia, and León is shaped by the relationship of Othello, Desdemona, and Cassio (with the diminished role of Iago in the novel played by Natalia's companion, Dato). What is important about this intertextual blending, however, is not the many differences (and some similarities) between *Othello* as text and the three characters of the novel, but the way that Marías maneuvers the narrative to reveal the foibles of León (Cassio) rather than emphasize the jealousy of Manur (Othello). To be sure, when Manur learns that León seems intent on pursuing Natalia, he confronts the singer and warns him to stand clear. Further, when Natalia eventually leaves Manur for León, her husband attempts suicide and later dies from the wounds. Hence the plot of *Othello* presides over the novel and reminds the reader of its underlying artifice. However, the intensity of the novel's meaning derives not from repositioning elements of the plot of *Othello* (or of any other opera), but from the recurrent focus on the inauthenticity of intimacy in León's life that is linked to the roles that he assumes.

This can be seen in a number of ways. First, when León becomes interested in Natalia he is performing the secondary role of Cassio in *Othello* in Madrid. Cassio, it will be remembered, functions largely as a pawn in Iago's game of revenge that inspires Othello's jealousy. Iago's rage at Othello for naming Cassio as his lieutenant (Iago had desired the position) grows at least in part from his view that Cassio lacks practical experience, that he knows only the theory of war through the texts he has read about it. As Iago puts it, Cassio has "never set a squadron in the field."[26] Like Cassio, León has never (metaphorically speaking) "set a squadron in the field"—he has only learned the theory of love as it has been textually defined for him. He has never felt the emotion or the passion of love in the reality of his life, but instead has assumed a role in which both are paramount. This is evident in his relationship with Berta, as we have seen, and is further demonstrated in his

---

26 William Shakespeare, *Othello* (Oxford: Oxford University Press, 2006), 1.1.21, p. 197.

encounters with prostitutes. Indeed, as he recalls returning home to Berta after long absences while on tour, he is scarcely inspired by the emotion of seeing her: "No tengo ilusión por Berta, cuando regreso a casa no me alegra demasiado verla, ni siento la necesidad ni el deseo de acostarme con ella en seguida. ... De hecho me ilusiona más convocar a una puta de lujo en mi habitación de lujo en algunas de mis soledades mayores de mis viajes musicales" (95) ("I don't feel excited about Berta; when I get home, I don't feel particularly glad to see her, nor do I feel any immediate need or desire to go to bed with her. ... The fact is that I find it more exciting to have a luxury call girl come up to my luxury room during some of the lonelier nights of my musical travels" [94–95]).

León's attraction to Natalia is no less awakened and sustained by textual association. While on the one hand, in his dream he relives with precision the events of his affair with Natalia and then sets about narrating it to us, on the other he tells us virtually nothing at all about the affair. When he stops to reflect on why he pursues Natalia, and even proclaims his introduction to her as a transformative moment, he is able to explain it only in the words and feelings that he has learned from opera. As he observes, "¿Por qué querré seguir viéndola a diario? Tal vez porque deseo ser como Liu y como Otello" (96) ("Why do I want to go on seeing her every day? Perhaps because I want to be like Liu or like Otello" [96]). The passion of Liu (from *Turandot*) and of Othello becomes fully fledged here as both source and patron of León's own passion. What compels León is not experience or feeling that he may have summoned forth in reality, but rather the feeling that he has learned in roles he has assumed. He cannot escape the pull of texts and the deep desire of the characters who reside there. Further, he asserts his belief that passion can be conjured and his life transformed by the stories (and passions) of others if only he can locate himself in their roles (though Liu, of course, is a female character, whose feeling he can never actually perform).

Marías has observed about *El hombre sentimental* that León never allows love to gain the presence and complexity in his narrative that readers might anticipate in a story that is ostensibly about love. As Marías writes, "*El hombre sentimental* es una historia de amor en la que el amor no se ve ni vive, sino que se anuncia y recuerda"[27] ("*The Man of Feeling* is a love story in which love is neither seen nor experienced, but announced and remembered").[28] Marías further notes that love beckons most urgently either in anticipation or in memory, and thus is the sentiment, as he puts it, "que exige

---

[27] Javier Marías, "Lo que no se ha cumplido," in *El hombre sentimental*, p. 172.
[28] Javier Marías, "Epilogue: Something Unfulfilled," in *The Man of Feeling*, p. 180.

mayores dosis de imaginación" ("Lo que no se ha cumplido" 172) ("that requires the largest dose of imagination" ["Epilogue" 181]). Yet while imagination may foster love and nourish its intensity, love can only exist for readers as part of a story. As Marías has pointed out on many occasions in both his essays and his fiction, in order to narrate the real, one has to imagine it.[29] And it is precisely here where León's narration is weighted down with irony. Unable to imagine his own feelings, he has mouthed the words of others from works of art that are instigated and sustained by someone else. As León puts it in perhaps the most synthetic passage of the novel, he perceives himself as:

> Un pobre tenor que tiene miedo de su propio relato o de sus propios sueños, como si utilizar palabras en vez de letra, vocablos no dictados, frases inventadas en vez de textos ya escritos, aprendidos, memorizados, repetitivos, paralizara su poderosa voz, que sólo ha conocido hasta ahora el estilo recitativo. Me resulta difícil hablar sin libreto. (45)

> A poor tenor who is afraid of his own story and of his own dreams, as if using words instead of lyrics, words that have not been dictated, invented phrases rather than repetitive written texts, learned, and memorized, had paralyzed his powerful voice, which up until now has only known the recitative style. I find it hard to speak without a libretto. (33–34)

For this reason León's love remains strikingly absent from his own story. Even when he addresses Natalia directly in his narrative and appears to speak with emotive intensity about his feelings of need and desire for her, he diminishes their authenticity by assimilating them into his operatic vision: "Pero tu muerte sería también la mía—le dije a esta misma mujer, y así, al igual que sucede en la opera, se lo he repetido también varias veces en mi sueño de esta mañana" (23) (" 'But your death would also be mine,' I said to this same woman and, just as happens in opera, I repeated these same words several times in this morning's dream" [12]).

---

[29] For example, in his essay "Los malditos detalles," Marías writes that "También lo real ha de ser imaginado" ("Also, the real must be imagined"), in *Mano de sombra* (Madrid: Alfaguara, 1997), p. 325; or in "Imaginar para creer," he praises the great works of Mann, Conrad, and Dickens and notes that in order to present various aspects of reality, these novelists not only have the ability to observe the world, "sino que además hay que imaginarlo" ("but also, one has to imagine it"), in *Literatura y fantasma* (Madrid: Alfaguara, 2001), p. 214. For further discussion of Marías's views on literature and imagination, see chapter II. For a discussion of imagination as it specifically applies to *El hombre sentimental*, see Alexis Grohmann, *Coming Into One's Own: The Novelistic Development of Javier Marias* (Amsterdam and New York: Rodopi, 2002), pp. 89–122.

Yet an authentic man of feeling does manage to emerge in Marías's novel—not the professional singer who finds it difficult to "speak without a libretto," but the banker whose rigid life of business deals and meetings seems to oppose all sentiment. Indeed, in their first encounter after being introduced in the hotel, León dismisses Manur as "pedante, correcto, sentencioso" (64) ("pedantic, correct, sententious" [58]), and views him more as an obstacle to be eliminated than a threat able to incite Natalia's passion. When Manur later warns León to remove himself from Natalia's life, his insistence seems divested of emotion of any kind. And when León comments on the ordinariness of the banker's marriage to Natalia, Manur in fact describes their relationship using the language of business: "En la mayoría de los matrimonios no se da la circunstancia de que uno de los cónyuges tenga—hizo una mínima pausa—comprado al otro, adquirido en propiedad. Mi mujer me pertenece en el sentido más riguroso de la palabra pertenecer ..." (126) (" 'It is not the case in most marriages that one of the spouses has,'—he paused for a split second—'bought the other, acquired them. My wife belongs to me in the strictest sense of the word 'belonging' ..." [133]).

Yet as the novel develops, Manur emerges not as a sterile and indifferent figure of material wealth, but as a man sustained and finally vanquished by desire. This desire becomes evident to León in two forms: first, through Manur's perseverance in his quest for Natalia's affection ("no he visto nunca a ninguna otra persona con tanta voluntad de perseverancia en su elección y en su amor" [130]) ("I have never seen anyone with such a will to persevere in his choice and in his love" [135]). Second, and most importantly, in his capacity to imagine love, to await signs of its disclosure, and to feel it. As Manur tells León at the end of their encounter in León's hotel room, "Tenga en cuenta que no hay vínculo más estrecho que el que anuda lo que es fingido, o aún es más, lo que nunca ha existido" (137) ("Bear in mind that there is no stronger bond than that which binds one to something unreal or, worse, something that has never existed" [146]). Manur is able to sustain passion that is not reciprocated because he can powerfully feel it, and thus live it through desire and imagination. In contrast, León is able to imagine passion only when playing his part in the opera.

León persistently stands apart from feeling, both in his life and in his narration. As he reflects on the story that he is telling, he rates his own voice as disconnected and indifferent. Without the words of others to draw upon, he stands largely impassive before life: "En estas páginas que he ido llenando (sin haber desayunado aún) reconozco una voz fría e invulnerable, como las de los pesimistas, que, lo mismo que no ven ninguna razón para vivir, tampoco ven ninguna para matarse o morir, ninguna para temer, ninguna para aguardar, ninguna para pensar ..." (59) ("In these pages that I have been filling (without yet having had any breakfast) I recognize a cold, invulnerable voice, the voice of the pessimist, who, just as he sees no reason to live, likewise sees no reason to kill himself, or to die, no reason to feel afraid, no reason to wait, no reason to think ..." [51]).

While León's narration allows him to do precisely what he seems to deny himself, "temer, aguardar, pensar" ("feeling afraid, waiting, and thinking"), the coldness of his self-knowledge underscores the opposing outcome of the story for these two men who are pursuing the same woman. When Manur learns that his wife has left him, he commits suicide. When León awakens on the morning of his dream and realizes that Natalia is gone, he tells a story. And to further mark the difference between the two men, León interweaves speculation on what might have happened the night Manur killed himself with his own thoughts on what he might dream the next night when he falls asleep. He imagines Manur's final thoughts and actions in the shadows of the evening when Manur seeks to kill himself, then links them to his own: "Manur se mira la mano en penumbra. Así, sentado, vestido de calle, le vienen ganas de aniquilarse. Mi mano está en penumbra. Pero no debéis preocuparos, yo sería incapaz de seguir su ejemplo" (166) ("Manur looks at his hand in the shadows. Then, sitting down, dressed to go out, he feels a desire to destroy himself. My hand is in the shadows. But don't worry, I would be incapable of following his example" [177]).

What is critical here, and what finally distinguishes León from Manur, lies in the narrator's final few words, "I would be incapable of following his example." León is ill-suited for killing himself because it is not a role he knows how to play in real life. There is no libretto to lay out the plot for him; he has become an indifferent Othello who has lost Natalia because she simply grew tired of him. The novel thus ends not within an opera through which León can recognize himself, but with him cast adrift in a dim reality that leaves him with neither expectation nor hope. He suggests in his narrative that he will become once again the dispassionate man he was before he met Natalia. In fact, of course, he will continue to be the man he has been all along, but which he has sought to disguise during the four years of his affair.

The epigram that prefaces *El hombre sentimental* comes from William Hazlitt, the great English essayist with whom Marías shares, among other things, an interest in Laurence Sterne's *Tristram Shandy*: "I think myself into love, and I dream myself out of love" (np).[30] For León, however, thinking and

---

30 The quote comes from Hazlitt's essay "On Dreams." See *The Miscellaneous Works of William Hazlitt*, Volume II (New York: Derby & Jackson, 1859), p. 155.

dreaming provide neither entry to love nor departure from it: love remains alien to his authentic being, though he is able to imagine its power when performing characters who exist only in texts. During the course of narrating the dream of his affair with Natalia he offers no explanation of why he pursued her to begin with, and he offers no hint that he will pursue her now that she is gone. What he found in Natalia, as well as what now he has lost, bears the marks of emotional flat-lining. He is unable to arouse affective lavishness outside of his performances on the stage, hence he fails to save either himself or Natalia from the chasm of insignificance that surrounds them. His lengthy dream of Natalia comes to constitute the story that he wishes to tell, yet what it actually means in the context of his life remains outside his vision and his consciousness. This blindness lies at the heart of the novel and creates its pervasive irony. In brief, as the novel tells us, León is unable to see because he is unable to feel.

IV

On Oxford, Redonda, and the Practice of Reading: *Todas las almas* and *Negra espalda del tiempo*

The two novels explored in this chapter, *Todas las almas* (1989) (*All Souls*, 1992) and *Negra espalda del tiempo* (1998) (*Dark Back of Time*, 2001), are two of the most intimately linked of all of Marías's works of fiction.[1] This intimacy obtains on many levels, even though nine years passed between the publication of the two works, and despite the fact that Marías wrote two other novels in the intervening period, *Corazón tan blanco* (1992) (*A Heart So White*, 1995) and *Mañana en la batalla piensa en mí* (1994) (*Tommorow in the Battle Think on Me*, 1996). To a large extent, Marías wrote *Negra* to set the record straight about statements he had seen in reviews and essays concerning the referential base of *Todas* in general, as well as comments from acquaintances about its overall autobiographical nature. Thus he sets out in *Negra* to clarify certain aspects of *Todas* that readers had misconstrued, to expand upon characters and ideas that were left ambiguous or incomplete, and to introduce new information that bears upon certain events and locations represented in the earlier novel. Additionally, he creates large sections in the novel that have little or nothing to do with Oxford and the cast of characters from *Todas*.

Marías also lays out a series of theoretical principles and queries about fiction in *Negra* that stand as complex and purposefully contradictory declarations of intention about the art of novel-writing and the nature of reading. While *Todas* hints at some of these ideas, and also offers a narrative that easily identifies with the formal tradition of novels written in the first person,

---

[1] The three volumes of Marías's trilogy, *Tu rostro mañana* (published in 2002, 2004, and 2007) form the other body of work that is closely related. The obvious difference from the perspective of creative intention between the two sets of novels lies in their origins: while the trilogy was designed to be a multi-volume endeavor, *Negra espalda del tiempo* was not even an afterthought to *Todas las almas* when Marías published *Todas* in 1989.

Negra is clearly different: it emerges as a hybrid that blends the voices of author and narrator, incorporates multiple graphic images into the text (including maps and photographs, among many others), and is so expansively nurtured by intertextual connections and references to real-life figures that it becomes uniquely positioned within Marías's body of work. At the same time, however, it displays many of the technical and thematic features that inform the most accomplished and sophisticated of Marías's writing, above all an emphasis on the ambiguities and intractable contradictions of storytelling.

Todas las almas

Todas las almas is the story of what the first-person (and unnamed) narrator of the novel describes as a brief perturbation in his life—his two-year stay as a visiting faculty member at the University of Oxford.[2] He carefully points out that this perturbation (which occurred two and a half years before his actual telling of it in the present) was not at the time, nor is it today, a source of compelling trauma or overwrought despair for him. As he puts it at the end of the novel, when reflecting upon the people whom he knew in Oxford and the nature of his time there:

> Ya no estoy perturbado, aunque mi perturbación de entonces no fuera gran cosa, fue leve y pasajera y articulada y lógica, como ya he dicho, una de

---

[2] In 1996 the father and daughter filmmaking team of Elías Querejeta (producer) and Gracia Querejeta (director) made *Todas las almas* into a movie entitled *El último viaje de Robert Rylands* (*Robert Rylands' Last Journey*). While Marías had granted his approval for the film to be made, he was infuriated with the outcome. In two articles published in November of 1996 in the Spanish newspaper *El País*, "El novelista va al cine" ("The Novelist Goes to the Movies") and "El novelista se sale del cine" ("The Novelist Leaves the Movies Behind"), reprinted in *Donde todo ha sucedido* (*Where Everything Has Occurred*) (Barcelona: Círculo de Lectores, 2005), pp. 217–19 and 220–22 respectively, Marías explains his objections to the film and claims that he will never again allow his work to be made into a movie. He argues that the Querejetas made fundamental changes for the movie version that miss completely what the novel is really about (e.g., they create a homosexual relationship between two male characters, Cromer Blake and Toby Rylands, which, for Marías, is not even implied in the novel), and further, they did not understand nor did they respect the work's artistic integrity. As Marías writes in "El novelista va al cine," "[*El último viaje de Robert Rylands*] tiene muy poco de la letra y nada del espíritu de *Todas las almas*" ("[*The Last Journey of Robert Rylands*] has little to do with the letter and nothing to do with the spirit of *All Souls*") (210). For further discussion of the movie version of *Todas* in relation to the novel, see Dona Kercher, "Children of the European Union, Crossing Gendered Channels: Javier Marías's novel, *Todas las almas*, and Gracia Querejeta's *El último viaje de Robert Rylands*," *Cine-Lit* 3 (1997): 100–12.

esas perturbaciones que no nos impiden seguir trabajando, ni conducirnos de manera sensata, ni ser formales, ni tratar con las demás personas como si no nos sucediera nada; una de esas perturbaciones que seguramente pasan inadvertidas para todo el mundo menos para el que la siente, una de esas que todos tenemos de vez en cuando. Está todo muy lejos. ...[3]

I'm not troubled now, and my sense of unease then was never really that serious, it was slight and transient, coherent and logical, as I said, the kind of malaise that does not keep us from our work, or from behaving sensibly, or being polite, or dealing with other people as if in fact nothing were happening to us; the kind of malaise that doubtless passes unnoticed by everyone except the person feeling it, a malaise we all experience from time to time. It all seems very far away. ...[4]

The narrator's apparent insouciance concerning his stay in Oxford, and his dismissal of its continuing pertinence to his life, would seem to create an obvious question: why make the effort to tell about it if, as the narrator implies, there exists a deep cleavage between his life today and his life then, with the further implication that the present bears felicitous significance and the past bears little. In other words, what is actually at stake in the narrator's story if it simply represents a mildly disquieting time in his past that scarcely shapes life for him in the present?

First of all, the narrator's statement is sustained by overarching irony. It comes near the end of his story which, we might logically conclude, he would have refrained from telling at all had he actually believed his own assertion of its insignificance. Further, his comments reflect a calculated blindness to the power of storytelling as a form of sense-giving, even as the very presence of his narrative affirms insight into what actually occurred during his stay in Oxford and the importance of recounting it. His heightened awareness of the past, and also of the necessity of telling about it, in fact forms the impetus and essence of the novel. As he puts it: "Pero ningún secreto puede ni debe ser guardado siempre para todo el mundo, sino que está obligado a encontrar al menos un destinatario una vez en la vida, una vez en la vida de ese secreto. ... Por eso nos condenamos siempre por lo que decimos. O por lo que nos dicen" (*Todas* 165–66) ("But no secret can or should be kept from everybody

---

[3] Javier Marías, *Todas las almas* (Barcelona: Anagrama, 1989), p. 239. All references to the novel in Spanish are to this edition.

[4] Javier Marías, *All Souls*, trans. Margaret Jull Costa (New York: New Directions Books, 1992), p. 207. All references to the English translation of the novel are to this edition, except where noted.

for ever; once in its life, once in the lifetime of that secret, it is obliged to find at least once recipient. ... That's why we always condemn ourselves by what we say. [Or by what others say to us]" [*All* 140].⁵ In other words, the narrator attaches consequence both to the telling and to the receiving of the tale, making the perturbation of the past more significant than he at first allows.

From the broader perspective of Marías's fiction as a whole, the narrative of *Todas* stands out for a number of reasons: it represents further development of the first-person narration of Marías's novels (which began with *El hombre sentimental*, as we have seen, and is sustained through all of his subsequent works); it presents a character (the narrator) who will reappear as the key figure in Marías's trilogy (*Tu rostro mañana*), though he is never named as such; it introduces into Marías's fiction the real-life figure John Gawsworth and the kingdom of Redonda, both of which will come to play an important role in Marías's life and writing.⁶ Further, it opens in explicit fashion what might be termed a "fictional/autobiographical perturbation" related to Marías that has created substantial theoretical discussion about the relation between authors and their works in general, and a more specific debate about which persons from real life (including Marías himself) can be linked to certain characters in *Todas*.⁷ Perhaps most importantly, it engen-

---

⁵ The translation into English for the bracketed segment of the Margaret Jull Costa edition reads "Not by what we do." While figuratively interesting, it misses the meaning linked to telling and narrating. I have given a more literal translation that captures the "telling" spirit of the quote and of the work as a whole.

⁶ Marías's relationship with the Kingdom of Redonda and John Gawsworth is lengthy and complex. One need only consult a search engine such as Google to discover thousands of entries that link Marías to both. Marías first writes about Redonda in his 1985 essay "El hombre que pudo ser rey," *Pasiones pasadas* (Madrid: Alfaguara, 1999), pp. 197–201. He discusses in some detail his interest in what he terms an obscure English writer who bears the title King of Redonda. Much of what he writes in this short essay is included in his digression in *Todas las almas* on Gawsworth, though with greater detail in the novel since Marías had since learned much more about him. For a brief overview of Marías and his link to Gawsworth, see Alexis Grohmann, *Coming Into One's Own. The Novelistic Development of Javier Marías* (Amsterdam and New York: Rodopi, 2002), pp. 153–55. In *Negra espalda del tiempo* (1998) Marías further explores Gawsworth and Redonda, both clarifying and convoluting the role of each in his work, his life, and the links between reality and fiction. For a compendium of Marías's writings on Redonda (with many references to Gawsworth) see the section in his *Aquella mitad del tiempo* (Barcelona: Círculo de Lectores, 2008) entitled "Redonda y sus nobles," which consists of thirteen columns that Marías wrote between 1990 and 2006 on the subject. It should also be noted that Marías includes a story by Gawsworth entitled "Cómo ocurrió" in his anthology of hard-to-find short stories, *Cuentos únicos* (Madrid: Ediciones Siruela, 1995).

⁷ For an excellent overview of the biographical foundation of the novel (including the specific connections between real-life figures in Oxford and characters in the novel, as

dered a second novel, *Negra espalda del tiempo* (1998) that is intended, at least in part, to contravene the biographical reading of *Todas* through clarification of Marías's intent. In other words, Marías (as author) sets out in *Negra* to guide the reader through the real-life and fictional connections of *Todas* by providing a metafictional and prescriptive commentary on the nature of telling and reading stories. As we shall see, however, *Negra espalda del tiempo* serves to deepen uncertainty rather than instill clarity concerning how to read *Todas* as well as how to read fiction as a whole. Indeed, it explores and enhances ambiguity as a critical component of storytelling, especially as it relates to the creation of narratives and the various ways in which they can be understood and used.

As might be expected in a novel by Marías, the narrator of *Todas* tells his story with many digressions. He recounts with varying degrees of detail his relationship with colleagues Toby Rylands and Cromer-Blake, who embrace his stay in Oxford and serve as mentors in the sometimes bizarre and arcane practices of the university (such as the etiquette of high table dinners for faculty and students); he describes his peripatetic adventures in the city that frequently include random meandering through the streets, during which he begins to recognize the many beggars of the city; he forges a more purposeful pattern of visiting antiquarian bookstores in his quest for rare books; he tells of his sexual (if not love) affair with Clare Bayes, the wife of one of his university colleagues. In the present time, as he writes about Oxford, the narrator no longer maintains contact with Clare, both Rylands and Cromer-

---

well as those characters that are completely "invented"), see Grohmann, *Coming Into One's Own*, pp. 123–48. See also Carmen Baugen, "Autor real y ficción en *Todas las almas, Corazón tan blanco, Mañana en la batalla piensa en mí* y *Negra espalda del tiempo*," in *Foro Hispánico* 20 (2001): 105–12. It should further be noted that many critics, especially in early reviews, characterized *Todas* as a *roman à clef*, seeing people from Oxford in nearly all the characters of the novel, especially those related to the University of Oxford. For a succinct discussion of the theoretical principles of biographical fiction, and the use of what has been termed "autoficción" in *Todas las almas*, see Manuel Alberca, "Las vueltas autobiográficas de Javier Marías," in *Javier Marías*, ed. Irene Andrés Suárez and Ana Casas (Madrid: Arco/Libros, 2005), pp. 49–72. The term "autoficción" generally refers to the ambiguous connections made between narrative fiction and an author's own life, with points of clear contact and points of divergence that may be found to be true or false if closer scrutiny of the author's life is undertaken. These types of connections are important in *Todas* (and in fiction as a whole) if the critical approach tends to emphasize the historical and the biographical aspects of the novel; otherwise, the intrinsic "truth" of the novel (i.e., its internal logic and consistency) moves to the fore as the critical point of reference. As we will see, the "autofictional" component of Marías's writing becomes more firmly pronounced in *Negra espalda del tiempo* as part of the structural and theoretical underpinning of the novel.

Blake have died, and the narrator himself has created a life in Madrid as a successful business man with a wife and young child. He occasionally communicates with a former colleague at the university, but has scant desire to return to the English city that he had abandoned two and a half years earlier. In other words, his relationship with Oxford seems to have been almost completely severed.

It is the nature of this severing, however, that has seeped into the consciousness of the narrator and allows him to understand why he should tell his story of Oxford. The temporal separation between the present of the narration and the events of the story is important—not because of the passage of time per se (it could have been two and a half months or two and a half years), but because the narrator has been able to distinguish between what it means to live a life and what it means to tell a story of that life.[8] As he notes at the beginning of his narrative, "El que aquí cuenta lo que vio y le ocurrió no es aquel que lo vio y al que le ocurrió, ni tampoco es su prolongación, ni su sombra, ni su heredero, ni su usurpador" (*Todas* 10) ("The person recounting here and now what he saw and what happened to him then is not the same person who saw those things and to whom those things happened; neither is he a prolongation of that person, his shadow, his heir or his usurper" [*All* 3]). While a part of the narrator's assertion here may be understood as an extra-textual allusion to the difference between authors and their narrators (i.e., Marías warns readers against biographical speculation),[9] the larger issue

---

[8] The distinction between living and telling is a critical one in Marías's novels. As his work develops, what in *Todas* stand largely as two sequential types of activities (i.e., the narrator has certain experiences in Oxford, then tells about his life there), in his later fiction becomes increasingly coincident. In *Tu rostro mañana*, living and telling become activities that are difficult to distinguish from one another, and indeed, each increasingly informs the other.

[9] In the "Author's Note" to the English translation, Marías writes the following: "Given that both the author and narrator of this novel spent two years in the same post at the University of Oxford, some statement may be in order on the part of the former, before he finally yields the floor to the latter, to the effect that any resemblance between any character in the novel (including the narrator, but excluding 'John Gawsworth') and any other person living or dead (including the author, but excluding Terence Ian Fytton Armstrong) is purely coincidental as is any resemblance between any event in the story and any historical event past or present" (np). The note is tantalizingly ironic, of course, since Marías knows that any resemblance is more than coincidental but less than fully biographical. From a theoretical and prescriptive point of view, as we have seen in chapter II, Marías often articulated in his theoretical writing that "one must imagine the real" in order to narrate it. It is this approach in Marías's fiction that collapses many of the distinctions between life and literature without eliminating them.

has to do with evoking the narrator's life from another time and another place. The distinction between what was lived and what is told will later grow blurred in Marías's fiction—he explores the topic more fully in *Negra espalda del tiempo*, and it becomes the content of the form of the three volumes of *Tu rostro mañana*. In *Todas*, however, he insists on the sequencing of living and telling. Hence, unlike many characters in contemporary fiction, who seek to live their lives as if they were telling a story (for example, Jean-Paul Sartre's Roquentin in *La Nausée* is a well-known case, or in Spain, the narrator of Carmen Martín Gaite's *El cuarto de atrás*), Marías emphasizes here the life that was lived, followed by the story that is told:

> Todo lo que nos sucede, todo lo que hablamos o nos es relatado, cuanto vemos con nuestros propios ojos o sale de nuestra lengua o entra por nuestros oídos, todo aquello a lo que asistimos (y de lo cual, por tanto, somos algo responsables), ha de tener un destinatario fuera de nosotros mismos. ... Cada cosa deberá contarse a alguien. ... Todo debe ser contado una vez al menos, aunque, como había dictaminado Rylands con su autoridad literaria, deba ser contado según los tiempos ... ese momento se presenta a veces (las más) de manera inmediata, inequívoca y apremiante, pero muchas otras veces se presenta sólo confusamente y al cabo de lustros o de decenios, como sucede con los mayores secretos. (*Todas* 165)

> Everything that happens to us, everything that we say or hear, everything we see with our own eyes or we articulate with our tongue, everything that enters through our ears, everything we are witness to (and for which we are therefore partly responsible) must find a recipient outside ourselves. ... Each thing must be told to someone. ... Everything must be told at least once although, as Rylands had determined with all the weight of literary authority behind him, it must be told when the time is right. ... That moment presents itself sometimes (usually) in an immediate unequivocal and urgent manner, but equally often, as is the case with the greatest secrets, it presents itself only dimly and only after decades have passed. (*All* 140)

What is important to bear in mind, of course, and what forms the foundation of the novel, is the way in which the narrator uses the story both to derive and to give meaning to the part of his life that the story is actually about. Such a posture confirms Marías's persistence in constructing narratives that are indeed about something other than themselves (that is to say, other than the play of fiction as a structure that refers only to itself), even as he is aware of the power of narration to shape that "aboutness" through both the blindness and insight of the narrator.

This of course returns us to what is at stake in the narrator's story—despite his assertions about Oxford as a minor perturbation, his stay there and the form in which he narrates it point to both intrinsic and contextual explorations of himself and others in circumstances narrowly defined in time and space. The narrator's story cannot be viewed as a quest in the traditional sense, however. Clearly he does not follow the well worn path of "once I was lost but now I am found." Nor can his story be seen as a memory narrative in which the narrator evokes the past through both voluntary and involuntary memory, provoked by objects, persons, and sensations that come to mind through desire or chance. For the most part the narrator simply has made the decision to reflect upon the past, and within that context (but from the perspective of the present), try to understand what he experienced in Oxford and why it might bear upon his life in Madrid. First of all, as Robert Spires has pointed out, the narrator's perturbation has more to do with crossing spatial borders than with navigating temporal ones.[10] In Oxford the narrator feels cast adrift, unanchored to a firm sense of identity or even to a specific desire to do something. As beginning and end point for his story, the city of Oxford (its university, its spaces, its inhabitants, and its traditions) becomes the cynosure for the narrator's exploration of his perturbation. It is not an easy space to pin down, but the narrator sets out to explore its many facets.

The fact that he actually finds himself living in Oxford gives a shock to the narrator unlike any other he has known. The city represents for him not only an unfamiliar space but also a strange and bewildering one. As he puts it, "Habiendo estado siempre en el mundo (habiendo pasado mi vida en el mundo), me veía de pronto *fuera del mundo,* como si se me hubiera trasladado a otro elemento, el agua" (*Todas* 70) ("Having always been in the world (having spent my life in the world) I suddenly found myself outside it, as if I'd been transplanted into another element, water perhaps" [*All* 56]). Madrid suits the narrator—it provides him a sense of affiliation and comfort that he not only understands but in which he feels rooted temporally and spatially. In contrast, Oxford is "inmutable e inhóspito y conservado en almíbar" (*Todas* 181) ("[an] immutable, inhospitable place, preserved in syrup" [*All* 154]). He feels less overtly marginalized than subtly estranged in a variety of ways from the many traditions of the city. Exclusion would entail a willful act of aggression by the inhabitants that he has not experienced, while estrangement (a feeling of not fitting in) compels him to live a life of in-betweenness. He remains unembraced rather than openly rejected, though his sense of not belonging is sharply felt. Shortly after his arrival in the city, for example, he recognizes the first obstacle that he must confront: "Aquí

---

[10] Robert Spires, *Post-Totalitarian Spanish Fiction* (Columbia and London: University of Missouri Press, 1996), pp. 223–24.

sólo cuentan las instituciones, y uno puede llegar a ser muy poderoso en tanto que miembro o representante de una institución, pero no se puede llegar a nada sin ellas o fuera de ellas" (*Todas* 82) ("The only things that count here are the institutions, and whilst you can achieve considerable power as a member or representative of one of those institutions, you can achieve nothing without them or outside them" [*All* 67]). While he opts to remain outside of the traditions and mores of the city ("¿Qué me importan los lazos establecidos en esta ciudad a la que no pertenezco y en la que no me voy a quedar?" [*Todas* 84]) ("What do I care about the ties of a city where I neither belong nor have any?" [*All* 68–69]), he nonetheless understands the need to establish at least a small coalition of private interests within the broad and open possibilities that he experiences during his tenure at the university. In other words, he must become something other than an observer of life in Oxford if he wishes to overcome the lack of intimacy that compels him to see himself as "un vivo muerto" (*Todas* 182) ("one of the living dead" [*All* 155]).

The narrator sets out to do this in a number of ways, many of which are fleetingly portrayed against the backdrop of a city indifferent to persons not born and bred into its quirky social exigencies. For example (and most importantly), in the narrator's portrayal of his relations with others he evokes a world of social connections seen briefly, superficially, and in fragments. Many of these are chance encounters that begin as a blur in the crowd and suddenly resonate and grow sharply focused, thus gaining short-lived significance. For example, one evening while taking the train from London to Oxford, he makes the customary transfer at Didcot station with many other passengers. The cold indifference among the travelers is palpable for the narrator: "En Inglaterra los desconocidos no suelen hablarse, ni siquiera en los trenes ni durante las largas esperas, y el silencio nocturno de la estación de Didcot es uno de los más extensos que yo he conocido. El silencio es tanto más extenso cuando está quebrado por voces o ruidos aislados y sin continuidad" (*Todas* 22–23) ("In England strangers rarely talk to each other, not even on trains or during long waits, and the night silence of Didcot station is one of the deepest I've ever known. The silence seems even deeper when broken by voices or by isolated, intermittent noises" [*All* 15]). Amid the crowd, however, the narrator sees a young woman waiting for the train to Oxford and chain-smoking like him. He observes her for several minutes and decides that he would not mind at all striking up a conversation. As the narrator evokes this scene in the present (i.e., his writing about it in Madrid), it is vividly recalled yet only vaguely familiar.

> He olvidado por completo su rostro aunque no sus colores (amarillo, azul, rosado, blanco, rojo), pero sé que es la mujer que al primer golpe de vista

más me ha conmovido a lo largo de mi juventud, aunque no se me escapa que este comentario sólo puede acompañar, según la tradición de la literatura y de la realidad, a aquellas mujeres que los hombres jóvenes no llegan a conocer. (*Todas* 24–25)

I've completely forgotten her face but not her colours (yellow, blue, pink, white, red), yet I know that during the whole of my youth she was the woman who made the greatest and most immediate impact on me, although I also know that, traditionally, in both literature and real life, such a remark can only be made of women whom young men never actually meet.

(*All* 17)

The narrator remembers sharing a compartment with her on the train, but cannot bring to mind what they might have spoken about or even if they spoke at all. When they arrive in Oxford, they leave the station separately, yet over the next several days the narrator continuously looks for her throughout the city. In fact he does encounter her again on the street—she walks by him and for an instant (but too late to stop) they recall their previous meeting ("¡En el tren! ¡En Didcot!" [*Todas* 26], she shouts from a distance; "On the Train! At Didcot" [*All* 19])—and that is the end of it. For the narrator, the incident is important precisely because of its inconsequence. His relationship begins with his observation of her from afar and ends with her fading into a crowd of people on the streets of Oxford. The narrator's physical separation from her underscores his own social aloofness and isolation in the city. Even though he sat with her on the train, nothing of their conversation remains with the narrator, hence any sense of connection to Oxford, any feeling of community remains deferred.

The episode at Didcot station is by no means the only one in which the narrator remains an observer, even when it appears that he actually participates in the local cultural scene. For example, one evening at a discotheque not far from his house he unexpectedly runs into a colleague from the university, who later introduces him to a young woman named Muriel. She lives in a working-class section of the city and is somewhat unattractive, but after a short time talking with her the narrator takes her to his house for a sexual encounter. He recounts the entire episode with Muriel as if he were observing it from the outside, disconnected from emotion or even physical desire. When she wants to be told that he loves her, the narrator obliges with a mechanical affirmation of his love for her, but he remains far removed from her emotionally, thinking about other things the entire time. What is important about the narrator's encounter with Muriel, as well as about other small and apparently innocuous incidents that take place in Oxford, grows from their representative value in the narrator's life: they function as a synecdoche for a range of characters and encounters that underscore the narrator's inability to discover (or create) the core of affection that he seeks. Indeed, it is his life without affect that compels him to seek out small intimacies even as each instance presents him with frustration and failure.

The most complicated example of how this unfolds in the novel, and also the most compelling attempt by the narrator to become more than a mere observer of life, centers on his relationship with Clare Bayes. The narrator meets Clare four months into his stay at Oxford during his first high table dinner. While he observes with some astonishment and remarks with heavy irony about what takes place at the dinner, his gaze often turns across the table to Clare, for whom he immediately feels a strong sexual attraction. Yet his initial objectification of her (she revealed "un escote de excelente gusto" [*Todas* 53]; "a tasteful glimpse of décolletage" [*All* 41]) turns toward a more complex relationship even before they speak to one another—she returns his gaze and thus converts him from observer to observed. This of course entails more than a visual connection with a stranger. Indeed, it suddenly allows the narrator to believe that he is more than an isolated subject living apart from all social interaction. He has become a self who exists for another.

But it is the nature of this self, which he only intuits in Clare's gaze, that must now be shaped and defined. First of all, her gaze allows him to contemplate himself as having a past in a space where he exists for others only as pure present. It permits him to think of himself as unique and discrete rather than simply as another soul cast adrift in the foreignness of Oxford. He will become in her eyes a self separate from others, with a past and a story of his own. As he notes concerning Clare:

> [L]a vi como alguien que pertenecía ya a mi pasado. ... [Y] me miraba como si me conociera de antiguo, casi como si fuera una de esas figuras devotas y secundarias que pueblan nuestra niñez y que no son capaces, más tarde, de mirarnos como a los adultos detestables que somos, sino que, para nuestra suerte, nos seguirán viendo niños eternamente con su ojo inerte deformado por la memoria. ... Así me miraba Clare Bayes, como si conociera mi infancia en Madrid y hubiera asistido en mi propia lengua a mis juegos con mis hermanos y a mis miedos nocturnos y a mis peleas estipuladas a la salida del colegio. Y ese verme así de ella me hizo a mí verla de similar manera. (*Todas* 62–64)

> I saw her as if she were someone who already belonged to my past. ... [A]nd she was looking at me as if she knew me of old, almost as if she were one of those faithful but ancillary figures from our childhood who, later on, are never able to see us as the detestable adults we've become but instead, fortunately for us, will only ever see us as the children we were, their inert

gaze distorted by memory. ... That was how Clare looked at me, as if she knew all about my childhood in Madrid and had witnessed in my own language my games with my brothers, my night-time fears and the inevitable after-school fights. And her seeing me like that made me see her in a similar way. (*All* 50–51)

While he comes to understand that his stay in Oxford may go largely unnoticed and unrecorded (as he sees it, "No dejaré ningún rastro" [*Todas* 84]; "I'll leave no trace" [*All* 69]), he nonetheless refuses to discard his stay there into the nullifying bin of existential despair. Hence his desire and need to become something other than mere object, disengaged from his surroundings and with no affirming presence: "No puedo permitirme disponer de todo mi tiempo y no tener en *quién* pensar, porque si lo hago, si no pienso en alguien sino sólo en *las cosas*, si no vivo mi estancia y mi vida en el conflicto con alguien o en su previsión o anticipación, acabaré no pensando en nada, desinteresado de cuanto me rodea y también de cuanto pueda provenir de mí" (*Todas* 84) ("I can't let myself have all this time at my disposal and not have someone to think about, because if I do that, if I think only about things rather than about another person, if I fail to live out my sojourn and my life here in conflict with another being or in expectation or anticipation of that, I'll end up thinking about nothing, as bored by my surroundings as by any thoughts that might arise in me" [*All* 69]).

With his sense of identity and self tied up hopefully with Clare Bayes, he pursues her as if it were both necessary and possible "to leave a trace." The two lovers meet fleetingly but frequently over the next several months, with their encounters marked by a pressing urgency in the narrator to confirm a self still only faintly detected but now contextualized in Oxford. As time passes, the short-lived encounters with other people in the city (such as with the young woman at Didcot or with Muriel at his house) serve only to intensify his awareness of isolation. He thus grows increasingly dependent on his contact with Clare for any sense of self and identity. When her young son becomes ill and the narrator cannot see her for nearly a month, her absence brings about "el auge de mi perturbación y de mi identidad brumosa" (*Todas* 115) ("my feeling of unease and my uncertain sense of identity reached crisis point" [*All* 96]). He has no solution for his unsettledness other than to increase his meandering walks through the city in order to fill his day.

Yet as much as he tries, and as often as he meets Clare in hotels outside Oxford or even in his office, intimacy remains a slippery illusion. For in most respects, Clare is little more than Muriel writ large, though the narrator fails to discern it clearly even as his narration reveals it fully. For example, throughout his one-night sexual encounter with Muriel, he thinks continuously of Clare, ruminating about the ways in which Muriel is not Clare, or perhaps is the un-Clare. Yet as the narrator tells the story of his affair, it grows more evident that their relationship stands as little more than a series of one-night encounters extended over a long period of time, and that the narrator returns to his role of detached observer rather than existential participant in the intimacies of Clare's life.

This is most strikingly exemplified one day when the narrator happens to be leaving the Ashmolean Museum in Oxford at the same time that Clare is entering with her son and father. With little else to do during his "quinta semana de mi Segundo y solitario Trinity" (*Todas* 184) ("fifth week of my second, solitary Trinity term" [*All* 157]), the narrator had been visiting an exhibition at the museum. When he sees Clare, he decides to re-enter the building and follow her and her family. She surreptitiously waves him away, but he decides to observe them as they visit the various exhibitions. It strikes the narrator later, as he watches the family eat at a restaurant, that Clare, her father, and her son bear a remarkable resemblance to one another; in fact the three seen together make the narrator sense both familial continuity and decline that he has yet to experience: "en los ojos oscuros y azules del niño Eric vi *la sensación de descenso que todos los hombres sienten más pronto o más tarde*" (*Todas* 195) ("in the child's deep blue eyes I glimpsed the slow downhill feeling that we all experience sooner or later" [*All* 167]). The narrator's observation here has as much to do with the similar physical appearance of the family members as it does with his own need for locating himself amid something outside himself. While he notes that the boy may represent a family in decline, the narrator above all endorses continuity as a form of existential affirmation even while recognizing death as a component of on-goingness. Ruth Christie has made the salient point about the narrator's view of the family in relation to his own standing in the world: "From now on the narrator makes it clear that his desire for Clare Bayes is a desire to share this sense of identity, which is none other than a sensation of falling, a knowing that one is like others and will die because they have died."[11]

But it is during an earlier conversation at the museum between Clare and her son, which the narrator believes was directed specifically at him, when he confirms his detachment from Clare and the community which still refuses to embrace him. As the narrator listens from afar, Clare comments on the significance of a statue that represents Marco Polo with Chinese features: "Mira, Eric, este es Marco Polo. Era un viajero italiano, y llegó hasta la China en el

---

[11] Ruth Christie, "Nostalgia for a Prescribed Identity in *Todas las almas* by Javier Marías," in *The Scripted Self: Textual Identities in Contemporary Spanish Narrative*, ed. Ruth Christie, Judith Drinkwater, John Macklin (Warminster: Aris & Phillips, 1995), p. 21.

siglo XIII ... se quedó allí tanto tiempo que se le puso cara de chino, ¿ves? Pero era italiano, de Venecia. Mira cómo tiene los ojos azules. Ningún verdadero chino tiene los ojos azules" (*Todas* 189–90) ("Oh look, Eric, it's Marco Polo, the Italian explorer. He first reached China in the thirteenth century ... he stayed there so long he ended up looking like a Chinaman, see? But he was really Italian, from Venice. Look, he's got blue eyes. No real Chinaman would have blue eyes" [*All* 162]). While Clare offers an apparently innocuous explanation of the statue to her son, the narrator believes that the remarks are meant to define him, to serve as a reminder that he occupies no permanent place in Oxford or in her life. Indeed, as the narrator has sensed all along, he is trapped among many amorphous identities in a space and in a relationship that allow him to exist but not to be: "y ella ha alzado la voz al hablar de la estatua para que yo comprenda que quien pasa demasiado tiempo en un sitio del que no procede acaba no siendo de ninguno de ellos, acaba con cara de chino y ojos azules, como Marco Polo en esa estatua" (*Todas* 191) ("And when she raised her voice to talk about the statue it was so that I should understand that someone who spends too much time in a place other than his homeland ends up belonging to neither place, ends up looking like a Chinaman with blue eyes, like the Marco Polo of this statue" [*All* 163]). Although his stay in Oxford will end shortly, when the academic year comes to a close, the directness of Clare's message is harshly corrosive: "[Ella] me sigue diciendo ... que me aleje, que me marche, que desaparezca ya, sin más espera, de Oxford y de su vida, en la que no he estado tanto" (*Todas* 191) ("she continues to tell me ... that I should go away, leave, disappear now, without delay, from Oxford and from her life, where I haven't spent so very long" [*All* 163–64]). Though he sees her one final time in Brighton before leaving for Spain, their weekend together confirms for him that all along he has been perceived merely as some thing—utilitarian, detached from Clare's emotions, and finally discarded.

It is precisely for this reason that the recurrent image of the garbage bin resonates in the narrator's life with such symbolic insistence. As many critics have pointed out, the narrator's solitary existence, his inability to identify socially and personally with the city of Oxford and the people who live there, create for him a void in which meaningful events remain beyond his reach. Hence the garbage bin in his house provides physical proof and temporal certainty that the narrator has existed in a specific place and on a specific day—a kind of micro-existential confirmation of his being within a macro-existential abyss. As he purposefully writes,

> Cuando uno está solo, cuando uno vive solo y además en el extranjero, se fija enormemente en el cubo de la basura, porque puede llegar a ser lo

único con lo que se mantiene una relación constante, o, aun es más, una relación de continuidad. Cada bolsa negra de plástico ... produce el efecto de la absoluta limpieza y la infinita posibilidad. Cuando se la coloca, a la noche, es ya la inauguración o promesa del nuevo día: está todo por suceder. Esa bolsa, ese cubo, son a veces los únicos testigos de lo que ocurre durante la jornada de un hombre solo, y es allí donde se van depositando los restos, los rastros de ese hombre a lo largo del día. ... La bolsa y el cubo son la prueba de que ese día ha existido. ... (*Todas* 87–88)

When you're alone, when you live alone and live, moreover, in a foreign country, you take more notice than usual of the rubbish bin, because at times it may be the only thing with which you maintain a constant, no, more than that, an ongoing relationship. Each black plastic bag ... evokes a sense of absolute cleanliness and infinite possibility. When you replace the plastic bag each night it signals the inauguration, the promise of a new day: everything is still to come. That bag, that bin, are sometimes the only witnesses to what happens during the day of a man on his own, and it is in that bag that the remains, the traces of the man are deposited throughout the day. ... The bag and bin are proof that this day existed. ... (*All* 71)

When he departs Oxford for the last time the garbage bin once again moves to the fore. His final act before locking his house is to empty the bin that has served as proof of his daily existence there, but now underscores the negation of that existence (or the affirmation of his non-existence once he has left). "I will not leave a trace," it will be remembered, is how he had understood his stay there all along.

But while the narrator claims to have left no mark of himself in Oxford, the question remains whether Oxford has left a mark on him. Despite his assertions to the contrary, and though his stay in the English city appears to have been less dramatically traumatic than persistently disquieting, what happened to the narrator two and a half years earlier has become inscribed in his psyche as both a memory and a story. This can be seen in two important ways. First, the image of the garbage bin triggers recollections of the past in which the negation of his self casts a haunting shadow over his life in Madrid: "Ahora ya no me fijo tanto, paso semanas y aun meses utilizando el cubo sin prestarle atención, es posible que no me fije en absoluto a más que de tarde en tarde, un segundo, como cuando se recuerda algo tan repudiado o extinto que se la ahuyenta en seguida para que no haya posibilidades de que vuelva a existir y para que se asemeje a lo que no existió" (*Todas* 107) ("I don't take much notice of the rubbish now, whole weeks and even months pass without my paying it any attention, it may be that I don't notice it at all or only very occasionally, just for a second, as you might recall something so long disowned or extinct that you banish it at once from your thoughts to preclude all possibility of its ever existing again or to make it seem like something that in fact never did exist, something that never took place" [*All* 89]). While in general physical objects in fiction derive their significance and solidity from the human context in which they are placed, the bin lingers as a reminder of his life in Oxford even though he no longer envisions it in that context. While at one time it served literally as a repository for the narrator's rubbish and symbolically as an accounting of his existence, it now retreats into insignificance as a daily link to the past. Still, it continues to ripple through his psyche as a ghostly reminder of the opaqueness of Oxford and of the deficiency of his life there.

The second aspect of his stay in Oxford that remains fixed in the narrator's life is more complexly woven into his story, and it has to do with John Gawsworth. The narrator's link to Gawsworth in *Todas* is convoluted but consequential. He first hears Gawsworth's name from a strange man named Alan Marriott, who appears to have been following him through Oxford during his search for rare books. Marriott finally approaches him one day to inquire if he would like to become a member of the Machen Company, a group of persons interested in the writing of Arthur Machen.[12] As the narrator learns from Marriott, one of Machen's writings was an introduction to *Above the River*, a narrative by a somewhat obscure twentieth-century writer named John Gawsworth, whose works are difficult to find even among sellers of rare books.

Since his meeting with Marriott the narrator has searched for the works of Gawsworth during his many visits to book dealers. It is not Gawsworth's writing per se that attracts the narrator, but rather the fascinating and tragic life that he seems to have led. Indeed, a long digression on Gawsworth appears in the middle of the narrator's story (including much of what is known about Gawsworth's life), along with two photographs—one of Gawsworth in military uniform from World War II and the other of his death mask from September of 1970. Although Gawsworth had fought in the war, befriended many literary figures of the day (e.g., Dylan Thomas, Henry Miller, Lawrence Durrell), written several books himself, and assumed the title Juan I, King of Redonda, he died in abject poverty among the beggars of London. Marías uses Gawsworth in the novel in two principal ways: first, he is a real-life figure who becomes fictionalized in the narrator's story through his possible affair with Clare Bayes's mother many years before. A man

---

[12] Arthur Machen (born as Arthur Llewelyn Jones) was a Welsh author (1863–1947) best known for his writings of fantasy and horror. John Gawsworth wrote a biography of Arthur Machen, which of course was of keen interest to Marías. Machen's horror fiction continues to be influential even today, with his best known work entitled *The Great God Pan* (1890).

named Terrence Armstrong (Gawsworth's real name) had carried on a passionate love affair with Clare's mother that led finally to her suicide, an event witnessed by Clare as a young girl as her mother leapt from a bridge into the Yamuna River in India. For Clare, the explicit image of her mother's suicide remains vivid, but Gawsworth himself has stood as a vague figure throughout her life, linked to the tragic ending of her mother but not in a permeable way to Clare's consciousness: "El no dejó ningún rastro" (*Todas* 216) ("He left no trace" [*All* 187]), she pointedly remarks to the narrator, thus establishing Gawsworth's connection to the narrator's perception of his own passage through Oxford and his relationship with Clare.

From the broader perspective of the novel, the mixing of a fictional character (Clare's mother) with a real-life figure (Gawsworth) is hardly noteworthy in Marías's fiction—indeed it begins with his first novel, *Los dominios del lobo*, where real-life actors playing roles in various movies blend with characters invented by Marías. What is important in *Todas*, however, is that the narrator at once desires and fears that Gawsworth's life might parallel his own, even as the narrator now knows that the two lives stand almost diametrically opposed to one another. The narrator's affair with Clare never attains the passion that lay at the heart of her mother's affair with Gawsworth—most obviously, rather than take her life because she cannot escape her family and run away with the narrator, Clare chooses to discard him in a dispassionate renunciation of whatever he might have meant to her. In this sense, the narrator realizes that he will come to embody Gawsworth as a point of reference without significance in Clare's life. During their last night together in Brighton, the narrator grasps the critical point: "Es verdad. Una vez que me haya ido, ¿qué importancia tendrá lo que acontezca ahora? No dejaré ningún rastro. Como Terry Armstrong" (*Todas* 217) ("It's true. Once I've left, what possible importance can what is happening now have? I'll leave no trace. Like Terry Armstrong" [*All* 188]). Further, the narrator feared at one time that he might end up like Gawsworth as he grows older. In his frequent wandering through Oxford he had come to identify with the beggars of the city—he crosses paths with them on many occasions, begins to recognize them as individuals, and wonders if they also recognize him as a lost soul not unlike themselves (e.g., pp. 115–20; [96–101]). In addition, as he points out, many of the beggars were once people of high accomplishment, not unlike himself. Thus when he identifies with Gawsworth, he not only envisions himself in the context of Clare and her mother but also in the context of Gawsworth's later life. The English writer lived out his final years in London, "durmiendo en los bancos de los parques y muriendo, olvidado y sin un penique, en un hospital" (*Todas* 124) ("sleeping on park benches and dying forgotten and penniless, in a hospital" [*All* 105]).

With this image of Gawsworth vividly evoked but perhaps only partially understood, the narrator is finally able to proclaim his difference from Gawsworth as he tells his tale in the present. Most importantly, he draws upon Gawsworth to separate himself from Oxford. As he pushes his young son in a baby carriage in Madrid, he recalls that Gawsworth too pushed a carriage through the streets of London near the end of his life. The difference between the two actions is not only profound for the narrator but also liberating: Gawsworth "empujaba su cochecito victoriano de niño por Shaftesbury Avenue, lleno de cerveza, con paso tranquilo hacia oscuridad" (241) ("pushed his Victorian pram full of beer bottles along Shaftesbury Avenue, before disappearing into the dusk at a leisurely pace" [209]). The narrator now fully understands that "a él [Gawsworth] me parezco menos, porque la vida se ha puesto al día por fin conmigo" (*Todas* 241) ("I am less like him now, because life has caught up with me" [*All* 209]).

The memories of Gawsworth, Clare, Muriel, and the beggars of Oxford have indeed remained with the narrator—they have left their mark on his life even though he claims to have left no mark of his stay in the city. Not unlike the opera singer León, protagonist and narrator of *El hombre sentimental*, the narrator of *Todas* reflects on a relationship (here, with Oxford and with Clare) that lacked intimacy and authenticity. His narrative stands less as a story of discovery than as one of exploration in which he evokes the perturbation of Oxford without embracing its deep resonance in his life. The narrator may have overcome the perturbation of his time there, as he insists in his narrative, but he has had to tell his story in order to do so. At home in Madrid, he no longer feels compelled to check the garbage bin to confirm his existence—instead he looks at the young soul in his baby carriage. The image of his son not only affirms the absolute presence of the present for him, but links him to Oxford and to Clare as a way of perceiving the continuity of a meaningful life and the persistence of his identity through time. What he lacks, however, is the vision to perceive fully that the perturbation of Oxford also constitutes part of that continuity—indeed, his story stands as striking confirmation of it.

Negra espalda del tiempo

In the first few pages of *Negra espalda del tiempo* (1998), the narrator lays out two oppositions which have long sustained the writing of prose fiction.[13]

---

[13] Gonzalo Díaz Migoyo refers to *Negra espalda del tiempo* as "lo más parecido a una novela sin serlo" ("the most like a novel without being one") in Julio Ortega's list of the

The first is the narrator's claim both to know and to preserve the difference between real and fictive worlds: "Creo no haber confundido todavía la ficción con la realidad"[14] ("I believe I've still never mistaken fiction for reality").[15] Much writing over the past four centuries in fact has warned readers of the ills which can befall those who perceive the referent of fiction as both real and operative in life outside of the text (Cervantes's Don Quijote or Flaubert's Emma Bovary easily come to mind), even when that fiction conveys with precision a specific reality that is presumed to exist before its representation in writing.[16] Hence the narrator of *Negra* seems to stand firmly on the ground of common sense (and tradition) when he asserts one world that is real and another that is make-believe, each always distinguishable from the other.

The second opposition raised in the novel—between the narrator of a work and its author—is an opposition quickly collapsed by the narrator, who

---

best Spanish novels of the twentieth century: "Las mejores novelas españolas del siglo XX," ed. Julio Ortega, *El Universal* (Caracas) (May 8, 1998), np. Díaz Migoyo's ironic subversion of genre here (i.e., a novel that perhaps is not really a novel, but which appears on the "best novels" list) echoes the multiple subversions of the truth and meaning of narrative which lie at the core of *Negra espalda del tiempo*. It should also be noted here that the title of the novel comes from Shakespeare's *The Tempest*, Act I, Scene II, in the words of Prospero: "What seest though in the dark backward and abysm of time?" In his column "La negra espalda del no venido" ("The Dark Back of the Future"), written a year and a half before the publication of his novel, Marías notes that he has used the phrase several times in his writing with the meaning of "el revés del tiempo, su negra espalda, su vuelco" ("The reverse of time, its dark back, its upending"), in *Literatura y fantasma* (Madrid: Alfaguara, 2001), p. 369. His initial interest in the phrase was piqued by Juan Benet, who saw in it a succinct but profound summary of the study of time by the world of science. Marías admits to thinking that he understood the phrase at first, but as he contemplated and contextualized it in his own writing, its meaning became more elusive. Uncertainty of course nurtures much of Marías's fiction (as it does the writing of Juan Benet), and in *Negra* the author/narrator inserts the phrase into the narrative on several occasions with a range of meanings related to the indeterminacy of time and how it is able to shape human understanding.

14   Javier Marías, *Negra espalda del tiempo* (Madrid: Alfaguara, 1998), p. 9. All references to the novel in Spanish are to this edition.

15   Javier Marías, *Dark Back of Time*, trans. Esther Allen (New York: New Directions, 2001), p. 7. All references to the novel in English are to this edition.

16   The best known examples of such writing, of course, emerge in nineteenth-century realism in works by authors such as Dickens, Balzac, Tolstoy, or Pérez Galdós. The idea of writers observing reality, and then reproducing it in their works, formed the technical and philosophical foundation for the novel during this period. Stendhal's famous idea that the novelist holds a mirror up to reality and then places in his work what is reflected in the mirror, is perhaps the best known definition of the novelistic intention of realistic fiction during this time.

claims not only to bear the name of the author (Javier Marías) but in fact **to be** the author of *Negra*: "... este relato, en el que el narrador y autor sí coincidimos y por tanto ya no sé si somos uno o si somos dos, al menos mientras escribo" (*Negra* 60) ("... the present narrative in which narrator and author do coincide and I no longer know if there is one of us or two, at least while I'm writing" [*Dark* 13]). In other words, rather than limit the various planes of divergence between narrator and author in the tradition, for example, of Marcel and Proust in Proust's *Remembrance of Things Past*, the "I" of *Negra* proclaims and celebrates their sameness. While this unity is affirmed within the novel itself and therefore makes readers somewhat wary of embracing it as a declaration of novelistic intention, the practical consequences become immediately transparent: the narrative proposes to integrate the real and the make-believe (although at this point in the novel there is no intimation of actually confusing the two) and, further, it seeks to give to the author/narrator authority to represent the real and to tell the truth about it.

It must be pointed out, however, that the author/narrator's intention here emerges less from a desire to engage a theoretical perplexity about the relationship of authors and narrators in general than to assure us that he (Marías) is not (contrary to what readers have persistently asserted) the narrator of his earlier novel, *Todas las almas*. In addition, Marías suggests that he has a more specific and pragmatic purpose in *Negra*: as real-life author and as the named narrator of the novel, he seeks forcefully to gain ownership over narrative meaning. His resolve to do this in fact thematizes and structures meaning in *Negra* and becomes the focus of much of the work in a variety of ways. Thus while the narrator's initial assertions about writing may be perceived as circumscribing narration in prose fiction in a general way, his explicit intention in *Negra* is shaped by circumstances far more personal and concrete—the general naïveté and always mistaken approach by readers of *Todas las almas* through which they viewed the novel as camouflaged fact about the University of Oxford and its faculty and, more narrowly, identified the life of the author (Marías) with the life of the first-person narrator. As Marías puts it in *Negra*: "De todas mis novelas hay una [*Todas las almas*] ... que invitó a sospechar que cuanto se contaba en ella tuviera su correspondencia en mi propia vida. ... *Todas las almas* se prestó también a la casi absoluta identificación entre su narrador sin nombre y su autor con nombre, Javier Marías ..." (*Negra* 16) ("Among my novels there is one [*All Souls*] ... that invited [readers] to suspect that whatever was recounted in it had its counterpart in my life. ... *All Souls* lent itself to the almost absolute identification of its nameless narrator with its named author, Javier Marías ..." [*Dark* 13]).

Much of *Negra* is shaped by instances both small and large in which readers have approached Marías to talk about his real life as if it were identical to the narrator's life as portrayed in *Todas*. For example, Marías notes in *Negra* that one evening after teaching his translation class at the Universidad Complutense in Madrid, a group of his students met with him to discuss some matters related to the class. Quite unexpectedly, he reports, one of the students asked him about his child. When he expressed surprise, responding with "What child?" and denying any knowledge of being a father, the students pressed him further: " 'Pero si lo cuentas en tu novela la que acaba de salir'—protestaron como si exhibieran una garantía" (*Negra* 33) (" 'But you say so in your novel, the one that's just come out,' they protested, as if producing an embossed guarantee" [*Dark* 28]). Not anticipating that he would have to explain that his novel is a fiction, he nonetheless offers that " 'Pero ese no soy yo, es el narrador de la novela, yo no estoy casado ni tengo ningún hijo, al menos que yo sepa. Y creo saberlo' " (*Negra* 34) (" 'But that isn't me, it's the novel's narrator, I'm not married and don't have any children, or any I know of. And I think I'd know' " [*Dark* 29]).

According to Marías (in *Negra*), the misreading of *Todas las almas* is not limited to students who may not have the training and experience to discern the traditional difference between authors and narrators. Indeed what gives pause to the author/narrator of *Negra* stems from the overt artlessness (or self-importance) of the Spanish faculty at Oxford, who have scrutinized the novel to determine their own presence in its plot and who, in many instances, claim to have discovered themselves there. For Marías such connections discovered by the faculty are not only crudely erroneous but intellectually astonishing:

> [Yo] suponía que haber dedicado buena parte de sus vidas a la enseñanza de la literatura (aunque fuera la española e hispanoamericana) les permitiría distinguir sin dificultad ni dudas una obra de ficción de unas memorias o un ensayo, y no tomarse a mal cualquier divagación impertinente o bufa exageración o fabulación mías sobre un lugar literario que sólo se correspondía a medias con el nombre de Oxford que yo le daba, o sobre unos personajes que ni los retrataban a ellos ni los caricaturizaban ni desde luego llevaban sus nombres, aunque sí ocuparan sus puestos, como mi narrador el mío. (*Negra* 45)

> I imagined that having dedicated a good part of their lives to teaching literature (even if it was Spanish or Latin American literature) they would be able, without doubts or difficulties, to distinguish between a work of fiction and a memoir or an essay, and not be upset by any brash digression or comical exaggeration or fabulation of mine with respect to a literary topos that only partially corresponded to the name of Oxford, which I gave it, and

to characters that did not represent or caricature them or, of course, bear their names, even if they did occupy the same posts, just as the narrator occupied mine. (*Dark* 37–38)

Marías is aware that many faculty members at Oxford have spoken of their role in the novel. He expresses concern that they might see it as "la novela de Oxford" (*Negra* 44) ("the Oxford novel" [*Black* 37]), and repeatedly assures us that his characters are fictional—even when, because of certain physical, biographical, or personal attributes, they might suggest a link to a person from real life in Oxford with whom the author was acquainted during his stay there. Fundamentally, however, *Negra* is expressly written as a response to this type of (mis)reading of *Todas las almas* and therefore may be viewed, at least in part, as a hybrid essay on the production of both truth and meaning in the novel.[17]

It is important to remember, however, that *Negra* is not an essay in any generic sense but a novel written about another novel. Marías uses *Todas las almas* as explicit referent of *Negra*: he incorporates characters from *Todas* into the text of his work, includes narrative fragments and photographic images extracted from the earlier novel, and purports to reveal about them what is true to life (reality) and what is not (fiction). Paradoxically, this intertextual focus of the narrative, rather than disentangle the real from the make-believe or allow the narrator to speak with certainty **for** the author and **as** the author, serves only to deepen the hermeneutic confusion of both works. But this of course is precisely the point. As *Negra* develops and the author/narrator seeks to achieve in practice what he has proposed in his theory about the real and the make-believe, his intertextual assemblage begets what might be termed the "hermeneutic consciousness" of the novel—those procedures suggested within the narrative through which the reader is led to understand and interpret the propositions of the text.[18] What is crucial in this instance,

---

[17] It is not my purpose here to draw out characters and events from *Todas las almas* and *Negra espalda del tiempo* which may or may not parallel closely the life of Marías. It is important to recognize, however, that autobiography as a narrative genre insinuates itself into both novels. For a discussion of aspects of Marías's life in relation to his writing of *Todas* in particular, see Inés Blanca, "Ficción autobiográfica en la narrativa española actual: *Todas las almas* de Javier Marías," in *Actas del Congreso en homenaje a Rosa Chacel*, ed. Martínez Latre and María Pilar (Logroño: Universidad de la Rioja, 1994), pp. 215–22. See also my discussion of *Todas las almas* earlier in this chapter.

[18] The idea of a hermeneutic consciousness generated within and by the text is by no means a novel concept in fiction. For a discussion of the conscience of narrative and its relationship to consciousness, see Cyrus Hamlin, "The Conscience of Narrative: Towards

however, is that the hermeneutic consciousness serves less to define interpretation than to convolute it (or perhaps more concretely, to define interpretation as convolution). Further, the concerns that generated Marías's perception of the misreading of *Todas* to begin with (the mixing of fiction and reality) grow increasingly confounded as *Negra* progresses, thus leaving authorial intention turned on its head.

Marías himself clearly sees the problem. Above all, it is difficult to prove the negative that *Todas* does not represent his life: "Lo que yo no podría ni puedo es demostrar que los hechos de la novela *no* me sucedieron a mí en mi vida, como es siempre imposible demostrar que uno *no* ha hecho algo o cometido un delito si se parte del supuesto contrario ..." (*Negra* 28) ("What I cannot and will never be able to do is demonstrate that the events of the novel did *not* happen to me in my life, since it is always impossible to demonstrate that you have *not* done something or committed some crime if the opposite is presumed ..." [*Dark* 24]). Still, he immerses himself in *Negra* as author and narrator with the hope and expectation that he will disabuse readers of their insistence on finding real-life incidents and persons behind every small story that constitutes *Todas*. Yet the very practice of novel-writing necessarily (and for Marías, joyously) hinders his position. He argues that storytelling always constructs and distorts life rather than reproduces it, and then announces to the reader that he understands how the context of his remarks (i.e., a work of fiction) can easily undermine their credibility as an expression of authorial intent: "me doy cuenta de que estoy poniendo involuntariamente en tela de juicio la veracidad de cuanto aquí estoy diciendo y seguiré contando ..." (*Negra* 28) ("I realize ... that I'm involuntarily putting into question the veracity of whatever I say here, and will go on saying ..." [*Dark* 24]).

It soon becomes apparent, however, that the hermeneutic consciousness of *Negra* is not constructed solely to set right the many misreadings of *Todas*. Indeed, while exploring the parameters of representation and meaning in the first few pages of the novel, the author/narrator also brings to the fore a closely related apprehension often voiced in contemporary fiction: the prickly postmodern concern with the ability of language to represent anything at all outside of itself, let alone to do so with mimetic adequacy: "Así, cualquiera cuenta una anécdota de lo que le ha sucedido y por el mero hecho de contarlo ya lo está deformando y tergiversando, la lengua no puede

---

a Hermeneutics of Transcendence," *New Literary History* 13 (1982): 205–29. For a discussion of how the role of the reader is shaped by the hermeneutic designs of the text, see Anna Whiteside and Michael Issacharoff, eds, *On Referring in Literature* (Bloomington and Indianapolis: Indiana University Press, 1987).

reproducir los hechos ni por lo tanto debería intentarlo ..." (*Negra* 9) ("Anyone can relate an anecdote about something that happened, and the simple fact of saying it distorts and twists it, language can't reproduce events and shouldn't attempt to ..." [*Dark* 7]). The narrator urges here not a separation of the real and the make-believe, as he first suggests, but rather a detachment of language from life altogether, thus hinting at the collapse of all linguistic creations into a vaguely framed ontological amorphousness:

> En realidad la vieja aspiración de cualquier cronista o superviviente, relatar lo ocurrido, dar cuenta de lo acaecido, dejar constancia de los hechos y delitos y hazañas, es una mera ilusión o quimera, o mejor dicho, la propia frase, ese propio concepto, son ya metafóricos y forman parte de la ficción. "Relatar lo ocurrido" es inconcebible y vano, o bien es sólo posible como invención. (*Negra* 10)

> The time-honored aspiration of any chronicler or survivor—to tell what happened, give an account of what took place, leave a record of events and crimes and exploits—is, in fact, a mere illusion or chimera, or, rather, the phrase and concept themselves are already metaphorical and partake of fiction. "To tell what happened" is inconceivable and futile, or possible only as invention. (*Dark* 8)

Hence any perceived confluence of the inside and the outside of the text, any intention to draw upon language to represent life as it really is, must be regarded as a vain chimera spawned by a writer's desire to appropriate the world and give it meaning. Such a posture for Marías of course stands as new fictional terrain in his novels. Though he had long explored in his writings (especially in his columns, as discussed in chapter I) the peculiar intricacies of telling stories, the material used to construct them, and the appropriation of stories by other storytellers into their own stories, he seems to assert here that "getting things right through language" (in history, in law, in testimonials) lies beyond the reach of narration.

The author/narrator's supposition that language distorts (rather than represents) the world is critical here for two reasons: first, it defines writing and reading within a postmodern context which undermines discourses claiming affiliation with the real; second, implicit in the negation of referentiality lies the affirmation of some "thing" outside of language which we are not able to lay hold of but which exists as a distinct ontological field. The denial of the capacity of language to represent reality, coupled with the author/narrator's earlier claims to distinguish between the real and the fictive and to tie the narrator and author to the same perceiving self, brings the narrative propositions in *Negra* full circle within the first few pages of the novel. This broad spectrum of views not only leaves the reader with mixed signals concerning both theoretical intention and novelistic praxis but establishes ambiguity and contradiction as narrative determinants.

The confusion is further thickened when the author/narrator proceeds to supplant his earlier assertions of textual inefficacy and ontological slipperiness with an expression of traditional narrative faith in the overriding referentiality of language. Most importantly, he proclaims that this faith will define the remainder of his discourse: "... voy a alinearme aquí con los que han pretendido [relatar lo ocurrido] alguna vez o han simulado lograrlo ..." (*Negra* 11) ("... I'm going to place myself on the side of those who have sometimes claimed to be telling what really happened or pretended to succeed in doing so ..." [*Dark* 8]). In other words, the narrator proposes to do something that others have sought to do (i.e., use language to represent life), but suspects that his intentions are diminished by the very discourses that he uses to define and illustrate them. This focus on language and failure lies at the core of the hermeneutic consciousness of *Negra* and, as the narrative progresses, buttresses the ironic foundation of the novel through which the reader is expected at once to believe and to doubt what is narrated.

Certainly, there is much to believe in *Negra* from a historical, biographical, and even cartographic perspective. For example, we learn about various members of the Spanish faculty at Oxford, and about British writers such as John Gawsworth, Matthew Shiel, Oloff de Wet, and Wilfred Ewart with such convincing evidence from outside the novel that we are swayed to use this information to understand more fully how these figures lived their lives and what they were "really" like.[19] Marías also inserts numerous graphic materials

---

[19] It should also be noted here that Marías devotes extensive narrative space in *Negra* to elaborating his relationship with the kingdom of Redonda. He includes several maps and an aerial photograph of the island, discusses the relationship of Shiel and Gawsworth to its history, and points to his own title among the Redondan aristocracy. What is important to bear in mind, however, has less to do with the factual representation of the island than with the way in which Marías uses it to enhance his general desire in *Negra* to confound the real and the invented and to show how his narrative persistently works to do so. As Isabel Cuñado has noted, Marías constructs the story of Redonda by weaving together fictional, historical, and legendary sources, which serve to reinforce the overall assertion of ambiguity and indeterminacy between narratives and their referents. Perhaps most pertinent to the construction of *Negra*, as Cuñado points out, is that, in addition to the myriad of people and events linked to the island, Redonda "se construye a partir de las biografías de los escritores que regentaron la isla" ("is constructed based on the biographies of the writers who ruled the island") in *El espectro de la herencia. La narrativa de Javier Marías* (Amsterdam and New York: Rodipi, 2004), p. 55. This gives to Redonda a peculiar geographical foundation that is always circumscribed by the literary figures and the legends attached to its narrative base.

into the novel with similar consequences for the reader—thirty-three pages of images in all in *Negra*, such as maps, letters, photographs, book covers, autographs, drawings, and newspaper clippings.[20] On the face of it, of course, these images serve to enhance the representational authenticity of the work. For example, the photos of Gawsworth, one of him in his military uniform and one of his death mask (both used previously in *Todas*), confirm his life and death beyond the novel, thus assuring us that even though he has appeared in Marías's fiction he is not a fictional character. A similar trajectory of inside and outside the fictional and the real can easily be seen in other graphic representations in the work: for example, the photograph of Marías's older brother as a young child (*Negra* 274; *Dark* 226), the sketch of his mother, Lola (*Negra* 272; *Dark* 224), a drawing of Gawsworth and Arthur Machen by Frederick Carter (*Negra* 159; *Dark* 133). While the author/narrator seems to know more about some of the figures represented in the images than he does about others, and while he admits that mystery surrounds certain parts of the life and death of some of the persons represented, the images serve to augment the lexical description of their lives provided by the narrator and thus solidify the representational aspect of *Negra* and the expressed intention to offer reliable biographical information to the reader about real-life people.

While the graphic materials thus seem to stabilize the lexical and referential foundation of *Negra* (which clearly forms the dominant part of the work) they also serve the more complex and ironic function of confounding this foundation. In other words, Marías wishes to have it, and indeed succeeds in having it, both ways. For example, the image on the dust jacket of Oloff de Wet's book, *The Valley of the Shadows* (1949) (*Negra* 330–31; *Dark* 274–75) bears a photograph of de Wet in tie and jacket. The author/narrator comments on the photograph, noting the obvious but also attributing to de Wet certain personality traits based on the image:

> Parece algo mayor que los treinta y seis años que quizá tenía, pero más por el tipo de físico recio y el respetable peinado con raya que porque se le adviertan estragos de su temeraria vida. Viéndolo así de aplomado nadie diría que había estado preso tanto tiempo ni que había padecido tormento. Los ojos claros poseen una penetrante mirada propia de ojos oscuros, y

---

[20] Graphic illustrations form an important part of Marías's recently published writings, and are also a central component of the early books published between 2000 and 2003 in Reino de Redonda, the publishing house founded by Marías in 2000. For more detailed information about the graphic aspects of Marías's writing, see Stephen Miller, "Graphic-Lexical Dialogue in Marías and Rivas," *Romance Quarterly* 51 (2004): 97–110.

ninguno de los dos se ve tuerto; sus facciones son muy correctas, un hombre bien parecido al que no cuesta imaginar de uniforme ni tampoco en siglos pasados, sobre todo en el XVII como corsario o noble o como ambas cosas en combinación nada infrecuente, o en el XIX más lejos, al otro lado del océano en el salvaje Oeste. (*Negra* 332–33)

> He appears somewhat older than thirty-six (his age then, perhaps) but more because of his robust physique and respectably parted hair than because of any noticeable ravages left by his reckless life. Seeing him so imperturbable, no one would ever guess he had been a prisoner for so long or that he'd been tortured. The clear eyes have a penetrating gaze typical of dark eyes, and neither looks sightless, his features are very correct: a fine-looking man easy to imagine in uniform or in some past century, particularly the seventeenth century, as a corsair or noble or both things together in a not infrequent combination, or in the nineteenth century, but farther away, across the ocean in the Wild West. (*Dark* 276)

In the long narrative that follows (nearly forty-five pages), the author/narrator inserts other graphic images (several clippings in English and German, a sketch of de Wet) and draws upon them to fill in the biographical information of what is known about this somewhat mysterious figure in real life. At the same time, though, Marías remarks on much that is not known, or on what is told from different points of view, and thus offers varying historical accounts of what de Wet actually did as a mercenary, pilot, and spy.

It is de Wet's book itself (*The Valley of the Fallen*), however, that summarizes the uncertainty of its own assertions and echoes the broader concerns that Marías voices throughout *Negra*. Below his photograph on the book jacket, parts of a German newspaper article are quoted (in English) about de Wet's life followed by a comment on the quotes: "This extract, described by Mr [*sic*] de Wet as 'founded on fact,' though 'in various respects slightly inaccurate,' is taken from the *Völkischer Beobachter*'s report of his trial in the People's Court at Berlin, when he was found guilty and condemned to death" (*Negra* 331; *Dark* 275). What stand out here in the context of *Negra*, of course, are the two juxtaposed phrases which, sequentially, establish fact and then undermine it. In other words, Marías uses the de Wet book as a parallel illustration of the truth and accuracy of what his own author/narrator proposes throughout *Negra* about *Todas las almas* specifically, and about narration and representation in general.

It is important to point out, however, that the long segment on de Wet does not entail a case of lying (in either a novelistic or a real-life context) but rather enables Marías to explore how readers perceive the relationship between texts and reality and between texts and other texts. Indeed, confirmation of the facts presented by Marías in *Negra* about many real-life figures is relatively easy to obtain from other sources, such as encyclopedias, literary dictionaries, and other biographical writings. Information offered by the author/narrator about certain parts of the life of Marías himself can also be corroborated from a perusal of other sources, including Marías's columns written for magazines and the press (as discussed in chapter I): for example, Marías discusses in *Negra* the death of his brother at age three and a half in 1949 (two years before Javier's birth); the suicide of his friend and fellow writer Alioch Coll in 1990; the passing away of his mother in 1977; and the death of his close friend and mentor Juan Benet in 1993. Marías's attachment to all of these people (even to his brother, whom he never knew) provides a powerful sentimental component to *Negra* that would seem to betray any notion that it can be viewed within postmodernism as a work of fiction that struggles to represent anything beyond its own construction.

At the same time, as we have seen, the author/narrator claims to have written *Negra* because real readers of *Todas* have incorrectly viewed themselves as the persons whom the story is really about. What is more, in many instances they have argued that the novel misrepresents them and therefore, at its core, the novel presents things that are not "true." Such allegations, of course, imply that novels have the obligation to convey truth from outside the novel and, further, that they stand firmly in a position to assert what that truth actually is. This is the case in *Negra*, for example, with the owners of Titles bookstore in Oxford, Ralph and Gillian Stone. In an interview in the magazine *Bookdealer* in 1993, the Stones claim to have been featured in a novel by Javier Marías.[21] Marías reproduces in the text of *Negra* a page from the Stone interview (in English) in which they confirm that, "We even appear in a Spanish novel by Xavier Marías, a nice young man who was at All Souls a few years ago and came into the shop regularly. He picked up on a habit some dons have of not seeing women, so that one might ask me a question, and I might refer to Gillian who might supply the answer. ... The book is called *All Souls* and we feature as Mr. and Mrs. Alabaster" (*Negra* 136; *Dark* 113).

What appears to perturb the author/narrator, however, emerges on two levels. First, he reproaches the Stones for their ill-considered confusion of fiction and reality, and for assuming that they play a direct role in the novel: "Lo extraordinario de la situación era que en aquella entrevista los Stone

---

[21] The author/narrator refers to the magazine as *Bookseller*, but the Sheila Markham interview of August 1993 seems to have appeared in a trade magazine called the *Bookdealer*. For the long narrative section on the Stones and the bookstore, see *Negra* 117–40; *Dark* 93–117.

discutían indirectamente con una novela, o bien le rebatían a un narrador ficticio lo que éste había observado sobre unos libreros asimismo ficticios, por mucho que hubieran tomado en préstamo algunos detalles o rasgos del matrimonio Stone de la realidad" (*Negra* 138) ("The extraordinary thing was that in this interview the Stones were indirectly arguing with a novel, or rather they were refuting what a fictitious narrator had observed about two booksellers who were also fictitious, however much they had borrowed certain details or traits from the Mr. and Mrs. Stone of reality" [*Dark* 115]). Second, the author/narrator deepens the criticism of real readers of *Todas* (and extends the irony of misreading) by contesting what the Stones had to say about him (Xavier Marías) as if he actually were the narrator of *Todas*. He even feels the need to refute the facts of their statement about the real-life Marías: "Por lo demás, y en contra de su creencia expresada sin vacilaciones en la entrevista, no sólo yo no había estado adscrito a All Souls durante mis años en Oxford, sino que por entonces jamás había pisado tan estricto y exclusivo *college*, ni lo pisé de hecho, hasta el pasado verano del 96. ... Pero al menos habían dicho que yo era un joven agradable, y eso es muy de agradecer, aunque sea retrospectivamente" (*Negra* 140) ("Furthermore, and despite the belief the Stones unhesitatingly expressed in the interview, I was not attached to All Souls during my years at Oxford, and not only that but had never set foot in that strict and exclusive college, and did not do so, in fact, until last summer, 1996. ... But at least they had said I was a nice young man, which is something to be very grateful for, even if retrospectively" [*Dark* 116–17]).

Clearly, however, as Marías assumes proprietary rights in *Negra* over what he has represented in *Todas* he assures us that *Todas* is always meant to be a fiction except in the few instances where he intended it to portray the real (e.g., the writer Gawsworth). Thus in a letter to Harvill Press, publisher of the English translation of *Todas*, he emphatically denies that his work is a *roman à clef*:

> Me sentí obligado a comunicarle a Harvill ... que en modo alguno era *Todas las almas* una novela en clave ni una narración autobiográfica sino una novela a secas y una obra de ficción; que no había en ella ningún miembro de la SubFacultad de Español de la Universidad de Oxford ni de ninguna otra persona real, viva o muerta, con la excepción de John Gawsworth, quien precisamente había sido tomado una vez más por lo más ficticio y menos preocupante del libro; que "algunos personajes tienen, a lo sumo, una mezcla de rasgos procedentes de más de una persona real y—principalmente—de mis propias invención o imaginación"; que "las situaciones y hechos descritos en la novela no son reales". ...
> (*Negra* 293–94)

> I felt obliged to communicate to Harvill ... that *All Souls* was not at all a *roman à clef* or an autobiographical account, but simply a novel *tout court*, and a work of fiction; that there was no accurate portrayal in it of the Sub-Faculty of Spanish at Oxford University or of any other real person, living or dead, with the exception of John Gawsworth, who, once again, had been taken for the most fictitious and least worrisome element in the book; that "certain characters have, at most, a mixture of traits taken from more than one real person and—primarily—from my own inventive faculty or imagination"; that "the situations and events described in the novel are not real". ... (*Dark* 242)

The intention of the author/narrator here, as elsewhere in the novel, is clearly laid out: *Negra* stands as an affirmation of truth, proscribes ambiguity at every turn, and offers itself as an authoritative gloss. Thus, on the face of it, Marías would seem to have set the record straight concerning the imagined and the real elements of *Todas*. And he has done so by rereading and rewriting the work, thus establishing for the readers of *Todas* the parameters within which meaning can be ascribed and conclusions drawn about the word/world paradox of writing. In the eyes of its author/narrator, then, *Negra* serves as the unvexed avatar of hermeneutic competency.

Yet ascribing determinacy to Marías's novels seems always to require, at the same time, a hedge against determinacy, a concurrent recognition of ambiguity or even contradiction. *Negra* proves to be no exception. For at the same time that the author/narrator proposes to "tell what happened" ("relatar lo ocurrido") in *Negra*, he voices opposition to two narrative traditions which have long granted fiction authority to pursue such a proposition. First, he challenges the premise that reliable representation and reference in narratives are able to produce historically determinate meanings because, it is believed, reality itself is historically determinate and representable; second, he sets out to undo the traditional linear modalities of storytelling, which seek to correlate narrative time with historical time. Hence Marías further confounds the propositional parameters of his narrative by laying one intention against a contrary one. While he claims, for example, that he will tell his story so that the real will be drawn out and made available to the reader, he eschews one of the principal strategies for doing so: the delineation of cause (beginning) and effect (end) within a determinate period of time. Indeed, from the very beginning of *Negra*, Marías proposes to let his narrative proceed in unpredictable directions, advancing as if free from origin or end as well as from design or control linked to time and purpose:

> ... los elementos de este relato que empiezo ahora son del todo azarosos y caprichosos, meramente episódicos y acumulativos ... así, no tienen por

qué formar un sentido ni constituyen un argumento o trama ni obedecen a una oculta armonía ni debe extraerse de ellos no ya una lección—tampoco de las verdaderas novelas se deberían quererlo ellas—, sino ni siquiera una historia con su principio y su espera y su silencio final. (*Negra* 11–12)

... the elements of the story I am now embarking upon are entirely capricious, determined by chance, merely episodic and cumulative ... and therefore have no reason to make any kind of sense or to constitute an argument or plot or to answer to some hidden harmony, and no lesson should be extracted from them (nor should any such thing be sought from real novels)—not even a story with its beginning and suspense and final silence. (*Dark* 9)

Within this scheme of narration, causal structure deliquesces into a liquid form which seems to meander from one small story to another, nearly all of which have the stories of *Todas* as referent. To a large extent, therefore, the hermeneutic competency of *Negra* in the context of storytelling serves to reinforce suspicions voiced early in the novel about narrative efficacy and creates a strong undercurrent of ambivalence that becomes more and more evident as the narrative progresses. For example, at the same time that the author/narrator marks through his own reading of *Todas las almas* the configuration of meaning in the novel, his writing of *Negra* confounds it. While he signals for a hermeneutics of certainty on the one hand (as we have seen, he believes that he has never confused reality and fiction), on the other the text becomes a repository for ambiguity. And while a range of common narrative techniques buttress uncertainty in *Negra* (fragmentation of the story line, absence of origin, mixing of time periods), the most compelling strategy for encoding meaning in the novel relates to the shaping of the hermeneutic consciousness of the first-person author/narrator. Most importantly, in place of the development of the self in *Negra* as a recollected and reconstructed consciousness with his own history and experiences, as in most first-person narratives, the focus of the discourse is transferred to the textuality of the self.[22] As the narrator puts it, "La sensación de que los libros me buscan no ha dejado de acompañarme, y todo lo que ha pasado a la vida desde mis ficticias páginas de *Todas las almas* ha acabado por tener también

---

[22] Robert Spires touches upon the importance of textuality in *Todas las almas*, focusing on the inherent contradiction between experience and representation. Spires rightly draws out the irresolution of the contradiction and links it to the larger matter of "perturbations" in discourse and in life. See *Post-Totalitarian Spanish Fiction* (Columbia and London: University of Missouri Press, 1996), pp. 223–34.

materialización en esa forma de libro, o de documento, o de foto, o de carta, o de título" (*Negra* 253) ("The feeling that books seek me out has stayed with me, and all that has emerged into real life from *All Souls'* fictional pages has finally materialized in that form, as well: in the form of a book, a document, a photo, a letter, a title" [*Dark* 208]).

The textualizing of the self not only impinges upon the direct role of experience and memory in the shaping of meaning for the narrator but, more critically, compels the referential context of *Negra* to become more overtly intertextual. The early shift of the narrative from the subjective (i.e., the author/narrator conveying what he believes at the beginning of *Negra*) to the textual perspective, imposes upon the reader an awareness of the narrative as narrative. Hence the story being told (which is, it must be remembered, a story about another story) assumes the role of context. The intertextual focus of *Negra* implicates the reader in the conscience of the narrative and the ethical concerns that it raises for both writing and reading, and thereby reveals the full consciousness of both novels as textually constituted artifacts. In this way—through conscience implemented as textualized consciousness—all of the myriad theoretical aspects of *Negra*, all of the digressions, images, and intercalated texts, are gathered into a discursive formation which shapes meaning through ever receding textual allusions and references. Such a recession gradually displaces the representational elements of the work and presses them into a labyrinth of tenuous and movable connections unpropped against life.

The textualizing of the author/narrator therefore confounds any possibility of his self emerging through the narration of his own story, which has been a long-held way within novelistic tradition of confirming one's existence. In other words, Javier Marías (the real-life Marías and also his embodiment as narrator) is wrapped in text and context and is no longer representable simply within the real or fictive dichotomy announced at the beginning of the novel. For his part, the narrator also gains a kind of polymorphous density through his over-determined affiliation with textual worlds. These worlds are at times co-opted from texts external to both *Todas* and *Negra* (such as maps, letters, photographs) and at times extracted directly from the earlier novel. In each case, however, the narrator drifts slowly away from his initial referential base linked to the perplexities of living, emphasizing instead the discursive foundation of storytelling linked to the complexities of narrating.

Since the textual impetus offered within *Negra* for writing the novel in the first place grows from misreading by "real" readers of the referentiality of *Todas*, and since writing in this context derives from the author/narrator's desire to set the record straight (i.e., to read "properly"), the hermeneutic consciousness forged in the novel turns at least in part upon the contingencies of reading. What confounds this consciousness is Marías's assertion of privilege as a reader, thus conferring upon himself an overriding interpretive authority that diminishes all others. In other words, what he declares as truth when he reads his earlier novel is transcribed to form the truth of *Negra*. His authority gains substance in and as the narrative elaboration of the novel as he assures the reader of the non-biographical construction of what many have taken for true-to-life reportage: "Poco de lo que en el libro se cuenta coincide con lo que yo viví o supe en Oxford ..." (*Negra* 17) ("Little of what is recounted in the book coincides with what I experienced or learned in Oxford ..." [*Dark* 13]). Marías's approach to his exegetic task, it must be remembered, grows from his initial intention to align himself with those who have sought to represent the real. But as the novel develops, his narrative instead fosters an ironic subversion of his intention. This subversion occurs in two different ways, one with a writerly focus and the other with a readerly one, but it is the coalescence of the two which creates and sustains the final posture of the work.

In his role as author/narrator, Marías perambulates amid the theoretical possibilities of writing with the expressed purpose of getting things right. Much of his narrative indeed rings true within the traditions of realism, but this is so in large part only if we embrace *Negra*, as Marías at first intends, as a vehicle for true representations and referential solidity. But as we have seen, the writing of *Negra* engenders a hermeneutic consciousness which controverts truth and stability at every turn, and the author/narrator grows increasingly aware of his dilemma as he writes. For example, when examining Wilfred Ewart's life and death, which covers nearly one hundred pages in the novel, the narrative takes into account eyewitness testimony and biographical information available from a variety of sources. Both the purpose and effect of the author/narrator's research is to validate with external documentation an internal assertion of truth—i.e., that the story of Ewart narrated in *Negra* is the proper one and that it is supported by the facts. Yet the accumulation of information (especially concerning Ewart's death in a hotel room in Mexico City) serves only to dilute what many had assumed to be the truth. The fiction/reality dichotomy becomes exemplarily inoperative here as the author/narrative comes to understand that the telling of the story serves only to soften the facts and to intensify the inherent contingencies when worlds inside and outside texts are commingled. His comment concerning the small detail of a spent bullet related to Ewart's death makes the critical point: "En verdad no importa mucho ese detalle, al fin y al cabo casi nada de esta muerte es explicable ..." (*Negra* 233) ("True, the detail doesn't much matter; in the end almost nothing about this death is explicable ..." [*Dark* 192]).

The indeterminacy of Ewart's story grows from epistemological matters related to methods of seeking out the truth (for instance, what "facts" can be validated, who validates them, why they are viewed as reliable), as well as from narrative issues linked to language and reference. Furthermore, narration is always configured by the distorting elements of temporality (as indicated in the title of the novel) and eventually reveals the truth not about what it purports to represent but about its own strategies of representation. As the author/narrator sees it, a single strategy comes to circumscribe all others: "para relatar lo ocurrido hay que haberlo imaginado antes" (*Negra* 196) ("to tell what has happened you have to have imagined it as well" [*Dark* 161]).[23] Imagination constructs and distorts "what has happened"; it is the crucible in which experience (the real) is transfigured and made the substance of the text.

While his writerly persona enunciates the ambivalence of representation and enables the ever-increasing textualizing of the self, it is Marías as reader, reflecting on the nature of writing, who enacts the certainty that underscores the ambivalence. He begins the novel with the confident assertion that fiction and reality occupy two separate ontological fields, but his own reading of *Todas*, textualized within and as *Negra*, compels him to retreat from such certainty. In fact, what starts out as a process to confirm the distinction serves only to question and finally to undermine it. As the author/narrator observes at the end of his novel, the two fields inevitably bleed into one another both discursively and perceptually:

> ... los hechos en sí no son nada, la lengua no puede reproducirlos como tampoco pueden las repeticiones reproducir con su filo el tiempo pasado o perdido ni resucitar al muerto que ya pasó y se perdió en ese tiempo. *Quién sabe además a estas alturas lo que se ha hecho real y lo que se ha hecho ficticio.* (*Negra* 396–97 [emphasis mine])

> ... facts in themselves are nothing, language cannot reproduce them just as any number of repetitions, with their sharp edges, cannot reproduce the time that is past or gone, or revive the dead who have already gone past us and been lost in that time. *And at this point who knows what has become real and what has become fictitious.* (*Dark* 330 [emphasis mine])

---

[23] This is a much cited idea in Marías's writing, as mentioned earlier in this chapter in reference to *Todas*. See also chapter I for a discussion of how it guides his theoretical approach to fiction and to the representation of the real. Marías cites Isak Dinesen as the source for his thinking on this matter—i.e., that one must imagine the real in order to write about it. See *Negra* 370; *Dark* 305.

Further, since the narrative self of *Negra* is embodied textually, and since the textuality of storytelling blends the real and the fictive, the reader turned author/narrator is necessarily transformed. While Marías, as reader of *Todas*, asserts the difference between his self and that of the narrator of *Todas*, he embraces the concrescence of the two in order to proclaim the truth-value of his new novel. Again in this instance, however, the narrator of *Negra* reveals the softness of his theoretical base and coerces a rethinking of his own role as narrator:

> Ahora que voy a parar y a no contar más durante algún tiempo, me acuerdo de lo que dije hace mucho, al hablar del narrador y el autor que tienen aquí el mismo nombre: ya no sé si somos uno o si somos dos, al menos mientras escribo. Ahora sé que de esos dos posibles tendría uno que ser ficticio.
> (*Negra* 403–04)

> I'm going to stop now and say no more for a while; I remember what I said long ago, in speaking of the narrator and the author who have the same name here: I said I no longer know if there is one of us or two, at least while I am writing. Now I know that of those two possible figures, one would have to be fictitious. (*Dark* 336)

From the very first pages of *Negra*, Marías constructs a hermeneutic superstructure which asserts the process of literary understanding as mutual, reciprocal, and common to both reader and narrator, even when gaps of knowledge and intention separate the tasks of one role from those of the other. Most importantly, however, and what permits coherence in the novel despite its digressive structure, is that hermeneutic consciousness is a questioning one that is deeply rooted in texts. Thus the role of the reader is to embrace the hermeneutic consciousness shaped by these texts, but to do so with skepticism. For this reason, *Negra* becomes both a reading and a rewriting of *Todas*, as well as an ironic discrediting of such a reading and rewriting.

Negra attempts to control interpretation while claiming that interpretation always remains open; it seeks to pin down events and texts while asserting (and showing) that these are always elusive, beyond representation. Such oppositional tensions lead to a pervasive sense of uncertainty in *Negra*, which, of course, is precisely the point. As author/narrator of *Negra*, Marías claims to come right out and tell us what he means, but in doing so he affirms that texts always mean more than their authors can ever intend or imagine. The same strategy informs the role that Marías assumes in *Negra* as reader of *Todas*, thus imposing on the real reader of *Negra* an obligation to enter into the hermeneutic consciousness of the novel so that by analogy or semblance the vision offered by the work will be affirmed. As the writer imagines reality into his text, and as the reader engages the text to decipher it, the coalescence of reading and writing reveals the articulated truth of the novel: "Y así nunca se sabe nada a ciencia cierta, y se cuenta todo figuradamente" (*Negra* 245) ("And nothing is known with certainty, and everything is told figuratively" [*Dark* 201]). This perspective in the ends reveals the double focus of the novel's message: writing and reading which pretend to precision bear within themselves the instruments of their own resistance, just as reading which seeks authority offends against the multiple meanings always inherent in texts, whether intended by authors or imposed by readers.

V

Two Shakespearean Novels

In *Corazón tan blanco* (1992) (*A Heart So White*, 1995) and *Mañana en la batalla piensa en mí* (1994) (*Tomorrow in the Battle Think on Me*, 1996), Marías continues to emphasize two important aspects of his fiction: intertextual connections with other works of literature and film (most explicitly with Shakespeare in these two novels), and the way in which storytelling lies at the heart of how we construct our understanding of the world. Each of the novels begins with a sudden and unexpected death, and thus contains elements of a mystery novel which invite the reader to expect intrigue and perhaps danger as the narrative progresses. In each case, however, and in typical fashion for Marías, the intrigue is generally deferred and the mystery turns out to be less tautly drawn than readers might have anticipated. In *Corazón tan blanco*, the narrator tells the story of the death unwillingly—he does not directly set out to discover more about it (for example, why it occurred or what were its consequences), and in fact, he resists finding out what actually happened several decades before. In contrast, the narrator of *Mañana en la batalla piensa en mí* desires to tell the story of the night of the death and to explore as well what happened afterward. In each novel the death serves as a perturbation in the life of the narrator, and in each case the telling of the story determines how such perturbations may persist or diminish over time.

Corazón tan blanco

The initial point of reference for readers of *Corazón tan blanco* is an intertextual one, and derives from the title of the novel itself. In an epigram preceding the narrative body of the work, Marías discloses the source of his title as a fragment of a quote from Shakespeare: "My hands are of your colour; but I shame to wear a heart so white," with an accompanying translation into Spanish, "Mis manos son de tu color; pero me avergüenzo de llevar un corazón tan blanco."[1] Marías omits the name of Shakespeare's work in

---

[1] Javier Marías, *Corazón tan blanco* (Barcelona: Anagrama, 1992), np. All references to the novel in Spanish are to this edition.

which the quote can be found (many readers will no doubt recognize it), but we learn, within the text of the novel, that Lady Macbeth speaks these words in Act II, Scene II of the well-known tragedy *Macbeth*, shortly after her husband tells her that he has murdered King Duncan. As Macbeth puts it concerning the murder when informing his wife of what he has done (and as the first-person narrator of *Corazón* later inserts into his own story), "I have done the deed." Sensing fear in her husband because of the crime he has committed, and concerned that he has not left the bloody daggers behind as evidence that is intended to implicate the King's servants, Lady Macbeth hurries to the scene of the murder, smears blood on the servants (who lie unconscious after being drugged), and leaves the daggers that will point to the servants' guilt. Upon returning to her husband, she then speaks the famous lines of the epigram of Marías's novel.

For the narrator of *Corazón*, the dialogue from *Macbeth* is highly pertinent to the story that he tells, and he reflects on its meaning on more than one occasion in the novel. Does Lady Macbeth mean to share the guilt of Duncan's assassination even though she did not "do the deed" herself; or is she expressing her innocence? Does she accept responsibility for instigating the murderous plot? Is she echoing the fear that she discerns in her husband, who has fled the King's chambers without following the agreed upon plan? The quote begets ambiguity (both in how Lady Macbeth perceives her husband and in her own response to the murder now that it actually has been carried out), and the narrator himself seems unable to pin down its meaning despite his efforts to do so.[2] For the reader of *Corazón*, of course, the quote (and title of the novel) becomes doubly baffling: first, the narrator is unable

---

[2] In an article entitled "Shakespeare indeciso" ("Shakespeare Undecided"), published in 1992, Marías discusses the difficulty he has always had in understanding Shakespeare. He refers specifically to the narrator of *Corazón* who, as Marías points out, devotes several pages to the discussion of certain lines from *Macbeth*—namely, those that form the epigram of his novel. Marías offers that he was convinced that he knew what the first part of the dialogue meant ("My hands are of your colour"): Lady Macbeth has the same blood of Duncan on her hands that her husband has on his. However, the second part of the phrase ("but I shame to bear a heart so white") remained beyond his grasp—does the line refer to her innocence, or perhaps to her fear? In the end, Marías expresses pleasure at the ambiguity of the meaning—it coincides with the uncertainty and contradiction that often characterizes his fiction. As he puts it concerning the *Macbeth* dialogue: "Pues supongo que es justamente en virtud de su comprensibilidad e ininteligibilidad simultáneas, de su indecisión última, por lo que ha acabado haciéndome el gran favor de convertirse también en el título de una novela, quizá para su desgracia" ("I suppose that it is precisely because of its simultaneous comprehensibility and unintelligibility, its final irresolution, that it has ended up doing me the great favor of also becoming the title of a novel, perhaps to its misfortune") (368), in *Literatura y fantasma* (Madrid: Alfaguara, 2001), pp. 363–68.

to explain clearly what Lady Macbeth meant to convey; and second, ambiguity of meaning (one of the recurrent traits of Marías's fiction as a whole) is sharply imposed on the narrator's story, thus casting uncertainty into the core of his narrative, which (not by chance) begins with a death.

The death that is recounted at the beginning of *Corazón*, however, is not a murder but a suicide—one that occurred nearly forty years before the present time of the narrator's story.[3] The narrator tells of the incident with dispassion in the first sentence of the novel: "... una de las niñas, cuando ya no era niña y no hacía mucho que había regresado de su viaje de bodas, entró en el cuarto de baño, se puso frente al espejo, se abrió la blusa, se quitó el sostén y se buscó el corazón con la punta de la pistola de su propio padre, que estaba en el comedor con parte de la familia y tres invitados" (*Corazón* 11) ("... one of the girls, when she wasn't a girl anymore and hadn't long been back from her honeymoon, went into the bathroom, stood in front of the mirror, unbuttoned her blouse, took off her bra and aimed her own father's gun at her heart, her father at the time was in the dining room with other members of the family and three guests").[4] What the narrator does not relate in the opening fragment of his story—the name of the woman who kills herself and why she does so—establishes for readers the structural familiarity of a mystery novel, with the coincident anticipation of a plot that progresses through small revelations toward final resolution.

Yet, as occurs in nearly all of Marías's fiction, expectations are at once embraced and deferred. On the one hand, while the mystery of the suicide shapes and to a large extent impels the plot, on the other the narrator prefaces his description of the suicide with an epistemological qualifier: "No he querido saber, pero he sabido" (*Corazón* 11) ("I did not want to know but I have since come to know" [*Heart* 3]), which underscores the larger conflict between his desire to discover what had happened and his corresponding resistance to actually finding out. The reason for his ambivalence lies within the plot itself and unfolds during the slow disclosure of its component parts over the course of the novel: the woman who shoots herself (Teresa) is at the time of the incident the wife of the narrator's father, Ranz. Ranz later marries Teresa's sister, Juana, who we eventually learn is the narrator's mother and who is now also deceased. It is also revealed, though much later in the narrative, that Ranz is a three-time widower: his first wife, whom he had met and

---

[3] It is not until the end of the novel, on page 259, when we learn that the narrator's name is Juan. By this time in the narrative he has taken on a somewhat nameless persona, and for this reason I will refer to him throughout simply as the narrator.

[4] Javier Marías, *A Heart So White*, trans. Margaret Jull Costa (New York: New Directions Books, 2000), p. 3. All references to the novel in English are to this edition.

married in Cuba, died in a fire not long after their wedding. The secret that the narrator finally reveals at the end of the novel in fact turns entirely upon the marriage of Ranz to his first wife—he had brutally murdered her in order to marry Teresa. During a moment of passion on their honeymoon, he revealed to Teresa what he had done, perhaps intending to demonstrate his passion and deep desire to be with her at any cost. Teresa's horror at Ranz's action led her to take her own life not long after learning the truth, either out of fear of living with a man capable of murder; or because of her own small role in the incident. She had told Ranz (though perhaps innocently) that the only way for their love affair to continue would be for his first wife to die.

Marías knows well the traditions of fictional genres, hence the structuring and pace of *Corazón* would seem to be intentionally unconventional: the narrator moves towards revealing the mystery at the same time that he seems to lose interest in it. The novel in fact builds laterally, one digression after another, gains coherence through repetition of scenes and sub-plots that parallel the main narrative story, and finally reveals the reason for the suicide near the end of the novel. Along the way, *Corazón* becomes a work about many different things: marriage, relationships, deceit, violence, the narrator's sense of self, and above all, as in much of Marías's fiction, it explores the nature, purpose, and consequences of storytelling: how stories represent and shape life and the ways in which, through reading and interpreting stories, we understand and give meaning to existence.[5]

In important ways *Corazón* echoes Marías's previous novel, *Todas las almas*—not only in narrative perspective (both are related by first-person narrators) but also in the life of the narrator himself. The unnamed narrator of *Todas las almas*, it will be recalled, recounts what he views as a brief perturbation in his life that left him somewhat adrift and without a strong sense of self-identity: his two-year tenure as a faculty member at the University of Oxford, where he taught interpretation and translation. In *Corazón*, the narrator earns his living as an interpreter/translator for international organizations, and though he does not set out to relate a perturbation, his narrative grows from a sense of foreboding that began to take shape on the day he was

---

[5] As occurs with most of his fiction, Marías claims that he himself was not certain where *Corazón* was taking him or what it was about until after he had finished it. In "Errar con brújula," written after the completion of *Corazón*, he notes that the novel is about "[e]l secreto y de su posible conveniencia, de la persuasión y la instigación, del matrimonio, de la responsabilidad de estar enterado, de la imposibilidad del saber y la imposibilidad de ignorar, de la sospecha, del hablar y el callar" ("secrets and their possible desirability, persuasion and instigation, marriage, the responsibility of being informed, the impossibility of knowing and the impossibility of choosing not to know, suspicion, speaking and keeping quiet") (109), in *Literatura y fantasma* (Madrid: Alfaguara, 2001), pp. 107–10.

married and became more sharply felt during the wedding reception, when his father asked him, "¿Y ahora qué?" (19) ("Now what?" [11]).[6] Although Ranz's question does not pertain directly to his own misfortune in three marriages, and although the narrator does not interpret it in that fashion at the time, the question nonetheless loops back again and again in the narrator's story to intimate the precariousness of marriage. Thus it can be linked opaquely to the narrator's desire to know and not to know about Teresa's suicide (it will be his own wife, Luisa, who finally convinces Ranz to talk about it), which in turn the narrator himself vaguely identifies with the strange uneasiness that has haunted him since his wedding:

> La verdad es que si en tiempos recientes he querido saber lo que sucedió hace mucho tiempo ha sido justamente a causa de mi matrimonio (pero más bien no he querido, y lo he sabido). Desde que lo contraje (y es un verbo en desuso, pero muy gráfico y útil) empecé a tener toda suerte de presentimientos de desastre, de forma parecida a como cuando se contrae una enfermedad, de las que jamás se sabe con certidumbre cuándo uno podrá curarse. (*Corazón* 17–18)

> The truth is that if, in recent times, I've wanted to know about what happened all those years ago, it's precisely because of my marriage (in fact, I did not want to know, but I have since come to know about it). Ever since I contracted matrimony (the verb has fallen into disuse, but is both highly graphic and useful) I've been filled by all kinds of presentiments of disaster, rather as you are when you contract an illness, the sort of illness from which you never know with any certainty when you will recover.
> (*Heart* 9–10)

The narrator does not wish here to identify marriage per se with illness, but rather reflects on how one must adapt to unsettledness often brought about by illness. Hence the sense of foreboding, which the narrator associates directly with the disruption of his life: "mi matrimonio vino a suspender mis hábitos y aun mis convicciones, y, lo que es más decisivo, también mi apreciación del mundo" (*Corazón* 18) ("my marriage disrupted my habits and even my beliefs and, more importantly still, my view of the world" [*Heart* 10]). Put more harshly, as indeed the narrator puts it, "Ya en el viaje de bodas era como si se hubiera perdido y no hubiera futuro abstracto, que es el que importa porque el presente no puede teñirlo ni asimilarlo" (*Corazón* 20) ("On

---

[6] This key sentence is written into the narrator's story early in the novel (page 19), but we do not discover its importance or who uttered it until much later, on page 90.

my honeymoon it was as if the future had disappeared and there was no abstract future at all, which is the only future that matters because the present can neither taint it nor assimilate it" [*Heart* 11–12]).

To some extent, therefore, the narrator sees his marriage as the containment of a life that he has lived with a largely open horizon of expectations, which must now be located on a shared rather than individual grid. Somewhat curiously, the joining of lives explicitly demanded by marriage, and the possible enrichment of each, is seen by the narrator as neither an assemblage of likenesses nor a meshing of oppositions. Rather, in a coldly clinical (and therefore scarcely romantic) manner, he perseverates on how "los dos contrayentes están exigiéndose una mutua abolición o aniquilamiento. ... El aniquilamiento de cada uno, de aquel que se conoció y al que se trató y se quiso, lleva aparejada la desaparición de sus respectivas casas, o en ella queda simbolizado" (*Corazón* 20) ("the two parties are, in fact, demanding of each other an act of mutual suppression or obliteration. ... The obliteration of each of the parties, of the person they knew, spent time with and loved, involves the disappearance of their respective homes, or is somehow symbolized by that" [*Heart* 12]). The narrator does not lament this disappearance (nor does he embrace it), but rather sets out to adapt to it. His way of understanding and expressing adaptation, as Ruth Christie has aptly pointed out, turns upon the view that the life he lives "is not necessarily either a following of the right path, nor a deviation from it, but simply a possibility."[7] Such thinking of course fits squarely within the overarching thematic concern of the novel that envisions life within the framework of many possible stories sustained by a diversity of plots.

Still, the premonition of disaster remains strong for the narrator, and it intensifies as he nears the end of his honeymoon: "[E]l segundo malestar" (*Corazón* 21) ("[T]he second feeling of unease" [*Heart* 13]), as he puts it, comes to the fore when Luisa takes ill in their hotel room in Havana. As the narrator notes, one of his worries since his wedding is rooted in "la amenaza de la enfermedad o la repentina muerte de quien iba a compartir conmigo la vida y el futuro concreto y el futuro abstracto, aunque yo tuviera la impresión de que este último se había acabado y mi vida estuviera ya mediada ..." (*Corazón* 21) ("the threat of an illness or sudden death overtaking the person with whom I was going to share my life as well as both the concrete and the abstract future, despite my impression that the latter was no more and that my

---

[7] Ruth Christie, "Self-Writing and 'lo que pudo ser' in *Corazón tan blanco* by Javier Marías," in *The Scripted Self: Textual Identities in Contemporary Spanish Narrative*, ed. Ruth Christie, Judith Drinkwater, and Johbn Macklin (Warminster: Aris & Phillips, 1995), p. 139.

life was already half over ..." [*Heart* 13]). In this sense, the narrator again seems to have committed himself to marry without passion but also without remorse. He demonstrates a kind of affective indifference to his life with Luisa but also a keen interest in comprehending it (does he really love Luisa or has he simply drifted into marriage?). His feelings are constituted more by cognition than by emotion, and to a large degree his initial perception of himself as living between wanting and not wanting to know about the suicide finds a corresponding condition within marriage of wanting and not wanting to love.

It is not by chance, of course, that many of the narrative digressions of *Corazón* (i.e., the many stories that are told) describe relationships and, specifically, marriage. Indeed, the narrator seeks to understand his marriage and draws into close proximity an array of other relationships that bear upon his own. These include, in varying degrees of detail, the stories of Guillermo and Miriam, the narrator's friend, of Miriam and an odd man whose name we never learn (it could be Nick, Jack, or perhaps Bill), and of Ranza and his wives. It is also not by chance that these relationships are generally bereft of intimacy and passion. Even when they suggest or beget violence they appear largely inauthentic. For example, when Luisa and the narrator near the end of their honeymoon in Havana and Luisa becomes ill, the couple stay in their room while Luisa lies down to rest. Thus begins the scene (and story) of Miriam and Guillermo, which plays out first on the street below and then in the hotel room next door to where the narrator and Luisa are staying. Outside the hotel, and looking up at the balcony where the narrator is standing while Luisa rests, Miriam at first mistakes the narrator for Guillermo; later the narrator listens to the couple arguing in the room beside theirs, where he learns about certain elements of their relationship and speculates about others.

The plot of their story is straightforward: Miriam, a Cuban, is the lover of Guillermo, a Spaniard who often visits Havana on business. Miriam has apparently accepted Guillermo's explanation that he is trying to leave his infirm wife in order to marry her. In fact, he tells her he has withheld medicines from his wife with the hope that she will soon die. Miriam's patience, however, has reached its limit, and she insists that Guillermo take action: "Se está muriendo pero no se muere desde hace un año. Mátala tú de una vez, tienes que sacarme de aquí" (*Corazón* 41) ("She been dyin' for a year now and still she never die. Why you don't just kill her? You got to get me out of here" [*Heart* 31]);[8] and later, "Si no la matas me mato yo. Tendrás

---

[8] The translation here, as in the next quotation, is meant to convey the Cuban collo-

una muerte, o ella o yo" (*Corazón* 51) ("If you don't kill her, I kill myself. Then you get one woman's death on your hands, either her or me" [*Heart* 41]). Although the narrator never returns to the plot of Miriam and Guillermo and thus we do not know the outcome of their story, he remarks that he is unable to determine whose side he might take in their argument even though he knows neither one of them: is Miriam simply looking for a way out of Cuba, for example, or has Guillermo been lying to her about his wife all along? For her part, Luisa, who has also been listening through the wall, offers that Guillermo will never abandon his wife and take up with Miriam.[9]

Within *Corazón* the story of Guillermo and Miriam redounds structurally and personally to the narrator himself. Above all, it intensifies the unease he feels in his own marriage—he wonders if Luisa has experienced trepidation like his own, if perhaps "también ella se sentía amenazada e inquieta por la pérdida de su futuro, o por su alcanzamiento" (*Corazón* 47) ("she also felt threatened by and concerned about the loss of her future, or by its sudden arrival" [*Heart* 37–38]). Further, the story calls forth the intertext of *Macbeth*, which conveys one of the central ideas voiced in the play: how one persuades and instigates another "to do the deed." In this instance, Miriam has urged Guillermo to kill his wife, with the threat of suicide or of taking matters into her own hands, of "doing the deed" herself. As the narrator notes concerning the determinant authority of language: "Una instigación no es nada más que palabras, traducibles palabras sin dueño que se repiten de voz en voz y de lengua en lengua y de siglo en siglo, las mismas siempre, instigando a los mismos actos desde que en el mundo no había nadie ni había lenguas ni tampoco oídos para escucharlas" (*Corazón* 81) ("An instigation is nothing but words, translatable, ownerless words that are passed from voice to voice and from language to language and from century to century, always the same, provoking people again and again to the same act for as long as there have been people and languages and ears in the world to hear them" [*Heart* 71]).

This idea clearly pertains to Guillermo and Miriam, but does not relate only to them. The narrator also affirms the presence and power of those who

---

quial Spanish of a Cuban woman who is perhaps not highly educated—hence the use of somewhat untraditional and improper grammar.

[9] It should also be noted here that much of the second chapter (or segment) of *Corazón* is derived from the short story "En el viaje de novios," published in *Cuando fui mortal* (Buenos Aires: Delbolsillo, 2007), pp. 31–36. As Ilse Logie has astutely pointed out, the story serves as an excellent example of how meaning changes when a story is inserted into a new narrative context—here, into a novel of which the short story forms only a small part. See Ilse Logie, "La traducción, emblema de la obra de Javier Marías," in *Foro Hispánico* 20 (2001): 67–76.

seek to obligate others to act, in a universal sense, just as Lady Macbeth instigated the murder of Duncan. But as the narrator reflects on his circumstances, he comes to see that language can be used to instigate any number of actions. For example, it can be used to instigate marriage:

> Fue Luisa quien primero me puso la mano en el hombro, pero creo que fui yo quien empezó a obligarla (a obligarla a quererme), aunque esa tarea no es nunca unívoca y es imposible que sea constante. ... Creo que yo empecé, sin embargo, y que hasta hace un año, hasta nuestro matrimonio al menos y nuestro viaje de novios, fui yo quien propuso todo lo que fue aceptado. ... (*Corazón* 83)

> It was Luisa who first put her hand on my shoulder, but I think that I was the one who first began to oblige her (to oblige her to love me), although that task is never one-sided and never constant. ... I think, however, that I was the one who began it and, until a year ago, at least until the time of our marriage and our honeymoon, I was the one who proposed everything that was subsequently accepted. ... (*Heart* 71)

However, words may also have a kind of unforeseen authority to compel actions where none seem to be intended. In this instance, the story of Guillermo and Miriam is imbricated thematically into several important plots of the novel: most obviously, into the narrator's honeymoon, but also into both the absence of passion in marriage as well as to its overflow that leads to violence; and most importantly, into the story of Ranz and his three wives and then back again to *Macbeth*.

The story of Ranz's wives is a complicated one, and the narrator learns about it in different parts from three different persons. First, he hears from Custardoy (a friend of both Ranz and the narrator) that Teresa committed suicide. Custardoy (as he tells it) believed that the narrator had known all along about the suicide when he casually mentioned to him one evening how strange it seemed that Ranz had been married three times. Second, following their honeymoon and during a work assignment in Geneva, the narrator and Luisa have dinner with Professor Villalobos, a friend of Ranz, who fills in the story of Ranz's life with more details, including his belief that Ranz's first wife was killed in a fire. What remains missing from the stories of both Custardoy and Villalobos, of course, has shaped the mystery of *Corazón* from the very beginning: the reasons why Teresa committed suicide almost forty years earlier. It is a story that has been deferred for a large part of the novel but that finally demands to be told, despite the narrator's ambivalent sentiments expressed in the first sentence of the work—"I did not want to know but I have since come to know. ..."

First of all, the story takes root in Ranz's honeymoon with Teresa, which helps to clarify the decision by the narrator to begin the story of his marriage to Luisa with incidents from his own honeymoon. Only later does he fill in the details of his relationship with Luisa—how they met, the nature of their work, and what has occurred during the first year or so of their marriage up to the present time of the novel. The final piece of Ranz's story is not told second hand by someone who has heard it from another (as with parts of the story told by Custardoy and Villalobos), but rather by Ranz himself. And much like what occurred on the narrator's honeymoon, when he listened through the wall as Miriam and Guillermo revealed details of their relationship, the narrator now listens next door in the bedroom of his own apartment as Ranz finally tells Luisa what caused Teresa to take her life not long after their honeymoon—that he had killed his first wife in her bed and then set the bed on fire (with cigarette ash) to hide the crime.

The story that Ranz relates to Luisa resonates throughout the novel and instigates the narrator's attempt to piece together a chain of cause and effect that might explain parts of his family life from the past as well as his sense of unease about his marriage in the present. First, Ranz's startling revelation compels the narrator to see anew his father's life as well as his own. While the narrator had known about his father's shady dealings in the underworld of forged and stolen art, and knew as well that Ranz had used his ties to the French regime to advance his illicit trafficking, he had not considered his father capable of murder. Further, the narrator draws forth images of his mother, of Teresa, and of his Cuban grandmother in an attempt to clarify the past and stabilize the present as he continues to adapt to marriage. In essence, the narrator's ambivalence toward what he has learned from Ranz's story serves both to nourish his unease and to diminish it. Yet as occurs throughout *Corazón*, significant lacunae remain in the story even as what Ranz tells seems to fill in the important gaps. For example, did Teresa kill herself because she lived in fear of a husband capable of such grotesque violence, or was her suicide a response to her guilt for suggesting to Ranz that his wife's death provided the only opportunity for her and Ranz to marry: " 'Nuestra única posibilidad es que un día muriera ella,' me dijo, 'y con eso no puede contarse' " (*Corazón* 279) (" 'Our one possibility is if she should die,' she said to me, 'and we can't rely on that' " [*Heart* 258]). In a fashion not uncommon in Marías's novels, the storytelling process moves to the fore at this point through double interpretive gestures—in this instance by both Ranz and the narrator. First, Ranz tells Luisa how he construed Teresa's words concerning the death of his first wife and also how he has continued to understand them over the years:

Recuerdo que al decirlo me puso la mano en el hombro y acercó su boca a mi oreja. No me lo susurró, no fue una insinuación, su mano en mi hombro y sus labios cercanos fueron un modo de consolarme y apaciguarme. Estoy seguro, he pensado mucho en cómo fue dicha esa frase, aunque hubo un tiempo en que la tomé por otra cosa. Era una frase de renuncia y no de inducción, era la frase de quien se retira y se da por vencido. Después de decir eso me dio un beso muy breve. Abandonaba el campo. (*Corazón* 279)

> I remember that when she said it, she placed her hand on my shoulder and her mouth close to my ear. She didn't whisper it to me, she didn't mean to make it sound like an insinuation, placing her hand on my shoulder and her lips close to my ear was a way of consoling or calming me, I'm sure of that, I've often thought about the way she spoke those words, although there was a time when I took them to mean something quite different. It was an expression of renunciation, not of inducement, they were the words of someone withdrawing, giving up. Afterwards she kissed me, very gently. She was withdrawing from the field. (*Heart* 258)

For Ranz, this glance cast into the depths of time brings to the present a vanished event about which he alone knew the truth: the murder of his wife. Importantly, though, Ranz offers not simply a recounting of the incident but a sorting out of Teresa's desires as well as his own. Teresea bears no responsibility, he assures Luisa—"she was withdrawing from the field." But as we know, though Ranz remains unaware, Luisa is not the only listener of Ranz's story, nor is Ranz the only interpreter of Teresa's words. The narrator's "reading" and understanding of the incident allows him to relate it to what stands most pertinent in his own life and narrative—in this instance, as elsewhere when he has listened to fragments of the story told by Custardoy and Villalobos about Teresa and Ranz, the narrator identifies with Ranz, and through him he ties together many of the smaller stories of the novel and the most compelling ideas associated with them.

As the narrator recounts how he listened to Ranz tell his story to Luisa, he comments within his narrative on what Ranz relates. For example, he quickly links Teresa's words about the death of Ranz's first wife to the notion of instigation, which, as we have seen, recurs throughout the novel: " 'La lengua en la oreja es también el beso que más convence,' pensé, 'la lengua que indaga y desarma, la que susurra y besa, la que casi obliga' " (*Corazón* 279) (" 'The tongue in the ear is always the most persuasive of kisses,' I thought, 'the tongue that probes and disarms, whispers and kisses, that almost obliges' " [*Heart* 258]). Further, and most importantly, the narrator explains his understanding of Ranz's story through the intertextual connection to *Macbeth*. Earlier in the novel, when he describes meeting Luisa for the first time while interpreting for a British woman diplomat and a male Spanish diplomat,[10] the narrator had perceived the link between Shakespeare's play and his concern with obligation. Bored with the banal dialogue between the two diplomats (and with Luisa sitting behind him as the second interpreter who would intervene to correct any mistranslations or ambiguities), the narrator begins to invent his own dialogue, which he translates as if it originated from the diplomats. Finally, he constructs a question of his own for the English woman while pretending that it came from her Spanish counterpart: "Si puedo preguntárselo y no es demasiado atrevimiento, usted, en su vida amorosa, ¿ha obligado a alguien a quererla?" (*Corazón* 74) ("If you don't mind my asking and you don't think I'm being too personal, have you, in your own experience of love, ever obliged anyone to love you?" [*Heart* 63]).

Fearing that he has exceeded diplomatic etiquette (after all, he has already invented dialogue passed on as translation), and that his career will be ruined, the narrator anticipates Luisa's intervention and the diplomat's anger at what she believed was a question posed by her Spanish interlocutor. Much to the narrator's surprise, however, the English woman offers a lengthy and personal response to the question, evoking a line from Shakespeare ("Los dormidos, y los muertos, no son sino como pinturas" (*Corazón* 76) ("The sleeping and the dead are but as pictures" [*Heart* 66]) to emphasize her point. The narrator now (in the present) knows the source of these lines, though he did not know at the time, and he links them to the broader behavior of obligation and instigation: "Ahora que sé que esa cita venía de *Macbeth* no puedo evitar darme cuenta (o quizá es recordar) de que también está a nuestra espalda quien nos instiga, también ese nos susurra al oído sin que lo veamos acaso, la lengua es su arma y es su instrumento ..." (*Corazón* 79) ("Now that I know the quotation comes from *Macbeth*, I can't help but realize (or perhaps remember) that also behind us, at our backs, is the person urging us on, the person who whispers in our ear, perhaps without our even seeing him, his tongue at once his weapon and instrument ..." [*Heart* 68]). Most importantly, he establishes in the same context the pairing of Lady Macbeth and Teresa that will come to light fully only near the end of the novel when Ranz tells his story to Luisa: "Ella (Lady Macbeth] oye la confesión de ese acto o hecho o hazaña, y lo que la hace verdadera cómplice no es haberlo instigado ... sino saber de ese acto

---

[10] As many critics have pointed out, it is not difficult to identify the two diplomats as Margaret Thatcher (Prime Minister of England from 1979 to 1990) and Felipe González (President of the Spanish Government from 1982 to 1996). See, for example, Rita de Maeseneer, "Sobre la traducción en 'Corazón tan blanco' de Javier Marías," in *Espéculo. Revista de Estudios Literarios*: http://www.ucm.es/info/especulo/numero14/jmarias.html.

y de su cumplimiento" (*Corazón* 80) ("She [Lady Macbeth] hears his confession of this deed or act or exploit and what really makes her an accomplice is not that she instigated it ... but the fact that she knew about that deed and its accomplishment" [*Heart* 69]).

In other words, while Ranz has denied Teresa's blame in the death of his first wife—he has interpreted the meaning of her words that mention death as purely without any intention to inspire action—the narrative of the novel itself seems already to have sanctioned the textual connections that envision Teresa as Ranz's accomplice. We might ask, of course, which perspective in the end does the work endorse, if any at all? The answer necessarily incorporates several matters related to structure and theme (such as memory, referentiality, interpretation), but primarily it turns upon the vision implicit in the novel that defines narrative truth in relation to the world not always as unknowable but as ordinarily elusive. While Ranz in this instance wants to lean upon the stable foundation of his memory and his inferential reasoning to protect Teresa, the narrator disperses any certainty concerning Ranz's judgment into the large epistemological stew in which "doing the deed" and "instigating the deed" bear like markings of culpability. In this sense, Ranz's story is unable to redeem what it entails (in brief, murder for love), nor does it provide higher insight into Teresa's suicide or Ranz's own actions—this is the expected recompense that the narrator has long awaited but in the end has not achieved.

Ranz's story of the murder of his first wife can be linked to other important aspects of the novel as well. It resembles (but does not duplicate) the encounter that the narrator listens to in Havana, where Miriam forcefully urges her lover to kill his wife. Further, Ranz's burning of his wife's bed with cigarettes in order to conceal her murder subtly elicits the moment in Havana when the narrator drops cigarette ash on the sheets where Luisa lies resting, though he quickly flicks it away. The story that Ranz tells also seems to vindicate the sense of unease that the narrator has felt since his wedding. The conversation with his father that day still haunts the narrator, though he cannot clearly discern why. Even as he fills in the final piece of the mystery concerning Teresa's suicide with Ranz's confession to Luisa, he feels no sharp moment of redemption, either for himself or for Ranz. Contrary to what might be anticipated (the narrator's horror at the murder and rejection of his father), the narrator moves from past to future with the sense of unease largely diminished at the end of the novel. As he notes in the final segment of the narrative:

> Ahora mi malestar se ha apaciguado y mis presentimientos ya no son tan desastrosos, y aunque aún no soy capaz de pensar como antes en el futuro

> abstracto, vuelvo a pensar vagamente, a errar con el pensamiento puesto en lo que ha de venir o puede venir, a preguntarme sin demasiada concreción ni interés por lo que será de nosotros mañana mismo o dentro de cinco o cuarenta años, por lo que no prevemos. (*Corazón* 293)

> My unease has dissipated somewhat and my presentiments of disaster have grown less disastrous and, although I'm still not capable of imagining, as I once was, an abstract future, I can once again allow myself to think vague thoughts, to let my thoughts drift over what will or might happen, to wonder without too much exactitude or intensity what will happen to us tomorrow or in five or forty years' time, to wonder about things we cannot foresee. (*Heart* 271)

The narrator's return to the future here is critical, above all because he has arrived there through his journey into the past. He has discovered that his veritable being, the one that existed (if only tenuously) before his marriage to Luisa, remains intact. Importantly, this being is one that he recognizes not solely in the past and not projected solely into the future, but in the rapport that binds past and future together. As the narrator puts it, "Sólo que también es verdad que a nada se le pasa el tiempo y todo está ahí, esperando a que se lo haga volver, como dijo Luisa" (*Corazón* 294) ("But it's also true that there is a time for everything and that it's all there, waiting for us to call it back, as Luisa said" [*Heart* 272]).

Ranz's story in many ways echoes the strategy that guides the narrator's telling of his own story, in which what is told seems always intermittent, with planned gaps amid the many digressions that compel conjecture concerning both truth and meaning. Marías typically offers an array of ethical and unethical choices for the characters of his novels, and *Corazón* is filled with them—from Ranz's decision to murder his wife, to Berta's acquiescence to sending a video of herself, undressed, to a man she does not know. Equally important, however, Marías induces the reader to reflect upon how the story that presents such choices can be told. Indeed, throughout his fiction we discern a serial persistence in scrutinizing narrators and the nature of their narrations. In *Corazón*, the emphasis on storytelling not only suggests how the reader might understand the various stories told intrinsically but also points to theoretical matters within the larger enterprise of how language, as the raw material of storytelling, functions to reflect or deform the world as it seeks to re-present it.

The story of Ranz—the more general one that is woven throughout the novel as well as the one that Ranz tells to Luisa about his first wife—serves metonymically to cover much of the theoretical ground. This can be seen in three particular instances related to Ranz's life: first, when he tells Teresa the secret about how he murdered his wife; second, when he advises the narrator on the day of his marriage not to tell secrets to Luisa; third, when he tells Luisa the secret of why Teresa killed herself (which of course includes the secret that originally he had told Teresa many years before). In several ways these three stories point to the slippery epistemological foundation of narration, as well as to the concurrent and necessary practice of making narrative usable in daily life. Furthermore, they underscore the decisive need for storytelling, which can be dangerous as well as liberating, but above all which makes human life existentially feasible to begin with. As the narrator puts it:

> Cada paso dado y cada palabra dicha por cualquier persona en cualquier circunstancia (en la vacilación o el convencimiento, en la sinceridad o el engaño) tienen repercusiones inimaginables que afectan a quien no nos conoce ni lo pretende, a quien no ha nacido o ignora que podrá padecernos, y se convierten literalmente en asunto de vida o muerte. ... (*Corazón* 92)

> Each step taken and each word spoken by anyone in any circumstances (hesitant or assured, sincere or false) have unimaginable repercussions that will affect someone who neither knows us nor wants to, someone who hasn't yet been born or doesn't know that they'll have to suffer us and become, literally, a matter of life and death. (*Heart* 80)

When Ranz speaks with the narrator on his wedding day he offers a single piece of advice: "Cuando tengas secretos o si ya los tienes, no se los cuentes [a Luisa]" (*Corazón* 101) ("If you ever do have any secrets or if you already have, don't tell her [Luisa]" [*Heart* 89]). While at first glance the advice seems to pertain primarily to secrets, it is most usefully understood in the context of "telling." That is to say, Ranz's admonition, and the later revelation of his own secrets, points to a representational efficacy deeply inherent in storytelling that defies easy labeling.[11] We might ask, of course, what kind of efficacy exists in storytelling and for what purpose may it be used? Does telling draw the teller, the reader (listener) and the world closer together, or does it instigate or demand a distancing among all three. Is it conceivable or

---

[11] As I have suggested throughout this study, Marías seems always to be a very modern writer and on occasion a postmodern writer. Often, he seems to want to be both. Some critics see *Corazón* as a prime example of postmodern writing in contemporary Spain, though in my view, this is one of his works in which he wants to have it both ways. For the postmodern argument, see, for example, Karen-Margrethe Simonsen, "*Corazón tan blanco*—a postmodern novel by Javier Marías," *Revista Hispánica Moderna* 52 (1999): 193–212.

even probable that narration is the instrument of cognition through which subjects shape their world and thus themselves, or does narration become the instrument of the demise of the self? Does the text (story) result from the referential activity of a reflecting subject or is the text an autonomous, perhaps not even causally coherent amassing of words into paradigms that produce multiple meanings among multiple readers? In theoretical reflections on these matters in a number of essays, Marías lays out how he embraces all of these perspectives.[12] In *Corazón*, he shows how these perspectives gain functionality within a work of narrative fiction.

Ranz's advice to his son above all implies that there is an "aboutness" to telling that impinges upon real life. Narration is not merely a play of language, a closed system of signs, or a text that derives from and speaks to other texts, as much postmodern thinking proposes. It is also connected referentially to the world in which we live, and it creates existential consequences within that world. What is often perplexing about Marías's writing, however (and what obtains in *Corazón*), is that the author does not seek to resolve certain theoretical tensions once and for all, nor does he necessarily resort to different contexts to explore discrepant or even contradictory ideas. Instead, he often asserts conflicting notions about storytelling within the same context. As his meta-textual commentary proposes in *Corazón* (through the voice of the narrator, of course), and as the referential base of the novel implies, he embraces representation of the real, deformation of the real, and imagination of the real in the same narrative breath.

For example, nearly all of *Corazón* derives from the narrator's life since his marriage to Luisa—what he has experienced or been told, new information that he has learned, and events that he has remembered. As he sees it, marriage above all is "una institución narrativa" (*Corazón* 146) ("a narrative institution" [*Heart* 133]), with the implication that couples speak to one another and thus use language to enhance intimacy. As the narrator asserts,

> La verdadera unidad de los matrimonios y aun de las parejas la traen las palabras, más que las palabras dichas—dichas voluntariamente—, las palabras que no se callan—que no se callan sin que nuestra voluntad intervenga—. No es tanto que entre dos personas que comparten la almohada no haya secretos porque así lo deciden ... cuanto que no es posible dejar de contar, y de relatar, y de comentar y enunciar, como si esa fuera la actividad primordial de los emparejados. ... (*Corazón* 145)

---

[12] For a discussion of how Marías lays out various theoretical positions in relation to literature in general, and narrative fiction in particular, see chapter I.

> Real togetherness in married couples and indeed in any couple comes from words, not just the words that are spoken—spoken voluntarily—but the words one doesn't keep to oneself—at least not without the intervention of the will. It isn't so much that there are no secrets between two people who share a pillow because that's what they decide ... rather it's impossible not to tell, to relate, to comment, to enunciate, as if that were the primordial activity of couples. ... (*Heart* 132)

The intimacy implied here relies upon the referential capacity of language to convey feeling and represent facts, with consequences that are located in real life but that are shaped by the act of telling. Such is the case with Teresa, as we have seen, who kills herself after Ranz tells her what he has done to his first wife: "Se mató por algo que yo le conté. Por algo que le había contado en nuestro viaje de bodas" (*Corazón* 265) ("She killed herself because of something I told her. Something I told her on our honeymoon" [*Heart* 245]). The narrator listens to Ranz telling Luisa about the outcome of his "telling," and then offers his own reflection on the power of language and its link to the real:

> ("I have done the deed", pensé, o acaso pensé "He sido yo", o lo pensé en mi lengua, "He hecho el hecho y he hecho la hazaña y he cometido el acto, el acto es un hecho y es una hazaña y por eso se cuenta más pronto o más tarde, he matado por ti y esa es mi hazaña y contártela ahora es mi obsequio, y me querrás más aún al saber lo que he hecho, aunque saberlo manche tu corazón tan blanco.") (*Corazón* 274)

> ("I have done the deed," I thought in English, or perhaps I thought, "It was me" or else I thought it in my own language, "I have done the deed and I have committed the act, the act is both deed and exploit, which is why, sooner or later, it has to be told, I have killed for you and that is my exploit and telling you now is my gift to you, and you will love me even more knowing what I have done, even though knowing it stains your heart so white.") (*Heart* 254)

The narrator further asserts the efficacy of language by drawing forth the importance of the unspoken, with the belief that not to speak represents a withholding of feeling, thought, and information found in the world that can be communicated through the referential capacity of language. Indeed, the narrator's decision to conceal his unease from Luisa for the entire year of their marriage stems directly from his belief that the telling of stories instigates change in the reality external to the stories: "Cuántas cosas se van no diciendo a lo largo de una vida o historia o relato, a veces sin querer o sin proponérselo. Yo no sólo había callado cuanto ya he enumerado, sino sobre todo el malestar y los presentimientos de desastre que me acompañan desde mi matrimonio, hace ya casi un año" (*Corazón* 230) ("How many things are left unsaid in the course of a lifetime or a story, sometimes without our meaning or choosing to do so? I'd kept silent not only about all the things I've mentioned above, but about the feelings of unease and the presentiments of disaster that have afflicted me ever since I got married, over a year ago" [*Heart* 212–13]). In brief, as the narrator succinctly notes: "Callar y hablar son formas de intervenir en el futuro" (*Corazón* 227) ("Keeping silent and speaking are ways of intervening in the future" [*Heart* 210]).

This referential insistence serves as one of the primary epistemological markers of the narrator's thinking in *Corazón*. He organizes the domain of his text around the belief that the characters of his narrative, as well as his own complicated and contradictory self, can be recognized by readers within narration through the relationship that each maintains with the world. As he notes, "quizá sea esto lo que nos lleva a leer novelas y crónicas y a ver películas, la búsqueda de la analogía, del símbolo, la búsqueda del reconocimiento, no del conocimiento" (*Corazón* 200) ("and perhaps that is what drives us to read novels and news reports and to go and see films, the search for analogy, for symbolism, the need for recognition rather than cognition" [*Heart* 185]). The narrator's observation here concerning readers' search for recognition steers the hermeneutic response to the text inevitably towards the world—and in the interaction between the two, readers recognize and discover something about themselves, understood as part of human nature.

But for Marías in *Corazón*, and in much of his other writing as well, this referential reciprocity can never operate smoothly or directly, if it is able to operate at all. On the one hand, he affirms referential stability—for example, when Villalobos tells Luisa and the narrator about the death of Teresa and subsequently about the heart attack that killed her father, the narrator believes his father's old friend, and notes that Villalobos, "Contó durante unos minutos. Contó con detalle. Contó. Contó" (*Corazón* 247) ("He talked for some minutes, he described it all in detail. He talked. He talked" [*Heart* 228]).[13] On the other hand, however, the narrator persistently convolutes and contradicts referential soundness, thus disallowing epistemological comfort in favor of linguistic precariousness. For example, the narrator affirms that the very act of narrating creates dissonance in relation to all that lies outside it. In other words (and paradoxically), while for the narrator language re-presents the real, it always and necessarily distorts it: "Contar deforma,

---

[13] While the translation of this sentence in the English version, *A Heart So White*, is not inaccurate, a more faithful (though perhaps less rhythmic) rendering for the verb "contó" would be either "He told" or "He recounted," thus keeping the implicit meaning of the verb close to the idea of "telling stories" that it connotes here.

contar los hechos deforma los hechos y los tergiversa y casi los niega, todo lo que se cuenta pasa a ser irreal y aproximativo aunque sea verídico" (*Corazón* 200–01) ("Recounting an event distorts it, recounting facts distorts and twists and almost negates them, everything that one recounts, however true, becomes unreal and approximate" [*Heart* 185]). However, it is not just a matter of twisting objects and events from real life into a pattern that diminishes and changes them but of how the telling of stories affects and constitutes the world. This larger set of narrative values and principles finally lies at the center of *Corazón*, though as typically occurs with Marías, this center seems both amorphous and movable.

First of all, Marías argues forcefully in *Corazón* for an Ur-truth that exists in the abstract but remains unrepresentable by the language of storytelling:

> ... la verdad no depende de que las cosas *fueran* o sucedieran, sino de que permanezcan ocultas y se desconozcan y no se cuenten, en cuanto se relatan o se manifiestan o muestran, aunque sea en lo que más real parece, en la televisión o el periódico, en lo que se llama la realidad o la vida o la vida real incluso. ... La verdad nunca resplandece, como dice la fórmula, porque la única verdad es la que no se conoce ni se transmite, la que no se traduce a palabras ni a imágenes, la encubierta y no averiguada, y quizá por eso se cuenta tanto o se cuenta todo, para que nunca haya ocurrido nada, una vez que se cuenta. (*Corazón* 201)

> ... the truth doesn't depend on things actually existing or happening, but on their remaining hidden or unknown or untold, as soon as they're related or shown or made manifest, even in a medium that seems real, on television or in the newspapers, in what is called reality or life or even real life. ... The truth never shines forth, as the saying goes, because the only truth is that which is known to no one and which remains untransmitted, that which is not translated into words or images, that which remains concealed and unverified, which is perhaps why we do not recount so much or even everything, to make sure that nothing has ever really happened, not once it's been told. (*Heart* 185–86)

Marías clearly posits here a postmodern perspective that deepens the divide between the word and the world, even implying that all hope is lost for language and narration. Do not tell stories, he seems to be saying, because stories steal what is real from the world in order to reconstitute it as other than it has been in the past or can become in the future. Furthermore, stories permeate our social being to such an insidious and even pernicious extent, and those who tell (and listen to) stories are so fully bound up by them, that both perception of the real and reception of stories become an indeterminate narrative mess:

> ... llega un momento en el que uno confunde lo que ha visto con lo que le han contado, lo que ha presenciado con lo que sabe, lo que le ha ocurrido con lo que ha leído, en realidad es milagroso que lo normal sea que distingamos, distinguimos bastante a fin de cuentas, y es raro, todas las historias que a lo largo de una vida se oyen y ven, con el cine, la televisión, el teatro, los periódicos, las novelas, se van acumulando todas y son confundibles. (*Corazón* 253)
>
> ... there comes a time when one confuses what one has seen with what people have told you, what one has witnessed with what one knows, what happened to one with what one has read; in fact it's a miracle that, normally speaking, we can distinguish between them, and it's odd, because all the stories that you hear and see throughout your lifetime, what with the movies, television, the theatre, newspapers, novels, they all accumulate and could easily become confused. (*Heart* 234)

This narrative vertigo would seem to leave the narrator and the reader (listener) with no way out, thus suggesting a deep nihilism that leads to the existential abandonment (if not despair) of both.

But Marías does not proffer nihilism in his writing. Though he may take pleasure in creating narrative ambiguities and epistemological uncertainties, his narrator in *Corazón* still seeks to use stories to figure things out about himself and the world. As Luisa reminds the narrator on more than one occasion, "Todo es contable" (*Corazón* 149; 259) ("Everything can be told" [*Heart* 136; 239]), and from the telling comes the meaning: "[las cosas contadas] pasan a formar parte de la analogía y el símbolo, y ya no son hechos, sino que se convierten en reconocimiento" (*Corazón* 201) ("[things that are told] become part of some analogy or symbolism, and are no longer facts, instead they become mere recognition" [*Heart* 186]). But in both cases narrative can be used to recognize the self as well as to show that things could be otherwise. Narration for Marías thus serves not to deny reality or even to diminish it, but to underscore the contingency that permeates all that we cognize and put into words. Contingency thus emerges as a virtue, and serves as a kind of movable anchor in which the world remains present through our recognition of it within the texts that we narrate.

Corazón is one of the most densely packed of Marías's novels (with repetitions, theoretical propositions, and of course with stories), and also one of the most representative.[14] The novel focuses on a narrator intent on discovering

---

[14] For a detailed study of the many repetitions in the novel, and how they function structurally and thematically, see Alexis Grohmann, *Coming Into One's Own: The Novel-*

things about himself and the world in which he lives—a narrator who hopes to solve a mystery that has aroused in him the sensation of unease and foreboding in his marriage, who frames both of these within a narrative that breaks into multiple stories, and who also comments specifically and theoretically on the nature of these stories. *Corazón* is a highly literary work, with Shakespeare hovering around and within it, hence it demands that the reader make intertextual connections that enhance its relationship to the real as well as to the literary. In the end, therefore, Marías shows in *Corazón* that narrative constitutes and is constituted by the world outside of it. The narrator of the novel not only asserts such a proposition, but within the narrative lives it as well.

Mañana en la batalla piensa en mí

Mañana en la batalla piensa en mí begins with a conclusion, in the form of an aphorism drawn from a specific event in the narrator's life. The event is a traumatic one: the sudden and unexpected death of Marta Téllez, a casual acquaintance with whom the narrator (Víctor Francés Sanz) is about to have a sexual relationship in her apartment while her husband is traveling abroad and her young son plays in the room next door. Víctor's recollection of what happened that night occupies approximately the first seventy pages of the novel, and is represented in sharp and abundant detail. Víctor had known Marta for only a few weeks; she felt ill after preparing dinner for the two of them earlier that evening; her two-year-old son, Eugenio, seemed to sense that Víctor's presence was odd, even threatening, and resisted going to sleep; Víctor remains uncertain about what to do when Marta feels ever more ill and slips closer to death. He sits on the bed with her as she dies (partially undressed, in readiness for their sexual liaison) and he ponders his situation for quite a while, realizing that no one knows he has been there (with the exception of Marta's son). Secure in his anonymity, and after much equivocation, he decides to leave the apartment, but not before setting out food for the now sleeping child for when he awakens the following morning.

The aphorism that pertains to this event (the first sentence of the novel) offers an apt summing up in the way of an introduction to Víctor's predicament: "Nadie piensa nunca que pueda ir a encontrarse con una muerta entre los brazos y que ya no verá más su rostro cuyo nombre recuerda"[15] ("No one

---

istic Development of Javier Marías (Amsterdam and New York: Rodopi, 2002), pp. 183–245.

[15] Javier Marías, *Mañana en la batalla piensa en mí* (Barcelona: Editorial Anagrama, 1994), p. 9. All references to the novel in Spanish are to this edition.

ever expects that they might some day find themselves with a dead woman in their arms, a woman whose face they will never see again, but whose name they will remember").[16] Víctor's observation at the beginning of his narrative constitutes both a response to what has occurred and a foreshadowing of what will shortly unfold: the shock of Marta's death, and the memory of it that lingers, cannot easily be erased, and it soon becomes evident to Marta's family that someone other than Marta and her son had been present in the apartment that evening. For Marta's family, therefore, a mystery remains to be solved—not only about how she died but with whom she had shared her final hours. In Víctor's case, he has observed a death for which he is not responsible, in circumstances where his actions nonetheless seem somewhat deceitful and illicit. His presence in the apartment has not been detected yet he has been unable to make a clean break from what has occurred. In fact, the easy escape from the events of that night that he had originally envisioned soon becomes riddled with the shards and fragments of disquietude—a lingering perturbation, nurtured by memory, that he is unable to suppress. More specifically, what happened that evening has begun to haunt him, and the way in which he understands this haunting will shape much of his subsequent behavior. In brief, during the following weeks he sets out to meet the members of Marta's family and to reconcile his desire for anonymity with his need for self-revelation and intimacy as he narrates Marta's story in the context of his own.

The relatively simple and straightforward recounting of Marta's death nonetheless raises pertinent ethical and moral questions for Víctor as well as highly personal ones. First, since his presence at Marta's apartment has not been discovered, the implicit question becomes for Víctor, why not simply sever himself from the events of that night? After all, his encounter with Marta was not built upon passion or an outpouring of love and commitment whose sudden disruption leaves him emotionally adrift. Why not continue to lead the life he has long been leading, since all that has been lost is a casual evening of anticipated pleasure with no expectation of a continuing relationship. Why not, then, simply avoid the messy perils of association with Marta's death (legal, moral, psychological, even financial) and continue to live his own life without interruption even as Marta's family will grieve and suffer? Why not, in brief, simply forget about it? The exploration of these questions forms the heart of Marías's novel, as Víctor sets out to work

---

[16] Javier Marías, *Tomorrow in the Battle Think on Me*, trans. Margaret Jull Costa (New York, San Diego and London: Harcourt Brace, 1996), p. 3. All references to the novel in English are to this edition.

through—to narrate—what he believes about himself and the way in which he chooses to construct his relationship with the world around him.

Following Marta's death, Víctor desires to know what happened in the subsequent hours and days: for example, when Marta's body was discovered; if her son was found in good health. But Víctor senses that more than mere curiosity has compelled him to seek out the next part of the story. As he notes, "Y sin embargo preveía que una vez averiguado eso tampoco podría reanudar sin más mis días y mis actividades, como si el vínculo establecido entre Marta Téllez y yo no fuera a romperse nunca, o fuera a tardar en hacerlo demasiado tiempo" (*Mañana* 81) ("And yet I foresaw that once I had found that out, I would still not be able to get back to my daily life and activities, as if the link established between Marta Téllez and myself would never break, or might take a while to do so" [*Tomorrow* 66]). The "link" that he seems unable to sever leads him to contemplate the continuity of Marta's death into his own life, a continuity which he understands as a haunting that is both pervasive and persistent.

It is not the case, however, that Marta's ghost presents itself either ethereally in Víctor's dreams or physically in his waking life. To be sure, *Mañana* is not a ghost story in which ghosts appear, for example, in the same way that the ghost of Captain Gregg appears in Marías's favorite movie, Joseph Mankiewicz's *The Ghost and Mrs. Muir* (1947).[17] Rather, Marta's presence now occupies Víctor's thoughts through his conception of haunting as an ambiguous element of time that is thickened by memory. After reflecting on the English verb "to haunt," and linking it to the Spanish verb, "encantar," Víctor makes the critical temporal point: "Tal vez el vínculo se limitara a eso, a una especie de encantamiento o *haunting*, que si bien se mira no es otra cosa que la condenación del recuerdo" (*Mañana* 82) ("Perhaps the link was merely that, a kind of enchantment or haunting, which, when you think about it, is just another name for the curse of memory" [*Tomorrow* 67]).

Haunting and memory thus become foundational components of *Mañana*, evoked and embraced by Víctor to give thematic and structural shape to his

---

17 Ghosts and haunting form a critical part of Marías's writing as a whole. He has written many articles in which "fantasmas" are critical—not necessarily as disembodied beings, but as a memory or specter related to past time. The titles of his collections of essays, for example, point to the importance of the ghostly (e.g. *Literatura y fantasma*, *Vida del fantasma*), while critics have also used the concept to describe a number of recurrent themes in Marías's work, including the importance of time and history, linked to the intentional disremembering that followed the Franco years. See, for example, Isabel Cuñado's study, *El espectro de la herencia: La narrativa de Javier Marías* (Amsterdam and New York: Rodopi, 2004).

story. Yet the matter of ghosts cannot be neatly bound to a particular tradition of representation or meaning. As Jo Labanyi has pointed out in her study of Spanish film and fiction of the post-Franco period, there are many kinds of ghosts with an equally broad range of ways to deal with them.[18] The presence of ghosts might create fear or panic in individuals or societies, and thus their presence may not be acknowledged at all. Indeed, their presence may be covered over, or their recognition may be deferred to another time. On the other hand, ghosts may create nostalgia for times and emotions that seem distant but remain desired; they may inhabit memory as a balm for healing or, in a broader context, may help enact social justice that has been denied by political and historical circumstances in which the past is held at bay.[19]

For Víctor, the haunting brought on by Marta's death is powerfully felt but not wholly understood. It has insinuated itself into his thoughts and deeds, but it also binds him to Marta well beyond the actual circumstances of her death per se. To a large degree, therefore, Víctor's sense of being haunted is merely (though importantly) a symptom of something else within his psychological and existential make-up. Indeed, the haunting could not have occurred had Víctor's character been other than it is. This character, which Víctor both reveals and constructs as he tells his story, is at once complex and tenuous, and is brought to light within important parts of his haunted self during the course of his narration. Had Víctor felt no sense of justice, guilt, or even curiosity, for example, he could have wiped clean Marta's death from his life, and

---

[18] Jo Labanyi, "History and Hauntology; or, What Does One Do with the Ghosts of the Past? Reflections on Spanish Film and Fiction of the Post-Franco Period," in *Disremembering the Past: The Politics of Memory in the Spanish Transition to Democracy*, ed. Joan Resina (Amsterdam and Atlanta: Rodopi, 2000), p. 65.

[19] The idea of holding the past at bay following the death of Francisco Franco in 1975, of not "remembering" what happened during the Civil War and the Franco years, forms a critical component of much writing during the transition to democracy in Spain during the late 1970s and early 1980s, and continues today. The many organizations set up to recover the unmarked bodies in mass graves from the Civil War, for example, or the passage by Parliament of the "Ley de memoria histórica" ("The Law of Historical Memory") in 2007, point to the tensions over how to treat the historical past in Spain and how to seek justice for those who suffered at the hands of the Franco regime. In his early fiction, as we have seen, Marías shows scant interest in exploring the recent Spanish past, or even in locating his characters and their actions in Spain. In his more recent fiction, however, and beginning especially with *Mañana*, Marías begins to incorporate some elements of recent Spanish history into the mainstream of his plot. In *Mañana*, for example, the siege of Madrid during the Civil War is referenced. The most intimate and detailed allusions to history, including a semi-autobiographical component related to his father, will later appear in Marías's trilogy, *Tu rostro mañana*.

her family would never know what happened the night she died. Even at the cemetery during Marta's funeral, before Víctor has immersed himself in the lives of the Téllez family, he retains his anonymity (his self-lessness) and remains, "nadie" (*Mañana* 106) ("no one" [*Tomorrow* 88]) to them as he observes the burial from a distance. What he has come to see over the course of his own lifetime in a general way, however, and what he perceived specifically during the course of the evening when Marta lay dying, is the existential need within time for continuity: "Marta debía de estar pendiente de cada segundo, contándolos mentalmente todos, pendiente de la continuidad que es la que nos da no solamente la vida, sino la sensación de vida, la que nos hace pensar y decirnos: 'Sigo pensando, o sigo diciendo, sigo leyendo o sigo viendo una película y por lo tanto estoy vivo'" (*Mañana* 37) ("Marta must be conscious of every second, mentally counting each one as it passed, aware of the continuity which gives us not only life, but the sense of being alive, the thing that makes us think and say to ourselves: 'I'm still thinking or I'm still speaking or I'm still reading or I'm still watching a film and therefore I must be alive'" [*Tomorrow* 27]). Following Marta's death, and as the haunting intensifies, Víctor comes to understand that he has a part to play, and a story to tell, about this existential continuity. Not only does he recognize that life must contain "el hilo de la continuidad" (*Mañana* 56) ("a thread of continuity" [*Tomorrow* 44]), but he realizes that in fact his role is to serve as that thread ("Yo me había convertido en el hilo" (*Mañana* 82) ("I had become the connecting thread" [*Tomorrow* 67]), with complicated entailments both for himself and for the members of Marta's family.

The importance of the relationship between haunting and Víctor's self-identity is further deepened by the literary contextualization of Víctor's dilemma in the title of the novel, which is woven into several passages throughout the work: "mañana en la batalla piensa en mí," derived from Shakespeare's *Richard III*.[20] The title of course serves as yet another literary and intellectual salutation in Marías's fiction to the English dramatist, one that in this instance is also packed with existential significance for Víctor.[21]

---

[20] The direct source of the influence of *Richard III* on Marías's novel is most likely a combination of drama and film. While Shakespeare's drama is clearly represented in the language of the novel, it is also clear that Marías knows at least one film version of the play, since it is playing on television two and a half years before the present time, on a night when Víctor has returned from spending an evening with a prostitute. For an insightful study of the film versions of the drama, see Elizabeth Scarlett, "Victors, Villains, and Ghosts: Filmic Intertextuality in Javier Marías's *Mañana en la batalla piensa en mí*," *Revista Canadiense de Estudios Hispánicos* 28 (2004): 391–410.

[21] Shakespeare's presence is felt in much of Marías's fiction, and lines from his drama

More specifically, the title alludes to Richard's dream the night before the battle of Bosworth, in which he is visited by many of the victims of his murderous ascent to the throne. His brother Clarence and wife Anne utter the key words that form the title of Marías's novel, which are later expanded by Víctor himself as Shakespeare's drama comes to bear fully on the overriding idea of haunting in the novel. When Víctor anticipates that Marta's husband may tell him things that he will be unable to bear but which may exorcise his haunting, he cites a flurry of lines from Richard's nightmare:

> Mañana en la batalla piensa en mí, y caiga tu espada sin filo. Mañana en la batalla piensa en mí, cuando fui mortal, y caiga herrumbrosa tu lanza. Pese yo mañana sobre tu alma, sea yo plomo en el interior de tu pecho y acaben tus días en sangrienta batalla. Mañana en la batalla piensa en mí, desespera y muere. (*Mañana* 190)
>
> Tomorrow in the battle think on me, and fall thy edgeless sword. Tomorrow in the battle think on me, when I was mortal, and let fall thy pointless lance. Let me sit heavy on thy soul tomorrow, let me be lead within thy bosom and at a bloody battle end thy days. Tomorrow in the battle think on me, despair and die. (*Tomorrow* 160–61)

These lines sustain the literary undercurrent through which the novel implicitly demands that readers account for other texts in *Mañana*, and serve as well to dramatize the perturbation in Víctor's life that he seems unable to set aside. To be sure, however, the fear that besets Richard III following his nightmare, and the incipient guilt that seeps into his consciousness, is not meant to find a mirror image in Víctor's perseverations on his own actions the night of Marta's death. Not only has Víctor not murdered anyone (though he worries that his inaction when Marta became ill may have hastened her death), but more importantly, his entire self-identity openly contradicts the British King's maniacal egotism and quest for power. Indeed, as a ghostwriter who pens words for others, he even proclaims his insouciance in a profession (writing) that breeds self-aggrandizement: he counts himself among those who are "No muy ambiciosos" (*Mañana* 112) ("[not] overly ambitious" [*Tomorrow* 93]) and who take on tasks "en las que la personalidad del que escribe no sólo debe borrarse, sino interpretar y encarnar la del prócer al que

---

give the title to several of Marías's works. In addition to *Mañana en la batalla piensa en mí*, which, as we have seen, comes from *Richard III*, see also *Corazón tan blanco* (*Macbeth*); *Negra espalda del tiempo* (*The Tempest*); and the short story collection, *Cuando fui mortal* (*Richard III*).

se sirve" (*Mañana* 112) ("in which the writer must not only erase his own personality, he must also interpret and embody the personality of the national hero he is serving" [*Tomorrow* 93]).

Marías's linking of Richard and Víctor, however, occurs not by means of a third-person narrator who imposes the relationship, but through Víctor himself, who continually embraces it. As Richard is haunted by what he has done in the past because of his forceful ambition, Víctor too is haunted, at least in part by what he failed to do, and by the guilt that remains with him. Hence Marta comes to be fully present in his life even though she is starkly absent. All that Víctor sets out to do after Marta's death, and some of what he has done before, are now framed by his desire at once to embrace his haunting and to rid himself of it, to sustain its presence and allow it to slip away with time. This tension leads him not only to act in certain ways that will place him physically within the sphere of Marta's family, but also to narrate a story that creates and sustains identity and meaning for himself. Such a focus locates *Mañana* squarely within the main literary and philosophical concerns that occupy much of Marías's fiction, with emphasis on storytelling again serving to limn the form and content of the novel.

As a ghostwriter, Víctor often assumes the perspective of other persons and thus regularly writes in someone else's voice. Following Marta's death, he takes the name of a friend, Ruibérriz de Torres, who is also a ghostwriter and who has arranged to begin a writing assignment contracted by Marta's father, Juan Téllez Orati, for the King of Spain. Víctor had previously undertaken jobs that Ruibérriz had passed his way and is accustomed to the literary and personal oblivion associated with such a role. In other words, he often embodies an identity other than his own, though in this case he finds himself twice removed from himself: "Así, él [Ruibérriz] es lo que se llama un negro en el lenguaje literario—en otras lenguas un escritor fantasma—, y yo he oficiado por tanto de negro del negro, o fantasma del fantasma si pensamos en las otras lenguas, doble fantasma y doble negro, doble nadie" (*Mañana* 110) ("He [Ruibérriz] is what is known in the literary world as a ghostwriter and I have therefore become the ghost of a ghost, a double ghost, a double no one" [*Tomorrow* 91]).[22] Thus he stands even further removed from speaking and living authentically as he becomes known to the Téllez family as Ruibérriz, "a double no one" in his words. But in many ways his entry into

---

22 It should be pointed out here that the English translation does not include the entire passage from the original Spanish. It avoids translating the word "negro" as another name for a ghostwriter in Spanish, thus losing the precise language used by Marías though not diminishing the meaning of the passage.

their lives is also doubly deceitful—he is not who they think he is, and he has come to know them for a purpose other than the one for which he was hired. However, during the course of the novel Víctor gradually insinuates himself into their confidence. He confesses to Luisa, Marta's sister, that he spent several hours with Marta in her apartment the evening of her death, later listens to Eduardo Deán, Marta's husband, explain why he was in London when Marta died, and finally comes to believe that he may pursue a serious personal relationship with Luisa in the future. To a large extent, therefore, the novel traces not a dramatic transformation in Víctor's life (there are no existential epiphanies or paroxysms of enlightenment—this is not the way in which Marías portrays his characters), but rather a slow-rolling change that grows from and within Víctor's narrative as he begins to embrace his role as the "thread of continuity" from Marta's past to his own future. Indeed, a small sense of authenticity previously unfelt in Víctor's life prevails at the end of the novel, though in typical fashion for Marías, the story of how he arrives at such a point follows many twists and digressions.

Víctor's story bears many of the markings of a hybrid narrative. It takes the form of a self-reflective confession while drawing as well on aspects of detective fiction and *film noir*—for example, the unexplained death of a woman, the mysterious absence of her husband, the presence of a stranger, the search for that stranger and revelations about the deceased, all highlighted by the movie broadcast on television at the time of Marta's death, William Wilder's *Double Indemnity*.[23] But in a twist to the genre, Víctor plays the role of detective in the novel while also constituting the mystery. He sets out to discover what occurred after he left Marta the night of her death, but his presence in the apartment as the unknown "other" forms the core of the mystery that her family wishes to solve. Thus his story discovers and reveals—a dual task for Víctor and for the art of his storytelling.

Víctor frequently contemplates the strange series of events that set in motion his introduction to the Téllez family, and as he does so he often reflects on life and the passing of time as a series of losses. As he sees it, the

---

[23] The repeated referencing of the movie in the novel suggests a sinister plot with potential danger, when in fact there is none in Víctor's relationship with Marta or with Marta's family. Víctor also refers on several occasions to the stars of the film, Fred MacMurray and Barbara Stanwyck, as if to suggest a tenuous relationship between himself and Marta with the film. While the Fred MacMurray character in the film (Walter Neff) does indeed narrate the story in the first person, as does Víctor in *Mañana*, little of the *noir* aspect of the film penetrates Víctor's narrative—though the hint of a potential relationship with Luisa creates a certain anticipation of the unseemly in the novel (which is not fulfilled) for the reader familiar with the film.

sheer accumulation of things over time cannot stand against oblivion within time. Indeed, time itself bears no intrinsic purpose but to defy memory and to erase what has constituted the small and large components of life that are able to give it persistent sustenance if not profound meaning. On several occasions Víctor contemplates the destructive authority of time as a form of physical and mental nihilism. For example, as he prepares to leave Marta's apartment not long after her death, he reflects on the difficulty of sustaining the raw composition of daily living:

> Tantas cosas suceden sin que nadie se entere ni las recuerde. De casi nada hay registro, los pensamientos y movimientos fugaces, los planes y los deseos, la duda secreta, las ensoñaciones, la crueldad y el insulto, las palabras dichas y oídas y luego negadas o malentendidas o tergiversadas ... todo se olvida o prescribe, cuanto se hace a solas y no se anota y también casi todo lo que no es solitario sino en compañía, cuán poco va quedando de cada individuo. ... Todo el tiempo es inútil. (*Mañana* 68–69)
>
> So many things happen without anyone realizing or remembering. There is almost no record of anything, fleeting thoughts and actions, plans and desires, secret doubts, fantasies, acts of cruelty and insults, words said and heard and later denied or misunderstood or distorted ... everything is forgotten or invalidated, whatever is done alone or not written down, along with everything that is done not alone but in company, how little remains of each individual. ... All time is useless. (*Tomorrow* 54–55)

Víctor later repeats this quote in relation to his ex-wife, Celia (*Mañana* 262–63; *Tomorrow* 222), with whom he has maintained only a distant relationship. In a bizarre evening two and a half years before the death of Marta, Víctor visits Celia's apartment (which he had shared with her during their marriage) to try to confirm whether a prostitute with whom he had spent the evening was actually Celia dressed in disguise. Still uncertain after having sex with her and dropping her off on the street, he later goes to the apartment and finds Celia in bed with another man. Apart from the shock that he causes in Celia (she awakens to see Víctor standing in the bedroom, in a flash of lightning that makes him appear as a ghost), the scene reinforces his belief that much of an individual's life fades into time and loss: "Cuán poco queda de mí en esta casa, de qué poco hay constancia" (*Mañana* 264) ("How little of me remains in that apartment, how little trace remains of anything" [*Tomorrow* 223]).

For Víctor, not only does much of what happens in life resist recollection and definition within a manageable form, but it also stands outside of perception. Víctor's story as a whole generally conforms to the belief that narratives have the capacity to (re)present life, but he also proposes that the sheer accretion of events inevitably resists cognition. Not unlike Marías's mentor, Juan Benet, whose novels assert the difficulty of piecing the disparate elements of life into a solid and coherent whole, Marías suggest in *Mañana* that much of life seeps into a cognitive void—not because of the incapacity of language to reference it but because large parts of it inevitably drift toward temporal oblivion.[24] As Víctor observes concerning Marta's son in one of the most densely synoptic passages of the novel:

> Todo es para todos como para él yo ahora, una figura casi desconocida que lo observa desde el umbral de su puerta sin que él se entere ni vaya a saberlo nunca ni vaya por tanto a poder acordarse, los dos viajando hacia nuestra difuminación lentamente. Es tanto más lo que sucede a nuestras espaldas, nuestra capacidad de conocimiento es minúscula ... no podemos estar más que en un sitio en cada momento, e incluso entonces a menudo ignoramos quiénes nos estarán contemplando o pensando en nosotros, quién está a punto de marcar nuestro número, quién de escribirnos, quién de querernos o de buscarnos ... quién de arrojarnos al revés del tiempo o a su negra espalda, como pienso y contemplo yo a este niño sabiendo más de él de lo que él sabrá nunca sobre el que fue esta noche. Yo debo ser eso, el revés de su tiempo, la negra espalda ... (*Mañana* 69)

> Everything is to everyone else what I am to him now, a vaguely familiar figure observing him from his bedroom door without him realizing it, without him ever knowing or finding out and rendering him, therefore, for ever incapable of recalling it, the two of us slowly travelling towards our own dissolution. So much else goes on behind our backs, our capacity for knowledge is so limited ... we cannot be in more than once place at once, and even then we often have no idea who might be watching us or thinking about us, who is about to dial our number, who is about to write to us, who is about to want us or seek us out ... who is going to hurl us over on to the reverse side of time, on to its dark back, just as I stand here thinking about and contemplating this child, knowing more than he will ever know about what happened tonight. That is what I must be for him, the reverse side of his time, its dark back. (*Tomorrow* 55)

Víctor clearly proposes here the difficulty of accounting for all that we experience in life and the impossibility of overcoming loss brought on by time. In this instance, the shadow of Marta's death will grow ever dimmer in the

---

[24] For more on the influence of Benet on Marías, and the role he played as intellectual mentor, see chapter I on Marías's short essays and newspaper columns.

life of her son; it will become part of his dark back of time. The questions thus emerge as the novel progresses, is there a way to prevent or diminish this loss; is it possible to rescue the past or at least to skim off the dross to retain something of value. While Marías clearly points to the inevitable erasure of things we once knew, and to our ignorance of what falls outside our circle of perception, his fiction does not suggest deep angst or despair about the matter. Indeed, he links the potential recording of lives (and especially the capacity to engage with those things that haunt us) to the nature and purpose of storytelling. As Víctor concludes on more than one occasion in *Mañana* (and as Marías asserts as the formative premise for all of his fiction), "el mundo depende de sus relatores" (*Mañana* 182) ("the world depends on its storytellers" [*Tomorrow* 154]).

Víctor's assertion of the pre-eminence of storytelling points to several critical ideas in the novel. First, it associates the contingencies of life with haunting. As Jo Labanyi has pointed out, ghosts are the "might have beens" of the past—they serve to shake what appear to be the solid foundations of "what was" by offering possible alternative constructs of "what could have been" (Labanyi, "History and Hauntology" 78). Víctor's own uncertainty about himself (for example, his work as a ghostwriter; his assuming of Ruibérriz's name; his ability to submerge himself in the identity of someone else) leads him to speculate about the "what if"s of the night Marta died and how they relate to the present as a form of haunting. After ruminating on how differently the night might have turned out had any number of other things occurred (for example, if her son had gone to sleep more quickly; if he had made love with Marta and left; if he had telephoned her husband when she felt ill), Víctor understands that what did not occur bears as powerfully on the present as what in fact did take place: "No, nada de esto sucedió, y pensar en lo que no sucedió ha de ser parte de mi encantamiento, no tengo por qué sacudirme estas voces y estos pensamientos sino que debo acostumbrarme a ellos mientras siga acechado o frecuentado o revisitado o *haunted*" (*Mañana* 182) ("No, none of that happened, and thinking about what didn't happen must be part of my bewitchment, there's no reason why I should try and shake off these voices and thoughts, I should instead get used to them, for as long as I remain watched or haunted or revisited" [*Tomorrow* 154]).

Conjecture forms a recurrent and substantive part of Marías's writing. It serves to shape both his style and technique (for example, it allows him to develop his characteristically long and complex sentences and to organize his many philosophical and structural digressions from the main plot line). Conjecture further serves to intensify the overarching thematic focus on contingency—life could be one way or another; disengagement from life may be as coercive as engagement; actions resisted may hold the same power as those taken. These ideas can be linked to the thinking of Marías's father, Julián Marías, as several critics have noted, and take shape in many of Marías's works of fiction.[25] They share as well an intimate philosophical position with Juan Benet, for whom the present consists of all that was not—"todo lo que nos queda es lo que un día no pasó," ("All that remains to us is what one day did not happen" [*my translation*], he writes in his best known novel, *Volverás a Región* (1967).[26] Benet offers a more nihilistic posture than Marías proposes in his fiction in general, but one which nonetheless captures the sharp contingency of how roads taken and not taken define the realities and potential realities of our lives.

In *Mañana* the key instances of "what could have been" in relation to "what was not" are inscribed in the stories of the two deceased women, Marta Téllez and Eva García, which are narrated by Víctor and Eduardo Deán respectively. In both cases, contingency gains prominence, but it is understood always through Marías's persistent framing of life within the nature and purpose of storytelling. In Víctor's story, as we have seen, the haunting presence of Marta's death leads him to speculate on "what if" within a wide range of possible outcomes. He thus digresses in his story from what actually occurred not only in order to contemplate alternative possibilities, but also to comment on how his own narrative shapes how Marta's death is first constituted and then received:

> Y estos pensamientos veloces tan sólo al caer, porque quizá Marta Téllez habría muerto de todas formas y habría muerto en el acto sin tiempo para el malestar ni el miedo ni la depresión ni el arrepentimiento. Pero no sucedió nada de esto, sino otra muerte no menos horrible ni menos ridícula, con un desconocido al lado cuando estábamos a punto de echar un polvo ... lo que al suceder no es grosero ni elevado ni gracioso ni triste puede ser triste o gracioso o elevado o grosero al contarse. ... (*Mañana* 181–82)

And she would have had those rapid thoughts only as she was falling, because perhaps Marta Téllez would have died anyway and would have died immediately with no time for feelings of malaise or fear or depression

---

[25] For example, see Alexis Grohmann, *Coming Into One's Own: The Novelistic Development of Javier Marías* (Amsterdam and New York: Rodopi, 2002), p. 265; and Ruth Christie, "Self-writing and 'lo que pudo ser' in *Corazón tan blanco* by Javier Marías," in *The Scripted Self: Textual Identities in Contemporary Spanish Narrative*, ed. Ruth Christie, Judith Drinkwater, and John Macklin (Warminster: Aris & Phillips, 1995), pp. 135–52.

[26] Juan Benet, *Volverás a Región* (Madrid: Destino, 1967), p. 245.

or regret. That did not happen, but a different death, no less horrible and no less ridiculous, with a stranger beside me, just as we were about to have it off ... [what] isn't coarse or elevated or funny or sad when it happens can be sad or funny or elevated or coarse when you tell it. ...
(*Tomorrow* 153–54).

In other words, while conjecture, speculation, and representation comprise the telling of the story that Víctor wishes to tell, the meaning lies not embedded in the events from real life that may have instigated the tale but rather in the form and tone created by the teller. What is more, Víctor proposes here, channeled through the implied voice of Marta, what Marías has conveyed in much of his writing about the nature of meaning: "las historias no pertenecen sólo al que asiste a ellas o al que las inventa, una vez contadas ya son de cualquiera, se repiten de boca en boca y se tergiversan y tuercen ..." (*Mañana* 182) ("stories do not belong only to those who were present or to those who invent them, once a story has been told, it's anyone's, it becomes common currency, it gets twisted and distorted" [*Tomorrow* 154]). In this way Marías makes the critical existential point that links life and narration: realities, narrators, and readers (or events, tellers, and listeners) coalesce to create meanings where there are none, and these meanings in turn become changeable as they form part of someone else's story told to other listeners or made available to other readers.

Víctor affirms the same idea when he finally tells Ruibérriz the story of Marta's death. Had the story been Ruibérriz's to tell, and had Víctor assumed the role of listener, the nature and meaning of Marta's death would have emerged as wholly different even if the facts of the matter had remained the same. In other words, when narrators and readers change, so too do the potential meanings of a story:

> De ser suyo el relato lo habría proclamado a los cuatro vientos desde el principio y habría sido una narración a mitad de camino entre lo macabro y jocoso, lo bufo y lo tenebroso, la muerte horrible y la muerte ridícula, lo que al suceder no es grosero ni elevado ni gracioso ni triste puede ser cualquiera de estas cosas cuando se cuenta, el mundo depende de sus relatores y también de los que oyen el cuento y lo condicionan a veces. ...
> (*Mañana* 299)

Had it been his story, he would have proclaimed it to the four winds right from the start and it would have become a story that was half-macabre and half-jocular, half-absurd and half-sinister, a horrible death and a ridiculous death, something which, when it happens, is neither vulgar nor elevated nor funny nor sad can be any of those things when someone makes a story out of it, the world depends on its storytellers as it does on those who hear the story and occasionally influence it. ... (*Tomorrow* 253)[27]

In the final part of the novel, Eduardo Deán tells Víctor what happened in London on the night that Marta lay dying in Madrid. To a large degree, Deán's story parallels thematically Víctor's own story. First of all, it creates for Deán an ethical and confessional dilemma similar to that experienced by Víctor who, it will be remembered, found himself deciding upon a course of action in which ethical and practical considerations created uncertainty about how to proceed following Marta's death. Further, Deán is haunted by the death of Eva García as he sets out to tell Víctor his story of what turned into an unexpected and dramatic evening. And in the same way that Víctor chose to tell his story to a particular interlocutor (Luisa) who might be capable of giving it the meaning that Víctor hoped his story would have, Deán determines that he must tell his story to Víctor, the only listener who might give to his narrative the meaning that he desires to convey.

Deán's experience with Eva is heavy with plot twists but straightforward in sentiment—until, that is, he learns of his wife's death nearly a full day (twenty hours) after it had occurred. Without the knowledge of either his wife or his co-workers back in Madrid, Deán has spent those twenty hours in London with Eva, helping her secure an abortion. As it turns out, Eva has lied about her pregnancy in order to entrap Deán in their relationship. He discovers the lie, however, when he visits her in the clinic where the abortion was to have been performed. He is first befuddled by her deception, then angry, and quickly renounces his affair with her. In fact, he becomes so livid that he attempts to strangle her later that evening as they ride together in a public bus along the streets of London. When he realizes he cannot carry out this act of violence and weakens his grasp around her neck, she escapes into the street, where she is struck and killed by a taxi as the bus continues on its way. With no witnesses linking Deán to Eva or to the accident, Deán simply remains on the bus, and now finds himself in a position not unlike Víctor's: he knows the details of a death for which he was present but for which he bears no direct responsibility. Hence the questions, not unlike the ones that Víctor faces following the death of Marta—what ethical and moral responsibility does he bear; what should he do now?

---

[27] In yet another use for storytelling in Marías's fiction, Víctor employs the potential story that he will tell about Marta as a form of collateral to obtain Ruibérriz's help in connecting him to Juan Téllez Orati. Víctor promises to tell Ruibérriz all that happened that night with Marta, and later pays off the debt by indeed telling the story.

Deán's story serves as an ironic iteration of the story told by Víctor (the irony grows from the time and coincidence of the incident and the deception of each spouse—Marta and Deán—that is revealed by the unanticipated death of the two women). More importantly, it addresses the concerns that Marías explores on a larger and more complicated scale with Víctor. First of all, much like Víctor, Deán is driven by the need to tell his story. When Luisa informs Víctor that Deán urgently wishes to meet with him, it is not because Deán wants to take revenge against Víctor for Marta's death, or even to learn more details about what happened to his wife. Indeed, he does not want to hear more of the story about Marta but rather to tell a story of his own. As Luisa notes when Víctor asks her, "¿Para qué me busca"? ("Why is he looking for me?"), she responds, "Creo que más que saber quiere contarte algo. ... Quiere que sepas algunas cosas, no sé cuáles" (*Mañana* 297) ("I think he's not so much interested in finding out anything as in telling you something. ... He wants you to know certain facts, I don't know what" [*Tomorrow* 252]). This in turn compels Víctor to ponder the possibility that Deán too is haunted by something, and that through his narration he may be able to diminish its hold over him: " 'Ah,' pensé 'también él quiere contar. También él está cansado, su sombra también lo fatiga' " (*Mañana* 297) (" 'Ah,' I thought, 'so he too has something to tell. He too is tired, weary of the shadows' " [*Tomorrow* 252]).

Beyond the focus on Deán's need to tell his story, the "what if" that shapes the episode moves it to the fore as an existential determinant. As Víctor has averred on several occasions, it is not possible to register or retain all that occurs in the context of one's life, but the "might have been" weighs heavily on Deán just as it has weighed on Víctor since the night of Marta's death. As Deán observes when explaining the haunting presence of Eva:

> También hay trato con lo que se pierde de vista, con lo imaginario y con lo que no acontece ("Y quizá también con los muertos"). Si yo no me hubiera inquietado, si yo no hubiera entrado en el hospital Eva habría venido al café a las dos horas con el rostro desencajado y andares débiles como una heroína que ha pasado su prueba y yo la habría consolado hasta el fin de mis días. ... (*Mañana* 351)
>
> There is a link too with what has been lost from sight, with what one imagines and with what never even happens ("With the dead too"). If I hadn't got worried, if I hadn't gone into the hospital, Eva would have come across to the café after two hours looking shaken and slightly unsteady on her feet, like a heroine who has passed her trial by fire and I would have consoled her then until the end of my days. ... (*Tomorrow* 297)

Yet it is not so much what Deán might have chosen to do differently, or might have done differently by chance (e.g., not entered the clinic, not discovered the false pregnancy), but what he must do now to place the twenty hours of his life in London following Marta's death in a different narrative frame: "Esas veinte horas habrían pasado a ser para él una especie de encantamiento o sueño que debe ser suprimido de nuestro recuerdo, como si ese período no lo hubiéramos vivido del todo, como si tuviéramos que volver a contarnos la historia o a releer un libro; y habrían pasado a ser un tiempo intolerable que puede desesperarnos" (*Mañana* 285–86) ("Those twenty hours would have become for him the kind of enchantment or dream that must be expunged from our memory, as if we had not really lived through that period of time, as if we had to re-tell the story or re-read a book; they would have come to represent a period of time we find unbearable, a source of despair" [*Tomorrow* 242]). In other words, what concerns Deán about that night is not only how forcefully it continues to haunt him, but equally important, how to deal with that haunting. And as occurs with Víctor, he chooses storytelling as a means of constituting and giving it meaning. The retelling of the story (narration and rereading of the book) relates not only to the idea of how we wish to live in a world comprised of "what might have been" and "what was not," but ultimately is linked to narration as a source of authenticity for life. This idea induces Víctor to tell the story that gives impetus to *Mañana* as a whole (i.e., it forms the narrative of the novel), and allows for the possibility of transforming the self in a world, as we have seen, that "depends on its storytellers."

The importance of narration and use of words to authenticate the self is further enhanced through the character known as "el único" ("the Only").[28] A thinly veiled incarnation of the King of Spain, Juan Carlos I, the Only is haunted in his own way—not by any specific event from his past (though his decisions often entail severe and violent consequences for those affected), but by the way in which his public persona, built upon words written for him by others, is suffused with deceit. The possibility of change now lies in the hands of Víctor who, as we have seen, assumed the role of ghostwriter for the King using the name of Ruibérriz. The Only desires from Víctor what others have failed to provide him: a discourse that will create an intriguing, strong, and even enigmatic image that will enhance his standing in the present and shape

---

[28] This character is designated with many names by Víctor in his narrative, in part as a playful allusion to the King of Spain, in part to emphasize the King's lack of true identity. These names include Only, Solo, Solus, el Solitario, Only You, Only the Lonely, and Llanero.

his reputation in history. In the Only's words, he seeks "cierta autenticidad" (*Mañana* 145) ("a degree of authenticity" [*Tomorrow* 121]) amid the many possibilities of how the self is constituted through language. While in the end Víctor fails to produce a narrative that will fulfill the Only's desire (Víctor is not much interested in carrying out his task; he remains more concerned with the Téllez family), his more tenuous link to the King through his role as "reader" (or viewer) also stands as the most intriguing one. And once again, intertextual storytelling moves to the fore as the basis for relating the self to the world.

On the night of Marta's death, as Víctor watched fragments of Fred MacMurray and Barbara Stanwyck in *Double Indemnity* on television, the Only, suffering from insomnia, watched Orson Welles's 1965 film *Campanadas a medianoche* (*Chimes at Midnight*) on a different channel (and, of course, in a different location). Hence the "thread of continuity" that Víctor represents in Marta's story extends outward, linking him as well to a sleepless night for the King. More importantly, the intertextual connection that forms a central component of *Mañana* as a whole links the Only to the movie, which represents the lives of Henry IV and Henry V of medieval Lancaster. Similar to Víctor, who had been unable to view all of *Double Indemnity*, the King had not watched the whole of *Chimes at Midnight* that evening. As a result, he has missed the critical point, not about the story told in the film but about the nature of storytelling. As Víctor observes,

> Él [único] había visto incompleta aquella película y había sentido instantánea y primaria envidia, sin acordarse ni darse cuenta de que los dos medievales Enriques de Lancaster se beneficiaban del paso de los siglos que ya por sí solos los hacían ficticios, objeto *sólo* de representación, ni siquiera de investigación o estudio, de ninguna otra cosa, tan nítidos y reconocibles como nunca lo son las personas o sólo en cambio los personajes. (*Mañana* 159)

> He had only seen part of that film and had experienced a feeling of instantaneous, primitive jealousy, forgetting or not realizing that the two medieval Henries of Lancaster had benefited from the passing of the centuries which had, by itself, made them into fictitious beings, objects of representation, nothing more, not even objects of investigation or study, leaving them clear and recognizable in a way that a person never is, but in a way that personages can be. (*Tomorrow* 134)

The King's real problem, in Víctor's view, is that "Él era aún persona ... y las personas son volubles e inestables y frágiles y se distraen de sus intereses por cualquier cosa traicionando o desdibujando así su carácter" (*Mañana* 159)

("He was still a person ... and people are voluble and unstable and fragile and easily distracted from their own affairs, thus betraying or blurring their character" [*Tomorrow* 134]).

The idea of blurring one's character is of course critical here, and provides the final connection between the Only and Víctor. For just as the King seeks to redefine himself by means of future narratives that he will use to create a more dramatic persona, so too Víctor wishes to sharpen his own image and to bring what has been a blurred, inauthentic character into clear focus. The process for doing so is not without obstacles, but it becomes the way in which Marías converts a novel of many digressions into a story with a thread of continuity. This process of course begins and ends with storytelling, defined by conceptual parameters in a world where stories never remain the property of the teller but rather are appropriated, transformed, and commingled with other stories yet to be told.

When Víctor finally finds himself alone with Marta's sister after a family luncheon, and is prepared to tell the story of what happened the night of Marta's death, he has already incorporated into his understanding of those events a number of other texts that will augment his own narration—most prominently, as we have seen, *Richard III*, *Chimes at Midnight*, and *Double Indemnity*.[29] The haunting of Richard III is pre-eminent, of course. Víctor had watched the movie on television two and a half years earlier and remains disturbed by the dream that besets Richard the night before he dies—hence the repetition in the novel of the words of the haunted King's victims: " 'Mañana en la batalla piensa en mí ... y caiga tu espada sin filo: desespera y muere.' 'Pese yo mañana sobre tu alma, sea yo plomo en el interior de tu pecho y acaben tus días en sangrienta batalla: caiga tu lanza.' 'Piensa en mí cuando fui mortal: desespera y muere' " (*Mañana* 246–47) (" 'Tomorrow in the battle think on me ... and fall thy edgeless sword: despair and die!' 'Let me sit heavy on thy soul tomorrow; let me be lead within thy bosom and in a bloody battle end thy days: let fall thy pointless lance.' 'Think on me when I was mortal: despair and die!' " [*Tomorrow* 208]). But Víctor also recalls Henry V from *Chimes at Midnight*, "Ese rey está agonizando y luego muere, atormentado por su pasado y por el futuro en el que no estará contenido"

---

[29] Víctor also includes a World War II British propaganda film in his story entitled *Spitfire* (1942), which he viewed on television, though he does not name the film directly. The film is pertinent because it reminds Víctor of war planes that he saw hanging from the ceiling of Eugenio's room the night of Marta's death, and which evoked memories of his own youth and interest in airplanes. Again here, Marías establishes a thread of continuity between characters where there seems to be none.

(*Mañana* 314) ("The King is dying and eventually does die, tormented by his past and by the future in which he will not participate" [*Tomorrow* 266]).

Faced with haunting in his real life, which is intensified by his evocation of other persons from other texts, Víctor's confession—both to us, the readers, as well as to Luisa—not only serves as an attempted cleansing of his guilt but also as an affirmation of how he wishes to understand what happened the night that Marta died and what meaning it affords his own place in the world. Equally important, he seeks to shape the way in which others will understand it as well. His telling of the story will thus reveal something about the events as well as something about himself and the way in which he wishes to claim authenticity for a self that has resisted both stability and permanence. When he meets with Luisa, he asserts his desire to tell his story, and in doing so, conveys the narrative position that frames the novel as a whole:

> Conté. Conté. Y al contar no tuve la sensación de salir de mi encantamiento del que aún no he salido ni quizá nunca salga, pero sí de empezar a mezclarlo con otro menos tenaz y más benigno. El que cuenta suele saber explicar bien las cosas y sabe explicarse, contar es lo mismo que convencer o hacerse entender o hacer ver y así todo puede ser comprendido, hasta lo más infame, todo perdonado cuando hay algo que perdonar, todo pasado por alto o asimilado y aun compadecido, esto ocurrió y hay que convivir con ello una vez que sabemos que *fue*, buscarle un lugar en nuestra conciencia y en nuestra memoria que no nos impida seguir viviendo porque sucediera y porque lo sepamos. (*Mañana* 278)

> I told the story, I told it all. And as I told the story, I did not feel as if I were stepping free from the spell I was under and from which I have still not escaped and perhaps never will escape, I felt, instead, as if it were beginning to mingle with another less tenacious, more benign spell. The person telling a story is usually able to explain things well and to explain himself, telling a story is tantamount to persuading someone or making oneself clear or making someone see one's point of view, that way everything becomes capable of being understood ... everything can be forgiven when there is something to forgive, everything can be overlooked or assimilated or even pitied, such and such happened and we have to learn to live with it once we know that it did happen, we have to find a place for it in our consciousness and in our memory where the fact that it happened and that we know about it will not prevent us from going on living. (*Tomorrow* 235)

Víctor's haunting has at once a pastness as well as presentness to it, and his narrative offers a sort of memory-knowledge that is only available within the story as he decides to tell it. His story is less remembered than continuously felt, and it is confounded by narration even though the narration is the sole way to diminish the presence of his psychological wound. While it is clear in the novel that Víctor wishes to protect himself, he is also prepared to expose himself. This will enable him not only to fill in the temporal blanks for others concerning the specific nature of Marta's death, but also to begin to delineate the profile of his own self, to reconstitute and establish a more fully authentic relationship with the world where, for the most part, he has lived as a ghost.

During the telling of his story near the end of the novel, Deán's evocation of Henry V's admonishment to Falstaff, within the context of narrating, affords an aphoristic summing up of *Mañana* while also showing how the self can be modified and given new form: "Nadie hace nada convencido de su injusticia, no al menos en el momento de hacerlo, contar tampoco, qué extraña misión es esa. ... Pero en realidad el que cuenta siempre cuenta más tarde, lo cual le permite añadir si quiere, para alejarse: 'Pero he dado la espalda a mi antiguo yo, ya no soy lo que fui ni tampoco el que fui, no me conozco ni me reconozco. Y yo no lo busqué, yo no lo quise' " (*Mañana* 363) ("No one does anything convinced of its injustice, not at least at the moment they do it, it's the same with telling a story, what a strange mission or task that is. ... But, in fact, the person telling the story always tells it later on, which allows him to add things if he wants, to distance himself: 'I have turned away my former self, I am not the thing I was nor the person I was, I neither know nor recognize myself. I did not seek it, I did not want it' " [*Tomorrow* 308]).[30] In the end, caught between experience and language (narration), Víctor opts not for one over the other, but for the pertinence of both. He allows the memory of Marta a place in his life, but sets out to make it usable rather than destructive. This can only be achieved by linking experience to storytelling—a technique that lies at the heart of Marías's fiction and is neatly encapsulated in his lapidary phrase, "lo real ha de ser imaginado" ("the real must be imagined").[31] For Marías, imagination and narration cannot be separated from the real, but rather form a necessary alliance with it that allows the self at once to be located in the world and to tell about it.

---

[30] A much longer version of this quote, again evoking the figures of Henry and Falstaff, is found earlier in the novel as well: *Mañana* 200; T*omorrow* 168–169.

[31] See, for example, his article "Los malditos detalles," in *Mano de sombra* (Madrid: Alfaguara, 1997), p. 325. For a more detailed discussion of this idea, see chapter II.

VI

Tu rostro mañana

Tu rostro mañana is best understood as a three-volume novel rather than three novels sutured together to form a trilogy.[1] Published over a period of five years (2002–2007), it tells the story of Jaime Deza, who first appears as narrator and main character of Marías's 1989 novel *Todas las almas* and who narrates each of the three volumes of *Rostro*. Deza thus provides the "thread of continuity" in the narrative that Marías envisions as a critical part of lives and stories, an idea first asserted by the narrator of *Mañana en la batalla piensa en mí* and echoed by Deza here: "Yo soy el río, soy el río y por tanto un hilo de continuidad entre vivos y muertos al igual que los cuentos que nos hablan de noche ..."[2] ("I am the river, I am the river and, therefore, a connecting thread between the living and the dead, just like the stories that speak to us in the night ...").[3]

To a large extent, *Rostro* is more culminant than innovative within Marías's body of writing. Indeed, many key aspects of the novel can be found in his previous fiction: he revisits in *Rostro* several characters first presented to a greater or lesser degree in earlier novels (e.g., Peter Wheeler, Esteban Custardoy, his father, Juan Deza); he inserts visual objects in the text, such as paintings, photographs, and posters, a strategy that has helped to shape other

---

[1] Each of the three volumes of *Tu rostro mañana* bears a subtitle: Volume I, *Fiebre y lanza*, (2002) (*Fever and Spear*, 2005); Volume II, *Baile y sueño* (2004) (*Dance and Dream*, 2006); Volume III, *Veneno y sombra y adiós* (2007) (*Poison, Shadow and Farewell*, 2009). The single main title of the novel, with varying subtitles, distinguishes Marías's three-volume work from other trilogies of recent vintage in Spain, such as Josefina Aldecoa's work, *Historia de una maestra* (1990); *Mujeres de negro* (1994); *La fuerza del destino* (1997).

[2] Javier Marías, *Tu rostro mañana. Fiebre y lanza* (Madrid: Alfaguara, 2002), p. 224. All references to *Fiebre y lanza* in Spanish are to this edition and noted in the text with the letters *FL*.

[3] Javier Marías, *Your Face Tomorrow. Fever and Spear*, trans. Margaret Jull Costa (New York: New Directions, 2002), p. 180. All references to *Fever and Spear* in English are to this edition and noted in the text with the letters *FS*.

works (e.g., *Negra espalda del tiempo*; *Miramientos*; *Vidas escritas*); he elaborates on a range of ideas related to truth, knowledge, interpretation, violence, and ethics; he continues to follow the digressive style and technique for which he has long been known in his writing. In brief, *Rostro* reveals the thinking of a mature Marías who asserts the potential of narration to define the world in the present as well as its capacity to reshape our understanding of the past. But equally important, Marías sets out in *Rostro* to show how storytelling can also be used to organize our actions and perception of the world in the future.

Marías has never embraced fully the technical, stylistic, or philosophical foundations of overtly experimental fiction or postmodern writing.[4] In *Rostro*, he again shows such reticence, even though he contemplates throughout the three volumes how strained the relationship can become between the narrated world of the text and the reality outside of the text that he purportedly sets out to represent. *Rostro* will not be confused, for example, with the innovative and sometimes bizarre avant-garde writing of the early twentieth century in Europe and America, or with the most recent hypertextual multimedia production of blogger-novelists and cyber writers. However, as Spanish writer Félix de Azúa has smartly pointed out, the novel fuses "elementos democráticos con la hipertécnica de una escritura para profesionales" ("democratic elements with the hypertechnique of writing for professionals").[5] In other words, not unlike in postmodern fiction, which often consists of a mélange of texts speaking to one another, Marías pays homage in *Rostro* to elements of popular culture in film and literature (e.g., from Ian Fleming to gangster movies and country and western music), much like he has done since his earliest referencing of Hollywood and the adventure novel in *Los dominios del lobo* and *Travesía del horizonte*. Further, he incorporates the high cultural artistic production of authors such as Shakespeare, T. S. Eliot, and Lope de Vega, to name only a few, as well as visual

---

[4] See, for example, Thomas Docherty's *Reading (Absent) Character* (Oxford: Oxford University Press, 1983) and his *Alterities* (Oxford: Oxford University Press, 1996), for a discussion of recent techniques in representation and character portrayal, which Marías has never embraced. See any number of books on postmodernism for how characters and their social worlds are constituted by postmodern authors: for example, the now classic text by Jean-François Lyotard, *The Postmodern Condition*, trans. Geoff Bennington and Brian Massumi (Minneapolis: University of Minnesota Press, 1984); or Zygmunt Bauman, *Postmodernity and Its Discontents* (Cambridge: Polity, 1997).

[5] Félix de Azúa, "Lanzas, espadas, rostros y nada," in *Allí donde uno diría que ya no puede haber nada. Tu rostro mañana de Javier Marías*, ed. Alexis Grohmann and Maarten Steenmeijer (Amsterdam and New York: Rodopi, 2009), p. 51.

elements of both popular and high cultures—such as the painting of Hans Baldung Grien, propaganda posters from World War II and the Spanish Civil War, and photographs of other writers and movie stars.[6] Taken together, these texts create a dense intertextual foundation for the novel that demands cultural knowledge and active participation by the reader in both seeing and understanding how the texts interact. What must be fully grasped, however, is that Marías incites the intertextual flooding of *Rostro* without diminishing the capacity of his novel to speak to and about the world outside itself. Indeed, he argues convincingly in the end for both dependency and intimacy between texts and lives.

In much of his fiction Marías seeks to incorporate both tellers and listeners of stories into the fabric of his narrative. They assume a variety of roles in multiple contexts, but above all they allow Marías to work through his ideas on writing while avoiding the compression of his views into a narrow scheme or a restrictive theoretical model. Somewhat unexpectedly, however, Marías's intense interest in exploring the art and practice of narrating does not generate texts that are highly self-referential. Nor do his novels follow the common pattern of metafiction in which the protagonist is a novelist in the midst of writing a novel, which turns out to be the very work that we are reading.[7] Instead, Marías generally proposes a double focus within his narrative that affirms the rich capacity of fiction to serve both as a form within which the representation of reality takes place, and as an object within reality: on the one hand he endows narrations (stories) with ontological substance "(las figuraciones [textos] ya son hechos" [*FL* 30]) ("imaginings [texts] are already facts" [*FS* 17]) by asserting that they exist in the world as a body of words within a text, and thus constitute part of our social reality. On the other hand, Marías proposes an interpretive function for narration through which he seeks to say something about the teller of a tale as well as the world in which the tale is told. As Deza notes in *Rostro*, the world that his story represents may well be both substantive and complex, but above all "las cosas no acaban de existir hasta que se las nombra" (*FL* 27) ("things only exist once

---

[6] For a thorough and very useful article on the numerous intertextual references in *Rostro*, undertaken with the helpful input of Javier Marías, see " 'Cito a menudo para mis adentros': citas y alusiones en *Tu rostro mañana* de Javier Marías," in Grohmann and Steenmeijer, *Allí donde uno diría*, pp. 303–66.

[7] For a more detailed study of metafiction in the Spanish novel of the twentieth century, see Robert Spires, *Beyond the Metafictional Mode: Directions in the Modern Spanish Novel* (Lexington: University Press of Kentucky, 1984), and Antonio Sobejano-Morán, *Metaficción española en la postmodernidad* (Kassel: Edition Reichenberger, 2003).

they have been named" [*FS* 14]), hence "[el relato es] casi lo único que cuenta" (*FL* 27) ("[the story is] almost the only thing that counts" [*FS* 14]). In this way Marías is able to engage the nature of narrative without either embracing unfettered representation (i.e., the mimetic traditions of realism) or yielding to opposing postmodern claims of pure configuration, even though he seems to propose the latter in at least some of his essays and novels. As Alexis Grohmann has shown, such thinking represents one of the fundamental paradoxes of Marías's fiction in general, and of *Rostro* in particular.[8] In other words, Marías seems to embrace, as storytellers have long understood, that the essential nature of telling tales is shaped by the contradictory paradigm of "it was and it was not."

While Marías clearly sets out to re-explore in *Rostro* many of the ideas that have been woven throughout much of his earlier writing, above all he is interested in showing how narration (storytelling) is both highly usable and frequently used in a range of social contexts. Indeed, this proposition constitutes the main premise of the novel and gives it both narrative and philosophical substance. It is embodied primarily by Jaime Deza, through whom Marías creates a "hermeneutic consciousness," whose primary role is at once to examine and embody the link between the text and the world outside of it.[9] From Deza's perspective (and also from the novel's) what begins as an uncertain connection between the stories and the lives explored, yields not only to a clear assertion of how each shapes the other but to the full elaboration of stories as what Kenneth Burke has called "equipment for living."[10] As Marías proposes throughout *Rostro*, the relation between texts and lives is always circumscribed by complexity, and sometimes it is fraught with danger. Most importantly, however, it is the reciprocity and influence of one upon the other that resonates in the novel as the center of human existence. As we shall see, Deza not only comes to comprehend this reciprocity but also to embrace it. Hence he might say of stories as Marianne Moore remarked about poetry, "these things are important not because a / high-sounding interpretation can be put upon them but because they are / useful."[11]

---

[8] Alexis Grohmann, "La literatura como paradoja," in Grohmann and Steenmeijer, *Allí donde uno diría*, pp. 161–69.

[9] For more on the idea of "hermeneutic consciousness," see chapter IV on *Todas las almas* and *Negra espalda del tiempo*, note 18.

[10] Kenneth Burke, "Literature as Equipment for Living," in Walter Sutton and Richard Foster (eds), *Modern Criticism: Theory and Practice* (New York: Odyssey Press, 1963), pp. 242–47.

[11] Marianne Moore, *The Complete Poems of Marianne Moore* (New York: Macmillan/Viking Press, 1967), p. 266.

The story of *Rostro* is narrated by Jaime Deza (also called Jacobo, Jack, and Jacques) who, for the most part, relates the activities of his recent past working in London, but with many digressions that explore the more distant past through the memories and stories of various characters. As Deza tells it, he had returned to England to work as a translator for the BBC during the break-up of his marriage. Following a dinner party in Oxford at the home of his old friend and Hispanist, Peter Wheeler, Deza receives an offer to join a group of people led by Bertram Tupra, whose work is linked to former secret service activities of MI6. While Deza is unable to discern the precise affiliation of this clandestine group to a higher chain of command, or even determine if it is government sponsored (as he puts it, "trabajaba en un país extranjero y un edificio sin nombre para no sabía quién"[12] ["I was working in a foreign country and in a building with no name and for whom I did not know"]),[13] he gradually assumes responsibility for questioning persons of potential interest to the group, or for listening to them answer questions posed by others. Further, he is often called upon to travel with Tupra or to attend social events where an individual under investigation by his office is present, and where he can scrutinize the person at close range. Deza's task then consists of writing a detailed report about the character traits of the persons he has observed. Most importantly, he speculates about future actions of people based upon the stories that he pieces together about their past, and his conclusions become part of the material stored in the files of the office. He is perceived by others in his group as a talented colleague, and he possesses the ability if not to predict the future, at least to create valued stories about likely behavior in diverse situations that have not yet occurred. In other words, Deza's task is deeply rooted in linking stories to life.

During the course of his work Deza listens to others narrate (or he reads a text of their narration) and offers analysis (interpretation) that gives concrete meaning to their story in the present and affords potential meaning for the future. It is the future "in reality" that concerns him, however, and he tells an imagined story about what may occur, to the extent that the future can be inferred from stories of the past. His job, in short, is to "contar lo que aún no era ni había sido, lo futuro y probable o tan sólo posible—la hipótesis—, es

---

12 Javier Marías, *Tu rostro mañana. Baile y sueño* (Madrid: Alfaguara, 2004), p. 403. All references to *Baile y sueño* in Spanish are to this edition and noted in the text with the letters *BS*.
13 Javier Marías, *Your Face Tomorrow. Dance and Dream*, trans. Margaret Jull Costa (New York: New Directions, 2006), p. 336. All references to *Dance and Dream* in English are to this edition and noted in the text with the letters *DD*.

decir, por intuir e imaginar e inventar; y por convencer de ello" (*FL* 22) ("[talk] about what did not exist and had not yet happened, the future and the probable or the merely possible—the hypothetical—that is, to intuit and imagine and invent; and to convince" [*FS* 10]). Listening, analyzing, and telling—the reception and giving of meaning—thus become the principal focus of Deza's life and work even as he ponders the practical value and moral legitimacy of what he does. In the end, after witnessing horrid acts of violence by Tupra (described primarily in volume two); after committing similar acts of violence himself when he threatens his ex-wife's lover, whom he fears is abusing her (related mainly in volume three); and finally, after seeing that the stories he creates in his job can be used to instigate violence and murder, Deza abandons his work in London and returns to Madrid, where he now narrates his story in the present.

Rostro begins with a peculiar warning from Deza (quoting advice from his friend and mentor, Peter Wheeler, as well as from his father, Juan Deza): "No debería uno contar nunca nada" (*FL* 13) ("One should never tell anyone anything" [*FS* 3]). This is unusual counsel for any writer to give, but it is particularly striking in the case of Marías, whose fictional and theoretical writing generally celebrates storytelling as the principal way in which we connect ourselves to the world and give it meaning. The narrator of *Mañana en la batalla piensa en mí*, as we have seen, succinctly makes the point that circumscribes Marías's writing as a whole: "el mundo depende de sus relatores y también de los que oyen el cuento"[14] ("the world depends on its storytellers as it does on those who hear the story").[15] Thus Deza's exhortation at the beginning of *Rostro* not to narrate, or to keep quiet, creates a confounding dissonance with the demand for telling stories that shapes Marías's idea of the world, informs his view of writing in general, and quite literally introduces the story that we are about to read in *Rostro*. Furthermore, it has the practical effect of focusing attention on the nature of narration in *Rostro*, and of intimating that telling stories is never as innocuous as it may seem.

Beyond the overarching paradox of this introduction to *Rostro*, and the ironic subversion of his own narrative that it implies, Marías's challenge to storytelling suggests a number of pertinent questions. Most pointedly, why

---

[14] Javier Marías, *Mañana en la batalla piensa en mí* (Barcelona: Editorial Anagrama, 1994), p. 299. References to the novel in Spanish are to this edition.

[15] Javier Marías, *Tomorrow in the Battle Think on Me*, trans. Margaret Jull Costa (New York, San Diego and London: Harcourt Brace, 1996), p. 253. References to the novel in English are to this edition.

would he begin a story of nearly sixteen hundred pages by warning against telling stories? Is it dangerous to do so, perhaps irrational or even futile? And further, how might such an admonition shape readers' expectations about what they are about to read? More narrowly, does the warning form part of the plot, offered as practical advice and aimed at a specific character or circumstance that will later be revealed? Does it function as a metafictional framing device that promotes the self-directed turn of the novel, thus making its referential base seem distant, perhaps even unpropped against life?

While the terseness of Marías's admonition initially gives no hint to readers suggesting how to proceed, and Marías himself clearly offers no unequivocal answers, assorted possibilities begin to register as the narrator constructs the context and lays bare the intentions of his assertion. Above all, what is proposed derives from the deeply rooted concern that gives shape to *Rostro* and resonates in much of the author's work. The concern might be summarized as follows within two main areas of inquiry explored throughout the novel. First, what is the capacity of stories (language and narration) to represent life? In many of his novels and essays, Marías conveys his ambivalence about the referential capacity of narration without despairing over the impossibility of ever getting it right. On the one hand his narrators seem to deny the potential of linking word and world in transparent reciprocity (for example, "por el mero hecho de contar [lo sucedido] ya lo está deformando y tergiversando"[16] ("the simple fact of saying it already distorts and twists it");[17] or, " 'Relatar lo ocurrido' es inconcebible y vano" (*Negra* 10) (" 'To tell what happened' is inconceivable and futile" [*Dark* 8]). On the other hand, however, Marías's narrator firmly sanctions the role of stories in establishing such a link: "Voy a alinearme con los que han pretendido [relatar lo ocurrido] alguna vez o han simulado lograrlo" (*Negra* 11) ("I'm going to align myself on the side of those who have sometimes claimed to be telling what really happened or pretended to succeed in doing so" [*Dark* 8]). Hence while malleability at the root of storytelling defines much of Marías's work, so too does the belief that in some ways (and in some circumstances) stories refer efficaciously to the world and in other ways they do not.

The second main area of inquiry embedded in Deza's admonition against storytelling turns upon the social circulation of stories (or more particularly in *Rostro*, their professional use by Deza's employer). The inference that

---

[16] Javier Marías, *Negra espalda del tiempo* (Madrid: Alfaguara, 1998), p. 9. All references to the novel in Spanish are to this edition.

[17] Javier Marías, *Dark Back of Time*, trans. Esther Allen (New York: New Directions, 2001), p. 7. All references to the novel in English are to this edition.

might be drawn relates to how the stories can be used—and how they might easily spin out of control. In other words, we should refrain from telling stories because, regardless of their perceived authenticity at any particular moment, what we say may be appropriated and folded into another story, which in turn is appropriated by another until our narrative stretches beyond its original context, intentions, and meaning to form part of someone else's story and thus serve someone else's interests. This process can be insidiously deceptive, even treacherous, for it implies misappropriation and misreading of original desire and turns authorial intention into a form of hermeneutic encroachment.

Yet this process is also inevitable, as Marías has shown in his previous work. *Negra espalda del tiempo*, as we have seen, is written expressly to correct the perceived misreading of the author's earlier novel, *Todas las almas* (1989), and serves in part as an attempt by Marías to gain ownership over the use of the text by other readers. With similar intentions, *Rostro* signals that readers must traverse the narrative terrain with care. The novel aggressively turns inward to explore the nature of storytelling and outward to consider how stories pertain to life when inserted into new texts and contexts. Further, the narrative explores how such a process transforms life in the present as well as the past, and how the narrator of this process is defined by what he narrates. It is precisely this transformative component of storytelling that gives substance to Deza's work and to Marías's novel, which sets out to narrate life in the past, present, and future. However, while throughout *Rostro* Deza pins down the intersection of external occurrences and narrative representations related to present and past time, his professional task is to link narration to the world of what has not yet happened: "todo está ahí a la vista, en realidad todo es visible desde muy pronto en las relaciones como en los relatos honrados, basta con atreverse a mirarlo, un solo instante encierra el germen de muchos años venideros y casi de nuestra historia entera …" (*FL* 51–52) ("everything is there on view, in fact, everything is visible very early on in a relationship just as it is in all honest, straightforward stories, you just have to look to see it, one single moment encapsulates the germ of many years to come, of almost our whole history …" [*FS* 35]). In this way stories are tied to our horizon of expectations through the principle of cause and effect, which in turn is pertinent to the structure of narration as well as to the predictability of human behavior.

In this sense, the power of storytelling determines not only how people are defined, but also how they live. Thus it is not a matter, as Victor Brombert has suggested in another context, of having to choose between living or telling, but rather of understanding that living and telling share the same vital plain.[18] For this reason Deza and his group are able to exploit the nature of stories—not only do they have a presence in the world (they exist in reality—in this case in the files of Tupra's operation—as linguistic texts); they also represent something outside themselves. More importantly, Deza and his colleagues also perceive stories as able to construct and transform individual lives because individuals see themselves in reality as components of narrations. This gives an ontological weight to stories whose function is not merely descriptive but fully existential. Thus *Rostro* can best be viewed as a hybrid text that grows from a postmodern perspective of how stories define and construct reality, as well as from a high modern understanding of texts in which narrative is able to represent the complexities of the world even as it helps to determine our perception of its shape. Indeed, there remains in *Rostro* a strong modernist belief implicit in storytelling through which individuals can be cognized, recognized, and ultimately known. Such a perspective ascribes a teleological movement to stories, through which causal formations produce foreseeable outcomes in narrations as well as in life.

The reasons to eschew the telling of stories remain paramount in the novel, however, despite the nature of Deza's work. These turn upon both theoretical and practical considerations, each linked to the other through the articulated intentions and uncertain consequences of narrating. In the first place, in his reflections on his own story, Deza perceives the frailty of his discourse even while asserting its power. He thus makes the critical point:

> sólo cuento cuando no hay más remedio o se me pide insistentemente. Porque ... aprendí que lo que tan sólo ocurre no nos afecta apenas o no más que lo que no ocurre, sino su relato (también el de lo que no ocurre), que es indefectiblemente impreciso, traicionero, aproximativo y en el fondo nulo, y sin embargo casi lo único que cuenta, lo decisivo, lo que nos trastorna el ánimo y nos desvía y envenena los pasos, y seguramente hace girar la perezosa y débil rueda del mundo. (*FL* 27)

> I only tell anyone anything when I have no alternative or if someone insists. For ... I learned that what merely happens to us barely affects us or, at least, no more than what does not happen, but it is the story (the story of what does not happen too), which, however imprecise, treacherous, approximate and downright useless, is nevertheless almost the only thing that counts, is the decisive factor, it is what troubles our soul and diverts

---

[18] Victor Brombert, "Opening Signals in Narrative," *New Literary History* 11 (1980): 489–502.

and poisons our footsteps, it is doubtless also what keeps the weak, lazy wheel of the world turning. (*FS* 14)

Deza claims the right here to distinguish between stories that are true and those that are invented, and in each case affirms the capacity of language to represent the world or to make things up about it. The distinction is critical, but curiously, not pertinent. While Marías clearly proposes to distinguish between what is real and what is not (with appropriate concessions to the shadowy terrain in between), in each case he bestows upon storytelling a referential substance that is available to the teller but not required to be used. For Marías, the distinction that bears greater pertinence here and in the playing out of our daily lives as well, grows from the dissonance between representation and being that makes of storytelling both a perception about reality and an object in reality that is imbued with social meaning and therefore has social consequence. In this way Deza recognizes the dual role of language speaking **about** the world and being **in** the world, and he affirms its ability to shape human activity (i.e., it "keeps the weak, lazy wheel of the world turning").

But the critical question raised by the narrative—why should one never tell stories?—remains partially unanswered here both in relation to what *Rostro* actually is (a novel) as well as what it purports to be about (a young man's ability to envision the future by telling a story about it). The novel hints at the answer, but to a large degree it must be inferred from the tensions between storytelling per se and how storytelling might be used. Two examples from the work will serve to make the point. The first grows from a principle firmly rooted in the legal system of the United States and summarized in the well-known Miranda warning aimed at protecting suspects from incriminating themselves: the right to remain silent; anything they say may be used against them. Or as Deza puts it, a person is granted the right "a no dañarse narrativamente" (*FL* 18) ("not to harm himself by his own narrative" [*FS* 7]).

It is here, of course, where the role of the listener/reader moves to the fore. But the process is defiantly ambiguous even if the desired outcome is not. In other words, the role of the listener in a legal case (and most specifically, the police who interrogate the suspect) is to embrace the referential authority of the narrative in order to move it teleologically to the desired conclusion. While it is possible (and even probable) that the narrator/defendant may tell multiple and contradictory stories, especially if trying to avoid arrest and prosecution, the principal inference to be drawn from the Miranda warning related to storytelling is not that it is difficult to distinguish between fact and fiction (thought this is often the case), but that the distinction can be framed and determined by language. That is to say, language is both perceived and used as a capable vehicle for referring to life. It is both effective and consequential, and it often determines the outcome of our lives as if it were reality itself rather than a pale representation of it. Hence Marías's admonition never to tell anything to anyone seems to grant a foundational realism to narrative through the implied adequacy of its representations. And as Miranda presupposes, these representations may be used in someone else's favor.

The second and more prominent example of the urgency to remain silent is linked to World War II and British slogans exhorting the country's citizens to be wary of supplying information to German spies unintentionally, and to the Spanish Civil War, where similar warnings are posted during the three years of the conflict. Marías inserts images of a series of posters into the narrative of his novel, each containing a relevant drawing linked to a mini-narrative warning against casual talk in public settings.[19] In this way the people of England are reminded during the war to "Think twice" before making calls from party-line telephones (*FL* 405; *FS* 320); to "be like dad—Keep Mum" (*FL* 405; *FS* 320); and always to bear in mind that "Careless talk costs lives" (*FL* 399; *FS* 316). In similar fashion, Spaniards during the Civil War are reminded that "el espía te oye";[20] "cuidado con lo que hablas" (*VSA* 581; *PSF* 450); and "No deis detalles sobre la situación de los frentes. Ni a los camaradas. Ni a los hermanos. Ni a las novias" (*VSA* 581; *PSF* 450). These repeated warnings to keep quiet, to avoid telling stories, are designed to enhance the preservation of safety and implicitly rest upon the ability of language to represent life. Even the most casual of stories may direct the enemy to something in real life that poses danger. As with the Miranda warning, therefore, language is perceived as an able vehicle of representation that is both usable and consequential.

On the face of it, however, Marías seems to want to use his stories and to reject them too. On the one hand, stories can draw out the real, convey its substance, and convict a criminal or aid the enemy: "loose lips sink ships." Hence storytelling can make people do things they would not otherwise do and, what is more, can make them become people they would not otherwise

---

[19] Images of the posters appear in volumes one and three of *Rostro*. In the Spanish edition the images are in color (except where the original is in black and white), while in the English edition of the novel all images are in black and white.

[20] Javier Marías, *Tu rostro mañana. Veneno y sombra y adiós* (Madrid: Alfaguara, 2007), p. 581. All references to *Veneno y sombra y adiós* in Spanish are to this edition and noted in the text with the letters *VSA*; *Your Face Tomorrow. Poison, Shadow and Farewell*, trans. Margaret Jull Costa (New York: New Directions, 2009), p. 450. All references to *Poison, Shadow and Farewell* in English are to this edition and noted in the text with the letters *PSF*.

become. As Deza remarks about one of his subjects, "en cierto sentido le importa más su historia, más el relato de esa vida que la vida misma" (*FL* 355) ("he is, in a sense, more concerned with his history, with the story of his life than with that life itself" [*FS* 288]). In this sense, stories can represent reality as well as transform it, and thus serve as an instrument of power for those who are able to use them for either redemptive or transgressive ends.

More specifically, it is through Deza's own story that the authority of narrative is revealed and its transformative power affirmed in *Rostro*. However, Deza's story actually begins before he is able to narrate it himself. As his colleagues do with everyone in his office, they compose a report on him for his file:

> "A veces lo veo como a un enigma. Y a veces creo que él también lo es para sí mismo. Entonces vuelvo a pensar que no se conoce mucho. Y que no se presta atención porque en realidad ha renunciado a ello, a entenderse. Se considera un caso perdido con el que no ha de malgastar reflexiones. Sabe que no se comprende y que no va a hacerlo. Y así, no se dedica a intentarlo. Creo que no se encierra peligro. Pero sí que hay que temerlo."
>
> (*VSA*: 500)

> "Sometimes he seems to me to be a complete enigma. And sometimes I think he's an enigma to himself. Then I go back to the idea that he doesn't know himself very well. And that he doesn't pay much attention to himself because he's given up understanding himself. He considers himself a lost cause upon whom it would be pointless to squander thought. He knows he doesn't understand himself and that he never will. And so he doesn't waste his time trying to do so. I don't think he's dangerous. But he is to be feared." (*PSF* 385)

Deza begins literally as a blank page, and is constituted as an enigma in a story told by someone else. But importantly, it is Deza himself who finally composes his own narration, and it is in the process of telling that he begins to understand how stories have the capacity to define his existence and change the lives of others.

During the course of the novel Deza comes to recognize that narrations (and in particular, those he creates himself) are powerfully influential. His epiphany does not come easily, but does come suddenly, when he realizes that what he has written has resulted in the murder of a young Russian man by Dick Dearlove, about whose capacity for violence Deza has written a report. Before this incident, and even after many months working for Tupra, Deza frequently reflected on the general nature of his work, unable to perceive its relation to anything outside of its own existence:

Me había pasado mucho tiempo dictaminando a diario con cada vez mayor soltura y despreocupación ... diciendo quién era de fiar y quién no, quién mataría y quién se dejaría matar y por qué, quién traicionaría y quién sería leal ... y qué probabilidades llevaba cada individuo en el interior de sus venas, igual que un novelista que sabe que lo que diga o cuente de sus personajes, o les atribuya o les haga hacer, no saldrá de su novela y no hará daño a nadie, porque por mucho que se los sienta vivos seguirán siendo ficción y nunca interferirán con ningún ser real. ... (*VSA* 550)

I had spent a long time passing judgment on a daily basis and with ever greater ease and unconcern ... saying who could be trusted and who could not, who would kill and who would allow himself to be killed and why, who would betray and who would remain loyal ... and what probabilities each individual carried in his veins, just like a novelist who knows that whatever his characters say or tell, whatever is attributed to them or whatever they are made to do, will go no further than his novel and will harm no one, because, however real they may seem, they will continue to be a fiction and will never interfere with anyone real. ... (*PSF* 424–25)

In other words, Deza had composed stories derived from real life, had conjectured about future behavior (and implicitly, about future stories), but believed that his stories remained largely disconnected from real-life actions. When one of his stories seems to be the impetus for Dearlove's act of violence, Deza suddenly grasps the concept that the real (the life of Dearlove) and the narrated (Deza's story about Dearlove) do not inhabit two distinct worlds. What is more, his awareness of this connection compels him to see that his stories bear an ethical burden, and that they place upon him as well the burden of responsibility. But as occurs throughout *Rostro* with the actions of nearly all of the characters, Dearlove's violence and Deza's responsibility are textualized within narrative expectations so that one is unable to be defined without the other.

As a task within his daily work for Tupra, the preparation of Dearlove's file was not unlike that of others that Deza had done before. Dearlove appeared to have a relevant connection with figures in the government, and his future behavior, when projected into a variety of possible contexts, drew attention for its potential importance should one of these contexts gain prominence. Tupra assigns Dearlove's case to Deza and poses the question that he wants Deza to answer in his report:

> Dime, Jack, ¿te parece que ese mamarracho, nuestro anfitrión de anoche, sí, ese cantante ridículo, te parece que sería capaz de matar? En alguna circunstancia extrema, si se sintiera muy amenazado, por ejemplo. ¿O bien que no podría en absoluto, que sería de los que bajan los brazos y se dejan

acuchillar, antes que asestar ellos su golpe? O por el contrario, ¿crees que sí podría, y aun en frío? (*FL* 342)

Tell me, Jack, what did you think of our buffoon of a host last night, yes, that ridiculous singer, do you think he would be capable of killing someone? In some extreme situation, for example, if he felt really threatened? Or would he be simply incapable of it, would he be the sort who would just give in and allow himself to be knifed to death, rather than get his blow in first? Or, on the contrary, do you think he could kill, even in cold blood? (*FS* 277)

For Deza, the answer depends not only upon situations in which Dearlove might find himself in the world, but also upon the potential plots in which Dearlove is willing to place himself in stories. In other words, Deza understands that the story of Dearlove's future must echo how Dearlove himself would want to have his story told and how he would wish to emplot his life.

As Deza sees it, Dearlove would avoid at all cost putting himself in unseemly situations, not because of potential danger but because of the type of story that could be engendered about him. As Deza puts it: "es un horror narrativo, o una repugnancia; es pavor a su historia arruinada por el desenlace, echada a perder para siempre, hundida. ... Dearlove sería capaz de matar por evitarse tal sino. Tal sino estético, argumental narrativo, como prefiera" (*FL* 353) ([it is] a narrative horror or disgust; a dread of having his story ruined by the ending, wrecked for ever, destroyed. ... Dearlove would be capable of killing in order to avoid such a fate. Or such an esthetic, dramaturgical or narrative doom, as you prefer" [*FS* 286–87]). In Deza's view, story must be understood here not only as a representation of some thing in reality, but as a thing itself able to configure Dearlove's actions. Dearlove stands among a large cohort of people, in Deza's view, who "sienten su vida como materia de un minucioso relato, andan instalados en ella pendientes de su hipotético o futuro cuento" (*FL* 361) ("who experience their life as if it were material for some detailed report, and they inhabit that life pending its hypothetical or future plot" [*FS* 293]). What becomes critical here, as elsewhere in the novel, is the process by which one is able to control one's own story, or the way in which it is appropriated and controlled by someone else for their own benefit.

Deza's realization that his story has been used to destroy Dearlove's life creates in him a paroxysm of guilt. His previous belief that his work was removed from reality, that somehow he was a creator of fictions with no standing in the world beyond their own existence, now yields to awareness of his moral responsibility for the outcome of a story which he had written. As Deza puts it, "[yo] describía y desciframos a personas de carne y hueso y sobre ellas pontificaba y vaticinaba, y tanto mi acierto como mi desacierto, veía ahora, podían tener consecuencias nefastas y condicionar su suerte en manos de alguien como Tupra" (*VSA* 550–51) ("I was describing and deciphering flesh-and-blood people and pontificating and making predictions about them, and I saw now that regardless of whether I was right or wrong, what I said could have disastrous consequences and determine their fate if placed in the hands of someone like Tupra" [*PSF* 425]). Deza finally understands here the transformative power of stories as they represent and shape the world. But equally important in this case, he perceives how his telling of the story—his responsibility for telling the story—is also able to transform the person who tells it. Shortly after the incident with Dearlove, Deza resigns from his group and returns to Spain, but he remains forever linked to a story that he had created and narrated with the expectation that it bore no consequence: "Y por lejana que más adelante quisiera ver y lograra ver y fuera a ver la vinculación ... a aquel chico ruso que ni siquiera sabía de mi existencia, como yo había desconocido la suya mientras le duró, lo habían matado por mi predicción o mi hipótesis o fabulación, por lo que había dicho y contado yo, y ahora habría de repetirme: '*For I am myself my own fever and pain*. Y así yo soy mi propio dolor y mi fiebre' " (*VSA* 551–52) ("And however tenuous I tried to make and succeeded in making that link later on ... that young Russian man who did not even know of my existence, just as I had known nothing of his while it lasted, had died because of my prediction or hypothesis or fantasy, because of what I had said and reported, and now, in my head, I would always have the words: 'For I am myself my own fever and pain' " [*PSF* 426]).

The transformation of Deza from naïve participant in a narrative enterprise whose relation to reality is unclear, to his understanding of how that enterprise is able to shape reality and ascribe responsibility to those who create the narrations, is indeed the most compelling humanization of textuality in Marías's novel. In the strictest metafictional sense, it explains how narrative in general, and how *Rostro* in particular, establishes its own complex relation with the social uses of discourse and thus with the social world of individuals whose lives it portrays. Marías does not seek to resolve here the theoretical dilemma of how language, as a system of signs located in reality, is also able to represent that reality, but rather he offers an epistemological perspective on what Marías proposes, as we have seen, is "el motor de la vida" (*FL* 409) ("the engine of life" [*FS* 333]): the cognitive demand for storytelling that resonates deeply in all human culture. But Deza's transformation in *Rostro* is not simply a movement from ignorance of the consequences of his activities to an enlightened understanding of how stories and life are tightly intertwined and mutually determinate. It is also seeing that his own life is wholly commensurate with the view of storytelling that he has come to espouse and that his own life, in reality, is also changeable. In other words, the transformation of Deza's life (as well as the potential change in his file created and held by Tupra) is not solely a narrative one that reaffirms the principal assertion of the novel, it is also fully existential. Indeed, he moves from someone "que no se conoce mucho" (*VSA* 500) ("that doesn't know himself very well" [*PSF* 385]) to someone who is able to proclaim to himself, as does Shakespeare's Henry IV in *Henry IV, Part II* (and quoted by Deza as he reflects on his metamorphosis): "No presumas que soy lo que fui. He dicho adios a mi antiguo yo" (*VSA* 455) ("Presume not that I am the thing I was. I have turn'd away my former self" [*PSF* 349–50]. This departure from his old self is linked to narration as well as to action.

The occasion for Deza's transformation turns upon his desire to protect his wife (from whom Deza is separated) from the abusive behavior of her lover, Esteban Custardoy. Deza's decision to remove Custardoy from his wife's life will involve violent behavior, which his file in Tupra's office suggests is possible, but which he himself is not convinced he is capable of. He has seen Tupra terrorize Rafael de la Garza (an employee of the Spanish Embassy in London and friend of Deza) with a sword in the bathroom of a nightclub (a prominent episode in volume two), and he has witnessed inconceivable acts of violence on a DVD at Tupras's home. These were recorded by unknown witnesses of the events and sold to Tupra's group for possible use against individuals in the future for one political reason or another. The acts of violence that Deza witnesses are the "poison" in the subtitle of volume three of *Rostro* and constitute a part of human behavior that makes Deza literally sick. In the case of Custardoy, Deza needs to convince himself of his capacity to act—and in the end he does so by reflecting on how life is defined by stories. Indeed, as occurs throughout the novel, action is possible for Deza only within the understanding that change is necessarily textualized.

When Deza first discovers that Custardoy is abusing his wife, he is uncertain how to proceed, and even contacts Tupra to seek his advice. Tupra lets Deza know, of course, that there is no ambiguity about what needs to be done: "*Just make sure he's out of the picture*" (*VSA* 436; *PSF* 345). Yet Deza conceives of the problem as well as its solution at first textually, in the context of his own work of trying to determine what will happen in the future. As he contemplates how to proceed, Deza wonders "Cuál es mi rostro ahora" (*VSA* 486) ("What face am I wearing now" [*PSF* 373]), and he places his possible course of action squarely within texts and the potential transformation of his story that will be recorded in his file.

Deza's eventual violent behavior to protect Luisa (he breaks Custardoy's hand with a fireplace poker, and warns him to leave Madrid and never to let Luisa know what has happened) of course has its parallel in Tupra's violent warning to de la Garza in volume two. For Deza, however, the impetus to act (as opposed to the form that the action will take) is understood through Shakespeare. In other words, Deza's movement toward violence, and hence his movement towards transforming himself from a being who narrates to a being who acts, is conceptualized wholly through textuality. As he decides how to intimidate Custardoy, how to move him "out of the picture" with Luisa, Deza calls to mind the words of Tupra: "Cada cual asiste a su relato, Jack, tú al tuyo y yo al mío" (*VSA* 493) ("We are all witnesses to our own story, Jack. You to yours and I to mine" [*PSF* 379]). And in this case, it is precisely Deza's insertion of Custardoy into Shakespeare's text (more specifically, into his understanding of Shakespeare's *Richard III*) that provides the impetus for Deza to attend to his own story.[21] Having already quoted the scene from the play earlier in the novel (*VSA* 466; *PSF* 358), Deza now paraphrases the passage as a way to justify an act of violence that had until now remained outside of his own reality but inside his narrations. This recontextualization of the famous words uttered by the ghost of Queen Anne to Richard III creates for Shakespeare's text, and thus for *Rostro*, a new meaning, which in turn textualizes Deza into a man whose acts emulate those of a story already told. As Deza puts it:

> Pero también he de evitarle a Luisa todo peligro y todo sufrimiento y tormento, para que su fantasma no deba decirle un día a este sujeto lo que el espectro de la Reina Ana le reprochó a su marido [Ricardo III] la víspera de la batalla, ni deba lanzarle luego la maldición que yo no cumplo cuando estoy en disposición de cumplirla: "Tu mujer, esa desdichada Luisa, tu mujer, Esteban, que nunca durmió una hora tranquila contigo ... caiga yo ahora como plomo sobre tu alma, y siente la punzada del alfiler en tu pecho: desespera y muere." (*VSA* 488)

> On the other hand, I must remove Luisa from all danger and suffering and torment, so that her ghost will not one day say to this man what Lady Anne's ghost said to her husband [Richard III] on the eve of battle, nor hurl at him the curse that I am failing to carry out despite being in a position to do so: "Thy wife, that wretched Luisa thy wife, that never slept a quiet hour with thee ... Let me sit heavy on thy soul, and may you feel the pinprick in your breast: despair and die." (*PSF* 374–75)

---

21 The scene between Queen Anne and Richard is of course not new in the fiction of Marías. It forms a critical part of *Mañana en la batalla piensa en mí*, and provides the title to that novel as well. See the chapter on *Mañana* for a discussion of how Shakespeare's play helps to shape the focus of the novel.

Deza's story, and therefore his transformation (i.e., the filling in of his file) is based neither on pure telling nor pure doing, but rather on the symbiosis of one with the other. He does not have to decide whether "to live or to tell"—for indeed he necessarily and always must do both. This is clear not only in the way that he achieves his new self but also in the way that he conceives it. For example, when Deza accompanied Tupra to the nightclub where eventually Tupra attacked de la Garza for trying to seduce the wife of one of his clients, Deza was frozen in horror as he watched Tupra nearly kill de la Garza. Deza had never witnessed such violence at close range, and certainly could not imagine that he would be capable of such action. Nonetheless he did nothing to prevent it. Following the incident, Deza confronts Tupra and forcefully announces that "No se puede ir por ahí pegando a la gente, no se puede ir matándola. Y menos si me involucras a mí en ello" (*BS* 407) ("You can't just go around beating people up, killing them. Especially not if you're going to involve me" [*DD* 339]). Tupra's response, "¿Por qué no se puede?" (*BS* 408) ("Why ... can't one do that?" [*DD* 339]) is unexpected, and leaves Deza unable to answer.[22] But in many ways, Tupra's question lies at the center of Deza's decision to protect Luisa, for it brings to the fore deeply hidden sentiments and capabilities of Deza to weave a story that falls within his narrated potential ("he is to be feared," according to his file), and a story that compels him to embrace the moral responsibility of his actions.

Several weeks after the incident with de la Garza, Deza returns to Spain, where the episode with Custardoy will unfold in Madrid. Before departing, however, Deza visits de la Garza in the embassy to see how he is recovering, and is stunned by de la Garza's display of absolute fear at Deza's presence. What surprises Deza, however, is his own reaction to de la Garza's horror:

> Imponer respeto, infundir temor, verse a uno mismo como peligro tenía su lado grato. Lo hacía a uno sentirse más confiado, más optimista, más fuerte. Lo hacía sentirse importante y—como decirlo dueño. Pero antes de coger el taxi también me dio tiempo a que aquella inesperada vanidad me repugnara. No es que esto último ahuyentara el engreimiento, sino que convivió con él. (*VSA* 300)

> Imposing respect, instilling fear, seeing oneself as a danger had its pleasurable side. It made one feel more confident, more optimistic, stronger. It made one feel important and—how can I put it—masterful. But before I

---

[22] Only much later in the novel, in *Veneno y sombra y adios* (volume three), does Deza reply to Tupra's question: "Porque no podría vivir nadie" (*VSA* 221) ("Because then it would be impossible for anyone to live" [*PSF* 168]).

hailed a taxi, there was time for me to find this unexpected vanity repugnant too. Not that the latter feeling drove out conceit, they lived alongside each other. (*PSF* 230)

As Deza later contemplates how to instill fear in Custardoy using violence, he considers his sense of justice within the contradictory emotions related to de la Garza's fear of him, and then inserts himself into a textual role that allows for his own transformation. And it is Shakespeare who once again provides the impetus: "Llevo una pistola y encierro peligro, ya no soy quien jamás dio miedo a nadie sabiéndolo, sino que no soy lo que soy, como Yago, o estoy empezando a no serlo" (*VSA* 455) ("I am carrying a pistol and I am dangerous, I am no longer the man who never knowingly frightened anyone; like Iago, I am not what I am, at least I am beginning not to be" [*PSF* 350]).

Deza's understanding of the textual nature of his violent action continues after he has left Custardoy with a broken hand and overwhelmed with fear. When he is visiting Luisa a few days later she receives a call from Custardoy, and Deza listens to the conversation as Custardoy tells Luisa that he is leaving Madrid even as she protests and claims that she does not understand. In the same way that he had prefigured the action of Dearlove through his story about the future, Deza understands that he has determined the story that he listens to as it unfolds on the telephone:

> Pero aquella escena en realidad la había preparado yo, casi la había configurado y dictado, como si fuera Wheeler, que sin duda dedicaba tiempo a la confección o composición de escogidos momentos, o, como si dijéramos, conducía sus numerosos tiempos vacíos o muertos hacia unas cuantas escenas prefiguradas y deliberados diálogos, su parte ya memorizada antes. Sólo que yo no intervenía en aquella conversación o bien era Custardoy quien había hablado por mí, al fin y al cabo no eran sus verdaderas palabras, sino las que yo lo había inducido a decir como un Yago, o lo había obligado a pronunciar. (*VSA* 542)

> But I had prepared that scene, almost set it up and dictated it, as if I were Wheeler, who doubtless devoted no small part of his time to the preparation or composition of prized moments, or, so to speak, to guiding his numerous empty or dead moments towards a few pre-planned and carefully considered dialogues in which he had, of course, memorized his own part. Except that I hadn't intervened in that conversation, or, rather, Custardoy had spoken for me, for he was, after all, not using his own words, but those which I, like an Iago, had led him to say or obliged him to pronounce. (*PSF* 418–19)

Deza exists here outside the story of Luisa and Custardoy as well as inside—he serves both as author and as the agent of its implementation. In other words, he has inserted himself into reality and into narration, which is what human beings do all the time. And this, of course, is entirely the point of Marías's novel.

The violence that surrounds Deza clearly forms an integral part of *Rostro*. As Isabel Cuñado has noted, "los tres volúmenes constituyen una amplia y sostenida reflexión sobre las circunstancias y efectos sociales de la violencia" ("the three volumes constitute a broad and sustained reflection on the circumstances and social effects of violence").[23] Both varying circumstances and specific effects of violence in the novel, as well as the complexity of its conceptualization, are represented in a number of ways, but appear most intensely through the four principal characters: Bertram Tupra and Jaime Deza, as we have seen, but also the two primary mentors of Deza, Peter Wheeler and Juan Deza, Jaime's father. Taken as a whole, the views on violence present certain ethical and moral dilemmas that are explored in detail in the work, though by no means resolved once and for all.

For Tupra, who studied medieval history at Oxford, physical violence (and its corollary, the fear created in the victim) functions overtly as an essential tool of the State. As he tells Deza, "El miedo es la mayor fuerza que existe" (*BS* 67) ("Fear is the greatest force that exists" [*DD* 48]). Violence is useful because it can be asserted against those whom the State wishes to intimidate and coerce, and also because it can be leveraged against those who have employed it against others in secret and often with impunity. Both of these instances of violent behavior are embodied in the long sequence involving de la Garza in the nightclub, when Tupra invites Deza to accompany him for an evening with the Italian Manoia and his wife. Although Deza is not told why Tupra has set out to cultivate Manoia, he deduces that Manoia works for the Italian Secret Service (SISMI), and later discovers, when Tupra shows him a series of violent scenes from real-life events that have secretly been taped, that Manoia has committed acts of torture and murder. From Tupra's perspective, the use of violence is most often intrinsic to circumstances that plainly call for it all along. In other words, Tupra's primary concern lies with how violence can best serve the interests at hand rather than the broader question of the moral or ethical justification of its use at the moment. Hence he often comments how violent acts can most effectively be carried out. With de la Garza, for example, he explains the importance of using the sword:

> Es el miedo, Jack. El miedo. ... El que uno mete ha de ser tan terrible que no haya lugar a asentarlo, a incorporarlo, a adaptarse ni a consentirlo, que

---

[23] Isabel Cuñado, "*Tu rostro mañana* y la ética de la memoria," in Grohmann and Steenmeijer, *Allí donde uno diría*, p. 235.

no pueda haber una estabilización ni una pausa para convivir con él, ni un segundo, para encajarlo y hacerle sitio, y así cejar un instante en el agotador esfuerzo por ahuyentarlo. Eso es lo que paraliza y desgasta, y consume toda energía, la incomprensión, la incredulidad, la negación, la lucha. (*BS* 390–91)

It's fear, Jack. Fear. … The fear you provoke has to be so terrible that there is no chance of the other person absorbing it or incorporating it, adapting to it or finding it bearable, there must be no point at which the fear stabilises, no pause so that the person can get used to it, not even for a second, or can assimilate and make room for it and thus, for a moment, cease the exhausting effort involved in fending it off. That is what paralyses and erodes and absorbs all their energy—incomprehension, incredulity, denial, struggle. (*DD* 324–25)

For Tupra, the act of violence must be forceful and immediate; it grows from pure physicality and stands as the embodiment of pain and fear. While the victim (de la Garza in this instance) struggles to mitigate the pain, Tupra seeks to impose the unfettered power of his will to control de la Garza not only in the present but in the future as well.

The pointed description of Tupra's acts of violence (his use of the sword, his dunking of de la Garza's head in the toilet) comes from Deza, of course, who himself is paralyzed by the violence that he had not anticipated and that he cannot prevent. At the same time, however, he is unable to turn away from it—he is equally fascinated and horrified by what he sees. Within the digressive style that shapes *Rostro* as a whole, the materiality of Deza's description is striking, and draws upon the full representational efficacy of language and storytelling (such as color, visual texture, sequencing for cause and effect) to enhance the reality of Tupra's actions. Deza's description here in fact seems to annul the narrative artifice that is generally found in *Rostro*, thus leaving no shock absorber to mitigate the utter realism of the scene and Deza's own reaction to it. In this way, Marías is able to focus clearly and precisely in the novel on the fundamental nature of violence that is deliberately committed, destructively anti-social, and degrading in its consequences.

But were Marías to leave the issue there, as simply a matter of fact, as a component of the plot or a trait of certain characters, Tupra's actions would bear scant interest beyond the way in which they endow his character with unforgiving brutality. What gives substance to the recurrent violence in the novel turns largely upon the suggestion that the capacity for violent action lies inherent in the human condition and perhaps is nurtured by human desire. Thus the harshness of Tupra's violence is not viewed merely as an individual act but is linked to the broad ideas expressed about violence that the novel examines. When Deza criticizes Tupra for his ruthless treatment of de la Garza and his overbearing use of brute force, Tupra's response to Deza makes the point:

> Me reprochas estupideces sin la menor importancia, vives en un mundo minúsculo que apenas existe, a resguardo de la violencia que ha sido la norma en todo tiempo y lo es en casi todas partes, es como tomar un interludio por la función entera, no tenéis ni idea, los que nunca salís de esta época ni de estos países nuestros en los que hasta anteayer mandó también la violencia. Lo que hice no fue nada. El mal menor. (*VSA* 54)

> You criticize me for some trifling, unimportant thing that I did, but you live in a tiny world that barely exists, sheltered from the violence that has always been the norm and still is in most parts of the world, it's like mistaking the interlude for the whole performance, you haven't a clue, you people who never step outside of your own time or travel beyond countries like ours in which, up until the day before yesterday, violence also ruled. What I did was nothing. The lesser of two evils. (*PSF* 34)

The critical moral question raised by Tupra is at once specific and universal: what are human beings capable of doing to one another, and what is the justification for doing so, to advance what they perceive to be "the lesser of two evils?" And further, is the perception of the lesser evil always tainted by parochial desire and political expediency, or do universal values rooted at the very core of human existence make certain forms of violence broadly unacceptable and always evil? While Marías does not explore per se the philosophical propositions that might lead to one conclusion or another, and certainly does not set out to resolve these matters in *Rostro* with a clearly wrought and definitive answer, he threads throughout the work a series of normative dilemmas related to ethical behavior. These dilemmas are linked intimately to Deza and his work for Tupra and how what he does relates to the moral fabric of our social existence.

The first and most visible instance of violence and justification, as we have seen, centers on Tupra's beating of de la Garza. On the one hand, Tupra offers a practical guide to the effective use of violence and fear, which Deza easily grasps: "el miedo que uno mete o infunde no debe ser conocido, ni casi ser imaginable. Si es un miedo convencional previsible, o cómo decirlo, trillado, el que lo padece será capaz de entenderlo, de ganar tiempo y con él costumbre, y quizá después de acometerlo" (*BS* 391) ("The fear that you provoke or instill cannot be a known or even an imaginable fear. If it's a conventional, predictable or, how can I put it, common-or-garden-variety fear, the person feeling the fear will be capable of understanding it, of gaining time and, eventually getting used to it, and perhaps, afterwards, even being able to tackle it" [*DD* 325]). As we have seen, Deza later uses Tupra's concept of violence to attain the same desired outcome with Custardoy that Tupra had achieved with de la Garza. Indeed, the physicality of the attacks in each case breaks through the victim's defenses so suddenly, and with such brutal force, that human dignity seems instantly to drain away. On the other hand, the justification that Tupra proposes for his actions is contextually explicit and highly utilitarian, related always to what he proffers as the social good. He thus draws to the fore the larger matter (in his view) of preserving the human community at the cost of diminishing the humanity of the individual. As Deza notes concerning the rationale that Tupra will evoke for the punishment that he may eventually inflict on the Italian Manoia:

> Hacía rato que sabía por dónde iba, "Fue necesario y evité así un mal mayor, o eso creía; maté a uno para que no mataran a diez, a diez para que no cayeran cien, a cien para salvar a mil," y así hasta el infinito, la vieja excusa que tantos llevarían siglos preparando y elaborando en sus sepulturas cristianas y no cristianas, a la espera del Juicio que no llegaba, cuantos aún creían en ese Juicio en la hora de su partida, casi todos los asesinos de la larga historia, y los instigadores. (*VSA* 216)

> I had known for some time now where he was heading. "I had to do it in order to avoid a greater evil, or so I believed; I killed one so that ten would not be killed, ten so that a hundred would not fall, a hundred in order to save a thousand," and so on, ad infinitum, the old excuse that so many would spend centuries preparing and elaborating in their Christian and non-Christian tombs, waiting for the Judgment that never comes, and many still believe in that Judgment at the hour of their departing, certainly almost all murderers and instigators of murder throughout history. (*PSF* 163)

Deza has been able to rationalize his work for Tupra, but his thinking is always embedded in a persistent unsettledness that reflects his unsure commitment to the entire enterprise as well as to his own duties within it. We see this, for example, in his conviction that he excels at his work but that his reports may end up as little more than a collection of hastily perused stories; it also appears in the ambivalence that compels him to turn away from the violence on Tupra's DVD and the beating of de la Garza, which at once repulses and attracts him. Early in his employment, as we have seen, Deza is troubled by his work not because of how it might cause harm to someone but, to the contrary, that it might not serve any purpose at all. From Tupra's perspective, however, Deza's work fits squarely within the vision and usefulness of their objective—to protect England, in a parochial sense, and to defend the good side of humanity more broadly conceived. As he tells Deza:

> Y nosotros queremos salvar vidas siempre. Andamos siempre haciendo cálculos, sopesando si vale la pena dejar morir ahora a una persona para que luego vivan muchas otras por eso. En primer lugar vidas británicas, claro, la prioridad se comprende. Como en la guerra. A todo debemos sacarle el máximo rendimiento, aunque haya que esperar varios años.
>
> (*VSA* 189)
>
> And we're always interested in saving lives. We're always making calculations, weighing up whether it's worth letting one person die now if that will mean many others will live. Our priority, understandably enough, is saving British lives. As it would be in time of war. We have to get the most benefit out of everything, even if that means waiting a few years. (*PSF* 142–43)

While Tupra mentors Deza in the practical nature of their professional work, resorting always to the "lesser evil" explanation rooted in situational ethics, there nonetheless remains a level of incommensurability between the violence of his actions and the loftiness of his goals. Deza perceives in Tupra a nearly pathological indifference to human worth that occasionally may be useful but that is always dangerous. For Deza, therefore, Tupra remains an enigma with a visceral transparency—he is certain of his convictions yet inscrutable beyond the frequently evoked lesser evil of what he does. For this reason, when Deza ponders the ethical and moral character of his work, with a desire to discern an overriding normative principle, he turns to what he has learned from the two most influential people in his life—his father, Juan, and his friend (and father figure), Peter Wheeler—who provide more universal balance and historical perspective to the thorny issues that he confronts. Through Wheeler and his father Deza gains perspective on violence, torture, murder, and revenge, which Deza realizes have become critical parts of his life.

Juan Deza affords insight into how violence impinges upon his life personally, as well as how he perceives its moral and ethical consideration more broadly.[24] During the Civil War he witnessed various forms of violence, heard stories told about violence, stood as a potential participant in violent actions, and found himself in a position to seek vengeance for the more slippery acts of moral violence (false accusations of treason) committed against him. He served in the Republican forces in Madrid during the conflict, and his reflections on what occurred there once again move storytelling to the fore in the novel. As he notes:

---

[24] For a discussion of some of the biographical elements of Marías's representation of Juan Deza here, see chapter I, concerning Marías's family, and also chapter IV, in particular the discussion of *Negra espalda del tiempo*.

"A mí me tocó ver lo de aquí, lo de Madrid", continuó mi padre, "y aún oí más de lo que vi, mucho más. No sé qué es peor, si escuchar el relato o presenciar el hecho. Quizá lo segundo resulta más insoportable y espanta más en el instante, pero también es más fácil borrarlo, o enturbiarlo y engañarse luego al respecto, convencerse de que no se vio lo que sí llegó a verse." (*BS* 299)

"It fell to me to see what went on here in Madrid," my father continued, "and I heard more than I saw, much more. I don't know which is worse, hearing an account or actually witnessing what happened. Perhaps, at the time, the latter is less bearable and more horrifying, but it's also easier to erase it or blur it and then deceive yourself about it, convince yourself that you didn't see what you saw." (*DD* 247)

What Juan Deza cannot erase from the past are two stories of violence which maintain a haunting presence in his life: one which he hears told on a streetcar, when during the war a Republican woman relates how she took a young child from his wealthy parents and threw him violently against a wall, killing him on the spot (*BS* 300–03; *DD* 248–50); the other concerns a story told by a well-known writer in his presence, about a friend named Emilio Marés, a prisoner held by the Nationalists in the Civil War who was tortured and killed in Ronda as if he were a bull—with banderillas, a lance, and the awarding of one of Marés's ears to the torturers (*BS* 315–20; *DD* 259–64).

While Juan Deza tells these stories in part to demonstrate the power of storytelling to sustain damage long after the actual occurrence of the incidents that they seek to represent, his more compelling engagement with violence is prescriptive and normative. On the one hand, his direct familiarity with violence, his understanding of how it can be used to inspire terror in war as well as in politics, does not lead him to eschew its situational justification. As he notes to his son about his role in the war, he is happy not to have killed anyone, "Pero eso no significa que no lo hubiera hecho, si no me hubiera quedado otro remedio. Si vosotros o vuestra madre hubierais estado amenazados de muerte y yo la hubiera podido impedir así, lo habría hecho, estoy seguro" (*VSA* 519–20) ("But that doesn't mean I wouldn't have if there'd been no other option. If any of you or your mother had been under threat of death and I could have prevented that, I'm sure I would have done so" [*PSF* 401]). Juan Deza's conviction that he is capable of killing others in order to protect his family echoes Tupra's utilitarian approach to violence in theory, but is narrowly drawn around personal responsibility rather than embedded in a political philosophy that sees the "lesser evil" with clarity and predicts his own comportment with certainty.

On the other hand, however, Juan Deza offers a broader philosophical view in which he envisions violence as a form of action whose inevitable result is self-perpetuation—a kind of ritualistic response to conflict that engenders a like response, which causes yet another, until virtually no end can be reached. In a prescriptive assertion of his own position, and which also defines the position of the novel as a whole, Juan Deza offers a historical example that addresses the point: "cuando se le declaró la Guerra a Hitler, y quizá no ha habido ocasión en que se hiciera más necesaria y justificable una guerra, el propio Churchill escribió al respecto que el mero hecho de haberse llegado a aquel punto y a aquel fracaso convertía a los responsables, por honrosos que fueran sus motivos, en culpables ante la Historia" (*BS* 335) ("when war was declared on Hitler, and it may be that there has never been an occasion when a war was more necessary or more justifiable, Churchill himself wrote that the mere fact of having come to that pass, to that state of failure, made those responsible, however honourable their motives, blameworthy before History" [*DD* 276–77]).

It is not that violence stands always on immoral ground but that its use represents a failure of other forms of social and political engagement. For those who understand the moral danger of violence, it may still be exercised, but (in contrast to Tupra's way of thinking) only within a restrained plan of action. As Juan Deza puts it based on his experience in the Civil War, "Quien ha vivido la violencia a diario durante una época de su vida no jugará nunca con ella, ni se la tomará a la ligera. La administrará, no ya con cuidado, con cautela extrema, sino con tacañería, con enorme avaricia. No se la permitirá, siempre que pueda ahorrársela, y eso casi siempre es posible" (*BS* 333) ("Anyone who, at some stage in his life, has lived with violence on a daily basis will never take any risks with it, never take it lightly. He'll administer it not just with care and with extreme caution, but in as stingy and miserly a way as he can. He won't allow himself to be violent, not as long as he can avoid it, and it almost always is avoidable" [*DD* 275–76]). For Juan Deza, any act of violence has the potential to make victims of us all, both those who bear the effects of violence and those who inflict it on others. Not only does it diminish the necessary empathy required to lessen the distance between people that is created by difference, but it lingers on in society, sometimes insidiously and often times overtly—but always in the stories told about it. Juan Deza has witnessed and experienced the persistent effects of violence and thus urges his son to be wary of its crippling harm to social well-being. As he notes, society must be "stingy" with violence while recognizing that violence will never be eradicated once and for all.

A similar idea shapes Juan Deza's response to his imprisonment following the Civil War, due to false accusations of treason made against him by his close friend Carlos Alonso del Real. Jaime Deza broaches the subject of his father's imprisonment at various points in the novel, hoping to discover details about the incident that his father has declined to reveal over the years. Jaime marvels at his father's decision to repudiate all acts of revenge against his friend, whose accusations not only resulted in his imprisonment but prevented him from securing a teaching position in Spain following his release. Such treachery would have consumed him, Jaime thinks—he would have demanded explanations for his friend's actions and sought some form of retribution once conditions permitted it following the death of Franco and the creation of a democratic Spain. Yet Juan Deza stands firm in his refusal. Rather than perpetuate the cycle of violence, he espouses a personal and philosophical position that allows him to break free from its corrosive hold:

> hay acciones tan abominables o tan despreciables que su mera comisión debería anular cualquier curiosidad posible por quienes las cometen, y no crearla ni suscitarla, como tan imbécilmente sucede hoy. Y así fue en mi caso, pese a que fuera *mi* caso, mi vida. Lo que aquel antiguo amigo había hecho conmigo era tan injustificable, y tan inadmisible y grave desde el punto de vista de la amistad, que todo él dejó de interesarme al instante: su presente, su futuro y también su pasado, aunque en él estuviera yo. Ya no necesitaba saber más, ni estaba dispuesto tampoco a ello. (*FL* 218–19)

> there are actions so abominable and so despicable that their mere commission should cancel out any possible curiosity we might have in those who committed them, rather than creating curiosity and provoking it, as is the imbecilic way of things now. And that was the case with me, even though it was *my* case, my life. What that former friend had done to me was so unjustifiable, so inadmissible and so grave from the point of view of friendship, that everything about him instantly ceased to interest me: his present, his future and his past too, even though I existed in that past. I didn't need to know anything more, and I had no wish to delve deeper. (*FS* 175)

For Jaime, such a posture produces both discord and admiration, but also plants the seed for the rejection of his own role in the perpetuation of violence in his work with Tupra. Not only has his father renounced retribution for his friend's act of betrayal, but he has adopted the larger moral view of the novel in relation to the use of storytelling and its relation to violence. Juan Deza articulates this position on both a personal and a historical level:

> Y en esa Guerra ... hubo tanta delación y tanto envenenamiento, tanto insultador, tanto difamador y enardecedor profesional, dedicados todos sin descanso a sembrar y fomentar el odio y la saña, la envidia, el anhelo de exterminación, en los dos bandos pero sobre todo en el de los vencedores pero en los dos. ... Y sin embargo estoy seguro de no haber dicho ni escrito

una palabra que pudiera perjudicar gravemente a nadie. Ni tampoco la dije después, en el ámbito estrictamente personal de mi vida posterior. Jamás traicioné un secreto ni una confidencia, por pequeños que fueran, ni conté lo que sabía por haberlo visto u oído, si podía hacer daño con ello y no necesitaba contarlo para salvar ni exonerar a nadie. Y es de eso, Jacobo, fíjate, de lo que estoy más contento. (*VSA* 522)

And in our War there was ... so much treachery and so much poison, so many slanderers, defamers, and professional rabble-rousers, all tirelessly dedicated to sowing and fomenting hatred and viciousness, envy, and a desire to exterminate, on both sides, especially on the winning side, but on both sides. ... And yet I'm sure that I never said or wrote a word that could have proved seriously prejudicial to anyone. Nor later either, in the strictly personal sphere of my life after that. I never gave away a secret or a confidence, however small, I never told anyone about what I knew from having seen or heard something if that might do harm and if I didn't need to tell it in order to save or exonerate someone. And that, Jacobo, is what pleases me most. (*PSF* 402–03)

Such a pronouncement evokes not only the unintentional disclosure of secrets through careless talk, which forms a part of volumes one and three of *Rostro*, but includes as well the purposeful effort to cause harm to others, with subsequent unintended consequences for those whose lives are incorporated into stories without their knowledge and without the opportunity to tell stories of their own. Juan Deza's position here allows him to affirm the pronouncement that links him to Peter Wheeler ("quizá no se debería contar nunca nada," [*BS* 305]; "Perhaps one should never tell anyone anything" [*DD* 251], he tells his son), but more importantly, he gives to Jaime a moral foundation for envisioning the world and for acting within it: "Eres mejor que yo," Jaime tells his father, "O si no es cuestión de mejor ni peor, entonces serás más astuto y más libre" (*FL* 219) ("You're a better man than I am ... Or if it isn't a question of better or worse, you're certainly freer and more astute" [*FS* 175]).

Peter Wheeler's influence on Jaime Deza speaks also to the role of violence in social and political interaction framed within the role and power of storytelling. During World War II, Wheeler had served in MI6 (the British intelligence agency) as part of a group who wrote reports on what acts individuals might be capable of committing in certain circumstances, and it was he who recruited Jaime into his current position with Tupra. What he has learned from his experiences, and what he conveys to Jaime, pertain explicitly to violence and to storytelling, and ultimately to the ethical considerations of both. While, during his years of friendship with Jaime, Wheeler has discussed many things, he has deferred telling the story of his duties in World

War II and, more specifically, the story of the death of his wife Valerie. It is through the telling of her story near the end of his own life, however, where we see the thinking of Wheeler resonate most deeply in Jaime and in the novel as a whole.

During the war Valerie worked for a clandestine group within MI6 called the Political Warfare Executive, which did not exist officially and was quickly dismantled immediately following the conflict. Its main purpose was to disseminate false information and propaganda about the enemy from a variety of sources and through any means available. As its director, Sefton Delmer, explained to all those who worked in the unit, "No hay ningún conducto obstruido de antemano. Cuanto más sucias mejor. Mentiras, escuchas, desfalcos, traición, falsificaciones, difamación, encizañamiento, falsos testimonios y acusaciones, tergiversación, cualquier cosa. Hasta el puro asesinato, no lo olvidéis" (*VSA* 617) ("I must warn you that in my unit we are up to all the dirty tricks we can devise. The dirtier the better. No holds barred. Lies, phone-tapping, embezzlement, treachery, forgery, defamation, disinformation, spreading dissension, making false statements and accusations, you name it. Even, don't forget, sheer murder" [*PSF* 477–78]). Ethical and moral considerations were cast aside, with the understanding that any activity aimed at undermining the German war effort fell within the bounds of admissible behavior. As Wheeler notes, a policy, practice, or specific activity of the group had only to promote the following:

> crear descontento y rencor entre la población, rebajar la moral de los combatientes, desunir a la tropa y propiciar deserciones, estaba por encima de cualquier otra consideración. No olvides, Jacobo, que aquella se vivió como una guerra de supervivencia. Y lo fue, lo era. ... Los tiempos de paz juzgan luego severamente los tiempos de guerra, y yo no sé hasta qué punto pueden. Son dos tiempos que se excluyen. ... (*VSA* 620)

> feed discontent and rancor among the population ... lower the morale of the combatants, spread disunity among the troops and encourage desertions, that was what mattered. Don't forget, Jacobo, the Second World War felt like a battle for survival. And it was, it really was. ... Times of peace judge times of war very harshly, and I'm not sure how far it's possible to make such a judgment. They are mutually exclusive. (*PSF* 480)

Some of the actions undertaken by a small section of the Political Warfare Executive, headed by a man whom Wheeler knew only as Jeffreys, were so subversive and violent that today, as Wheeler notes, the persons who carried them out would be considered terrorists (*VSA* 635; *PSF* 491). None of what Wheeler tells Deza about his and Valerie's past activities is either new or shocking for Deza. Nor is the moral justification that sanctions these activities—the idea of killing one to save ten, the imposition of situational ethics that demand certain actions for the survival of oneself or of the group, and the principle of lesser evil, are all embraced by Wheeler with the conviction that the horrific violence of the war required unfettered efforts to end the conflict in any way possible. And furthermore, in Wheeler's view, historical judgments of violent actions bear scant validity when made outside the context of their occurrence.

Yet the haunting caused by events that linger beyond their occurrence may also sustain moral regret whose persistence can be dangerous, and even fatal, for those involved. Such was the case with Wheeler's wife. One of the assignments she undertook during the war included planting information about a Nazi officer named Rendel, who had married into an Austrian family she had befriended during summer vacations long before the war began. While the information proved to be effective in destroying Rendel's career (it asserted his distant Jewish heritage), the unintended consequences of Valerie's action led to the persecution and demise of her friend's family. Racked with guilt after learning of the tragic outcome of the story that she had planted in Germany, Valerie commited suicide not long after the war ended.

What is important about Valerie's story within *Rostro*, however, turns upon the two principal concerns of narration and morality. Valerie had told a story about Rendel that was appropriated by others to form part of another story, which was then used to create an outcome in reality that Valerie had never intended. Indeed, as we have seen repeated time and again throughout Marías's writing, once a story is placed amid the public, the teller loses control of the tale—how it is used, and how and what it means. As Wheeler notes, "Es lo malo que tiene el contar" (*VSA* 658) ("That's the trouble with telling anything" [*PSF* 509]). For Wheeler, of course, the tale that Valerie told during the war led to the unintended loss of the woman he loved. But for Deza, in the present, it evokes the nature of his work with Tupra and what he has finally begun to see as the unintended consequences of his own stories. Wheeler reminds Deza that once the tale leaves the hands of the teller it no longer belongs to him, nor can he be held responsible for how it is used: "Nadie puede controlar la utilización que se hace de sus ideas y de sus palabras, ni prever enteramente sus consecuencias últimas. En general en la vida. En ningún caso" (*VSA* 608) ("You can't control what use other people might make of your ideas or words, nor entirely foresee the ultimate consequences of what you say. In life in general. Never" [*PSF* 471]). Furthermore, Wheeler sees in Deza the capacity to accept unintended consequences, a conclusion already reached by Tupra and Wheeler when they invited him to work in his current job: "A diferencia de Valerie, tú sí podrás vivir con lo tuyo, te lo aseguro, o con lo que has hecho tuyo. Por extraño que resulte, en algunos aspectos te conozco a ti mejor que a ella. A ti te hemos estudiado, a ella no llegamos a tiempo" (*VSA* 608) ("I can assure you that, unlike Valerie, you *can* live with what's happened to you. Strange though it may seem, in some respects I know you better than I knew her. We've studied you, but in her case, we were too late" [*PSF* 471]).

As it turns out, of course, Deza can no longer justify the work that he has done with Tupra, and therefore resigns his position. What is ultimately important about Deza's decision, however, is what he is now able to see about himself and about the world. He has confronted a moral and ethical dilemma related to violence which he had not understood before but which has been defined by others and which he now discerns fully: the certainty with which Tupra acts in a world of violence, using violence of his own; the historical justification for violence offered by Wheeler, who can no longer understand that justification completely with the passing of time; the hypothetical violence of which his father might have been capable in order to protect his family, but the certainty he asserts that he never killed anyone during the Civil War or said anything that would lead to another's death. Above all, however, he admires his father's decision not to seek revenge against the friend who had betrayed him. In the end, Deza's decision to abandon his job, and thus to reject the violence associated with it, does not suggest that he has forsworn utilitarian ethics in favor of purely normative ones. To the contrary, he seems to embrace Wheeler's pronouncement about human conduct in war and in peace as well as his father's assertion that he is capable of violence in particular circumstances. Nor does his decision to remove himself from violence mean that violence will be mitigated or the moral challenges linked to it will be resolved. Indeed, it is not redemption that Deza has sought but rather understanding—both of himself and of the world. An aversion to his role in Dearlove's killing of the young Russian man provided the situational impetus for his resignation, but the more profound cause arose from the dreariness of his life in a job that he really knew little about even as he seemed to carry it out with great success. As he puts it,

> A mí me estaban ocurriendo cosas que había callado en la distancia: había perdido pie sin duda, o asideros, juicio, me dedicaba a una tarea cuyas consecuencias ignoraba o incluso si las había, a cambio de un salario sospechoso por alto; se me habían introducido venenos desconocidos hasta entonces, y en efecto llevaba una existencia más fantasmal cada día, inmerso en el estado onírico del que vive en país ajeno y empieza a no pensar siempre en su lengua. ... (*VSA* 329)
>
> Things were happening to me about which I, being far away, had said nothing: I had clearly lost my footing or lost both grip and judgment,

employed as I was in a job about whose consequences I knew nothing, not even if it had any consequences, and being paid a suspiciously large salary too; I had, by then, been injected with strange poisons and was leading an existence that grew ghostlier by the day, immersed in the dream-like state of one who lives in another country and is starting not always to think in his own language. ... (*PSF* 251–52)

Deza's decision to leave his employment is thus as existential as it is ethical. He now lives alone in Madrid and can only wonder what his face will be like in the future as he narrates the story of his past.

Tu rostro mañana is a complex novel that is **about** many things pertinent to the life of Jaime Deza: violence, espionage, morality, Bertram Tupra, Peter Wheeler, his father, the Spanish Civil War, among others. It is also the novel, within the entire body of Marías's fiction, in which history and memory, and for the author himself, the autobiographical, play the most prominent role. But at every turn the novel is framed by a single, overarching belief: that storytelling always defines and often determines the nature of human existence. As Wheeler affirms to Deza:

> hablar, contar, decirse, comentar, murmurar, y pasarse información, criticar, darse noticias, cotillear, difamar, calumniar y rumorear, referirse sucesos y relatarse ocurrencias, tenerse al tanto y hacerse saber, y por supuesto también bromear y mentir. Esa es la rueda que mueve el mundo, Jacobo, por encima de cualquier otra cosa; ese es el motor de la vida, el que nunca se agota ni se para jamás, ese es su verdadero aliento. (*FL* 409)

> talking, telling, saying, commenting, gossiping, passing on information, criticizing, exchanging news, tattle-taling, defaming, slandering and spreading rumours, describing and relating events, keeping up to date and putting others in the picture, and, of course, joking and lying. That is the wheel that moves the world, Jacobo, more than anything else; that is the engine of life, the one that never becomes exhausted and never stops, that is its life's breath. (*FS* 332–33)

The challenge that must be faced by all of human society, but one which Deza assumes as the business of his daily life, is how to make use of this "motor de la vida." What role does "talking, telling, saying" play in the ethical engagement with others? Can "telling" be used morally to instigate action that, on the face of it, seems violent and immoral? Can telling ultimately serve to show that human dignity does not exist in degrees, and that it cannot be traded away in order to promote one political perspective or another? These questions beget no definitive answers in *Rostro*, of course, but the exploration of their complexity constitutes the narrative substance of

Marías's novel. As a reader of others' stories, as interpreter of behavior and giver of meaning, Jaime Deza must "conocer hoy sus rostros mañana, por así decir: saber ya desde ahora como serían en el mañana esos rostros" (*FL* 465) ("[know] today what face they would wear tomorrow … to know right now what their face would be like tomorrow" [*FS* 378]). He cannot really know "esos rostros" in the strictest sense, but he can imagine them by creating a plot in the future rooted in both reference and narration of the past. Deza constantly searches for a "usable future" (to paraphrase Henry Steele Commager's famous dictum about history),[25] and his search compels him to observe life and to absorb its stories. In Deza's view, life and story cannot be separated; one cannot exist without the nurturing authority of the other.

Deza's task is to tell a story with an end that has yet to occur, analogous but ultimately opposed to the historian's task of emplotting time that has already passed. There is a profound dissonance to this task, somewhat akin to inquiring of an individual, "Where were you next week?" Telling begets a reality that entails other texts that are useful and necessary to the way in which we position ourselves in life and the way in which we are positioned by others—hence the danger of narrating anything at all. But as Marías sees it (and also as he tells it), we are surrounded by stories and we are connoisseurs of stories. They fulfill our need to talk about the world and they insert themselves into the world as objects with their own social standing. This is not only a position that Deza asserts throughout *Rostro* but also one that gives shape to his life. Indeed, narration is a mode of consciousness for Deza that allows for reflection about the world and also engenders action within it. The entire enterprise of Deza's group is rooted in a belief in the transformative authority of stories already narrated and those that are yet to be told. In the end, stories are at once powerful and transcendent for Deza, and herein lies their danger as well as their redemption. Which of these traits marks Deza's own story as he narrates it in and as *Rostro*? That is a matter no longer under his control, as Marías himself fully understands. Its fate now rests in the hands of his readers.

---

[25] Henry Steele Commager, *The Search for a Usable Past and Other Essays* (New York: Knopf, 1967).

VII

Other Writings

Non-fiction Sketches: *Vidas escritas* **and** *Miramientos*

Vidas escritas (1992) (*Written Lives*, 2006) and *Miramientos* (*Glimpses*) (1999) have in common at least one authorial intention: Marías's desire to write brief sketches about writers whom he finds intriguing. While on the face of it the two books share certain elements of composition (for example, photographic images of the writers in *Miramientos*; both photographs and drawings of authors in *Vidas*), the differences between the two texts are pronounced. Most notably, in *Vidas* Marías comments solely on non-Spanish writers who are deceased, using biographical and other information to form the content of his narrative, while in *Miramientos* he focuses exclusively on Spanish-language authors and comments only on the images inserted in the text, with no external information. In this way he offers a purely impressionistic "glimpse" of several writers no longer alive, some of whom he has known. To emphasize the occasionally playful perspective of the book, he also includes a section of photos of himself, with comments in the same fashion as those made about the dead authors.[1]

---

[1] *Vidas escritas* includes the following writers, with photographs or drawings of each: Faulkner, Conrad, Dinesen, Joyce, Tomasi de Lampedusa, James (Henry), Conan Doyle, Stevenson, Turgenev, Mann, Nabokov, Rilke, Lowry, Madame du Deffand, Kipling, Rimbaud, Djuna Barnes, Wilde, Mishima, Sterne. The 2006 translation, *Written Lives*, includes the same writers, but frequently uses different photographs. It also appends a section not found in the Spanish version entitled "Fugitive Women," with photographs and drawings of Lady Hester Stanhope, Vernon Lee, Adah Isaacs Menken, Violet Hunt, Julie de Lespinasse, and Emily Brontë. Both of the volumes contain a final section ("Artistas perfectos"), with photographs of 27 writers and brief sketches (most often, only a few lines) of what Marías "sees" in the photos, both physical and personality traits that emerge from the images. This last section of *Vidas escritas* serves as the model for the whole of *Miramientos*, which contains brief sketches of authors based solely on the photos provided, without the benefit of biographical or bibliographical information.

Vidas escritas

Vidas is not the first time that Marías has written brief biographical introductions to authors. As he notes in the prologue, the idea for the volume came from his edition of *Cuentos únicos* (*Singular Stories*) (1989), in which he put together an odd collection of short stories written originally in English by relatively obscure authors, with brief biographical sketches about each.[2] Somewhat curiously, as he explains in the prologue of *Vidas escritas*, many readers concluded that he had invented the authors as well as the stories of *Cuentos únicos*. As he notes, "La verdad es que si se leían todas seguidas, esas brevísimas biografías formaban un relato más, seguramente no menos único y espectral que los otros"[3] ("The fact is that, when read together, these briefest of brief biographies constituted another story, doubtless as unique and spectral as the stories themselves").[4]

For the content of *Vidas*, Marías chose to include well known authors and to write a biographical anecdote about each, but with no claim to complete accuracy. In other words, while he includes a bibliography at the end of the book that underscores his extensive reading and preparation for writing about each of the authors, and in this way seeks to authenticate in traditional fashion the non-fictional nature of his writing, his view of narration in general as it relates to the real, forms the underlying foundation of the volume. As he has expressed on numerous occasions in his essays, as well as in his fictions, the real must be imagined—narration does not reproduce the real but rather distorts and transforms it in every case, thus leaving contingency as a narrative determinant.[5] Hence the idea in *Vidas*, as he writes, "era

---

[2] The first edition of *Cuentos únicos* was published by Ediciones Siruela. The collection was reissued in 2004 by Marías's publishing house, Reino de Redonda, with three additional stories and the nineteen original ones. The collection was published again in 2008 by Debolsillo. The stories were all written in English and translated into Spanish for the collection, with the exception of an apocryphal story written by Marías himself, "La canción de Lord Rendall," and attributed to the English writer James Denham. This story is also included in Marías's collection of his own stories, *Mientras ellas duermen* (1990), with an explanatory note on its origin. Among the authors included in *Cuentos únicos* are E.F. Benson, "La otra cama," Martin Armstrong, "El fumador de pipa," Oswell Blakeston, "El miedo del lago," and Richard Hughes, "El fantasma." All of the stories are gothic, horror, and ghost tales, to which Marías has shown a particular affinity in his writing as well as his reading.

[3] Javier Marías, *Vidas escritas* (Madrid: Ediciones Siruela, 1992), p. 11. All references to the work in Spanish are to this edition.

[4] Javier Marías, *Written Lives*, trans. Margaret Jull Costa (New York: New Directions, 2006), p. 1. All references to the work in English are to this edition.

[5] See, for example, Marías's essay "Los malditos detalles," where he asserts that

... tratar a esos literatos conocidos de todos como a personajes de ficción, que probablemente es la manera, por otro lado, en que todos los escritores desean íntimamente verse tratados, con independencia de su celebridad u olvido" (*Vidas* 11) ("was to treat these well-known literary figures as if they were fictional characters, which may well be how all writers, whether famous or obscure, would secretly like to be treated" [*Written* 1–2]).

It is also important to point out, as Marías himself notes in his prologue (though his tongue seems to be planted firmly in his cheek), that the exclusion of Spanish authors from *Vidas* stems from his own feelings of non-Spanishness. Such a large number of critics and Spanish authors have criticized Marías for his Anglophilic passions, and as he suggests here, so many have publicly challenged his Spanishness (not only by pointing out his strong attachment to English language and literature but even by questioning his Spanish citizenship), that he felt certain inhibitions about discussing writers from his own country, even though there are many whom he admires.[6] He tells the stories in *Vidas* with a mixture of "afecto y guasa" (*Vidas* 12) ("affection and humour" [*Written* 2]), and further notes that he has derived great pleasure from the undertaking. Indeed, as he writes in the prologue to the English translation of the volume (not included in the Spanish edition), "With the passage of time, I have come to realise that, although I have enjoyed writing all my books, this was the one with which I had the most fun. Perhaps because these 'lives' were not just 'written' but 'read' " (*Written* 4).

The full pleasure of the book (for Marías as well as for his readers) derives largely from the author's open and subjective perspective on the writers, sustained by a foundation of biographical materials, letters, and documents. Marías perceives quirks and absurdities that shape his view of one author or another (e.g., Joseph Conrad's denial that he had written something when he clearly had; Ivan Turgenev's bizarre, murderous relatives; Malcolm Lowry's drunkenness; Rimbaud's lack of personal hygiene; Isak Dinesen's strange dinner with Marilyn Monroe and Arthur Miller; T.S. Eliot's meticulous grooming habits), and he intersperses these with other information garnered

---

"También lo real ha de ser imaginado" ("The real must also be imagined"), in *Mano de sombra* (Madrid: Alfaguara, 1997), p. 325; or in *Negra espalda del tiempo*, where he insists that "para relatar lo ocurrido hay que haberlo imaginado antes" (Madrid: Alfaguara, 1998), p. 196 ("to tell what has happened you have to have imagined it as well"), *Dark Back of Time*, trans. Esther Allen (New York: New Directions), p. 161.

[6] Specifically, Marías names "March, Bernal Diaz, Cervantes, Quevedo, Torres Villarroel, Larra, Valle-Inclán, Aleixandre," among the deceased authors, without mentioning living Spanish writers (*Vidas* 12; *Written* 2).

from his reading. None of these pieces of information provides new facts per se about an individual author but rather they become part of the sketch (or on occasion, caricature) of each. Marías relates essential traits as if the authors were characters in a short story who might later be given greater substance and developed into the main character of a novel. Indeed, in these written lives ("microbiographical" portraits, according to one reviewer),[7] Marías portrays the authors as if he had created them himself, as if they were indebted to him for their very being as a personage in a fiction. He clearly finds the authors intriguing, most of whom led lives filled with substantial torment. He draws them on the canvas of biography, but with the brush strokes of a narrator creating a fiction who is generally sympathetic to his creations but eager to point out their foibles and eccentricities.

A few examples from *Vidas* demonstrate the approach and technique that Marías uses throughout the volume—one about an author whom Marías greatly admires (Laurence Sterne) and another for whom he demonstrates scant sympathy (James Joyce). It was Sterne's fate, as Marías points out, to be born into the poor side of a privileged family (his father never rose above the rank of standard-bearer in the army), but from his father Laurence seems to have acquired a sense of humor that would propel him to success in his writing as well as in his social engagements. It even allowed him, on occasion, to reach a level of renown among the aristocracy, as when he dined, for example, with the Duke of York, brother of the Prince of Wales. Marías sees Sterne above all as an amusing and amiable man whose publication of the first two volumes of *Tristram Shandy* in 1759 allowed him to pursue what he seemed most to want—a life of fun and diversion. While there can be little doubt that Marías admires *Tristram Shandy* for any number of reasons (perhaps most notably, the work grows from what Sterne himself viewed as progressive digressions, and thus in many ways bears the mark of Marías's own way of novel writing), his respect for Sterne as an enormously imaginative writer appears to be matched in this microbiography by his affection for him as a marvelous character.

In contrast, Marías finds little about James Joyce to admire or to praise. As a character, Joyce is created here in much the same fashion that he had described himself in a letter to his wife, Nora, cited by Marías, "un hombre celoso, solitario, insatisfecho" (*Vidas* 33) "a jealous, lonely, dissatisfied … man" [*Written* 22])—though Marías's portrait of him is even less complimentary. Marías's subtitle of the Joyce section, "en sus gestos" (*Vidas* 33) ("in his

---

[7] James Berger, Review of *Written Lives*. http://www.sfgate.com/cgi-bin/article.cgi?f=/c/a2006/03/26/RVG97HQD0Q1.DTL

poses" [*Written* 33]), points to an inauthentic figure who became convinced at an early age of his own genius and transcendent purpose (for example, as reported by Marías, he once asked his brother Stanislaus, "¿No te parece que existe cierta semejanza entre el misterio de la Misa y lo que yo estoy intentando hacer?" (*Vidas* 33) ("Don't you think there is a certain resemblance between the mystery of the Mass and what I am trying to do?" [*Written* 23]). Further, as Marías points out, Joyce never hesitated in embracing the reverence in which he was held for so many years. Yet for Marías, Joyce was a repressed, even perverse individual (in letters to his wife his pornographic curiosity and directness about sexual matters is somewhat startling), unable to reveal feelings or intimacy. Marías has never praised Joyce as a novelist. Here, he diminishes him as a person who could be mean-spirited and disturbingly rude, and whose life developed as one long pose playing the role of a genius.

Miramientos

In the final section of *Vidas*, "Artistas perfectos" ("Perfect Artists"), Marías inserts photographs (or photographs of paintings and sculptures) of well-known writers accompanied by thumb-nail sketches of the images that portray the writers. This approach (a commentary on a specific image rather than a general biographical sketch) provides the working model for *Miramientos*, in which Marías inserts forty-four photographs of fifteen authors from Spain and Latin America, all of whom are deceased.[8] In each case Marías offers a glimpse into the image on the page through a brief

---

[8] Javier Marías, *Miramientos* (Madrid: Alfaguara, 1997). Marías includes the following authors (and more than one photograph in each case) in the book: Ramón del Valle-Inclán; Jorge Luis Borges; Vicente Aleixandre; Juan Benet; Adolfo Bioy Casares; Federico García Lorca; Victoria Ocampo; Fernando Savater; Guillermo Cabrera Infante; Pablo Neruda; Eduardo Mendoza; Antonio Martínez Sarrión; Luis Cernuda; Horacio Quiroga; and an "autorretrato" ("self-portrait"), with six photographs of himself. Marías also alludes in this volume to the same issue of Spanishness that he addresses in the prologue to *Vidas*: the idea that many critics and writers from Spain do not view him as authentically "Spanish." He addresses the criticism by embracing it: "en lo que respecta a mi convencimiento antes citado [mi falta de españolidad], he pasado al otro extremo, y ahora, desde mi condicion definitivamente extraterritorial, creo tener tanto derecho a hablar de los escritores de mi país de origen como de los de cualquier otro sitio. Todos me son igual de propios y ajenos" ("as to my conviction previously cited [my non-Spanishness], I have moved to the other extreme, and now, in my definitive extraterritorial condition, I believe I have as much right to speak about writers from my country of origin as about those from any place. All are equally fellow countrymen and foreigners" (11).

narrative description of what he sees. The interspersing of photographs on each author does not disrupt Marías's writing but in fact becomes the occasion for it. The idea of "seeing" in its most expansive sense (including attributing and interpreting) is critical here, for to a large degree Marías envisions photography as an art of imitation as well as imagination in much the same way as he views literature. In each case, Marías does not perceive the image as a reflection or replica of the real, nor does it stand disconnected from the world outside it. Instead, he envisions it as an object in reality, and imagines how it says something about the figure in reality that it at once represents and shapes.

Throughout *Miramientos* the photographs are not so much speaking pictures as they are pictures to which Marías himself seems to speak. The photographs illustrate and inform, as does the narrative that accompanies them. As he puts it in his prologue, he is writing about "rostros y actitudes" ("faces and attitudes") (*Miramientos* 13), while explicitly excluding biographical and literary information that form the core of his sketches in *Vidas*. Even in those cases where he possessed extensive information and knowledge about a writer (such as with Juan Benet and, of course, with himself), he sought to "forget" what he knew ("quizá sin éxito"; "perhaps without success" [*Miramientos* 13], as he notes) in order to "centrarme sólo en lo que veía" ("concentrate only on what I saw") (*Miramientos* 14). In this sense, he allows himself to see and imagine in the same breath, an approach that then continues in his written commentaries, where he has "desdeñado y rehuido todo intento de objetividad, o su simulacro" ("rejected and avoided all attempts at objectivity, or something like it") (*Miramientos* 14). Still, Marías is not interested in the theory either of photography or of narrative here—his "glimpses" constitute imaginative seeing and thus parallel his fiction as an imagining of the real and as a configuring transformation of it.

That Marías both sees and imagines the photographs in this collection is easily discerned by perusing a few of the "glimpses" themselves. For example, he includes two images of Ramón del Valle-Inclán. In the first, of Valle-Inclán seated in a chair, he offers a description of the author as presented physically in the image: he points to the long beard, the position of the hand, the author's eyes turned toward the camera, and flowing hair. In the second photograph, of Valle-Inclán walking on a sidewalk, Marías calls attention to the right arm positioned behind Valle-Inclán's back (as with the first photograph he mentions the missing left arm), to the spats on his shoes, the crease in his pants, and his buttoned coat. Marías "sees" these elements of the photograph (as can the reader, especially after Marías draws attention to them), and notes how the image of Valle-Inclán takes shape within its particular composition. But Marías also "imagines" the Valle-Inclán of the two photographs—in the first, he suggests that Valle-Inclán did not have time to turn fully toward the camera, and that he conveys surprise at the camera's presence. In the same breath, however, he offers that the surprise has been contrived, as if Valle-Inclán knew precisely what image of himself he wished to have created. Marías perceives irony in the photograph, as well as "un hombre capacitado para divertirse en cualquier instante, se ve en los ojos juveniles y vivos" ("a man with the capacity to enjoy himself at any moment, which can be seen in his youthful and lively eyes") (*Miramientos* 21). In the second photograph, Marías suggests that Valle-Inclán is satisfied with himself, seemingly with no worries that particular day, certainly not in a provocative mood to assert, as he had before, that "Los españoles nos dividimos en dos grandes bandos: uno, de Ramón del Valle-Inclán, y el otro, todos los demás" ("We Spaniards divide ourselves into two large factions: one, consisting of Ramón del Valle-Inclán, and the other, everyone else") (*Miramientos* 22).

With Jorge Luis Borges, Marías includes two contrasting photographs—one from when Borges was relatively young and still able to see; the other, of a much older and blind Borges. Marías again draws out the physical and the visible: for example, in the first photograph, the color of Borges's jacket, the size of the lapels, the button that holds his jacket closed, the pair of glasses in his hands. In the second photograph, the form and color of his hair, the size of his lower lip, his elongated nose. But here, and throughout the volume, Marías is at his most insightful when seeing beyond the physical. In the first photograph, "se le nota incómodo, efímero. ... Tiene un aire aseado y levemente dominguero, como si se hubiera pasado el día con la conciencia dominante de que iba a ser fotografiado, el acontecimiento de la jornada" ("he seems uncomfortable, ephemeral. ... He has a well-groomed air, wearing perhaps his Sunday best, as if the main thing on his mind was that he would be photographed, the event of the day") (*Miramientos* 25). In the second, Marías notes that with age (and blindness) Borges's photograph conveys a different attitude as a reflection of his changed psychological profile: "A estas alturas de su vida Borges ya estará acostumbrado [a que saquen su foto] y no posa, entre otros motivos porque no puede controlar lo invisible ni sentirse herido por quienes lo inmortalizan. ... [S]e lo nota más seguro de sí mismo" ("At this phase of his life Borges is probably accustomed [to having his photograph taken] and he doesn't pose, among other reasons because he can't control what he cannot see or feel wounded by those who immortalize him. ... [O]ne can see that he is more sure of himself") (*Miramientos* 28).

Marías's self-study at the end of the book, with six photographs, adheres to the same pattern of seeing and configuring the image at hand, though it would seem that Marías brings to his text both blindness and insight unavailable when he writes about the other authors. The photographs range from Marías at twenty-three years of age to forty-five (with varying physical attributes noted in each). The author is more ironic, and somewhat more humorous here than elsewhere. He seems to peruse the photographs rather than study them, almost knowing at a glance what he will draw from each. These impressions begin with what he sees as an air of romanticism so intense in the first photograph that it must be contrived—as he writes, "es muy posible que ese joven de ojos plácidos y algo orientales fuera un bribón, un fingidor, un farsante" ("it is highly possible that that young man with placid and somewhat oriental eyes is a rogue, a pretender, a sham") (*Miramientos* 119). Continuing through the images, Marías assesses his appearance as a false revolutionary with round glasses in the second photograph, and later his Lee Marvin or Jack Palance "tough-guy" look in the fifth. Marías clearly conveys here that he knows himself, but also that he is able to imagine the image of himself as he provides a "glimpse" of Javier Marías to the public.

Neither *Vidas* nor *Miramientos* has garnered broad critical attention (reviews are generally positive, with some dissenting voices about accuracy and insights offered by the author in *Vidas*). What is modestly important about the two works, however, is that they provide a few more fragments to the total production of Marías's writing, and thus serve to expand and enhance our understanding of his writerly profile.

Other Fiction: *Mientras ellas duermen, Cuando fui mortal,* and *El monarca del tiempo*

Marías is not a short-story writer by preference, and perhaps by nature. Many of his stories are contracted pieces with specifications concerning length or subject matter, hence their original publication did not stem from a desire by the author to produce a cohesive collection of short stories. For example, eleven of the twelve stories of *Cuando fui mortal* (1996) (*When I Was Mortal*, 2000) were commissioned for magazines and compilations of short stories with a thematic focus on one subject or another: "Domingo de carne" ("Flesh Sunday") grew from a request to write a story related to summer; "En el tiempo indeciso" ("In Uncertain Time") resulted from an assigned theme on football; "Prismáticos rotos" ("Broken Binoculars"), from a request to write about Madrid.[9] Two of the pieces from *Mientras ellas duermen*, "El espejo

---

[9] Javier Marías, *Cuando fui mortal* (Buenos Aires: Debolsillo, 1996). All references to the work in Spanish are to this edition. *When I Was Mortal*, trans. Margaret Jull Costa

del mártir" ("The Mirror of the Martyr") and "Portento, maldición" ("Wonder, Curse") were included in Marías's hybrid text *El monarca del tiempo* (*The Monarch of Time*) (1978) and reprinted in *Mientras ellas duermen* as stand-alone short stories.[10] It is not the case, however, that Marías sees the short story as a genre with diminished stature or scant merit in relation to the novel, or even that he derives little pleasure from writing stories. As he notes in the prologue to *Cuando fui mortal*, "... sólo concibo escribir algo si me divierto, y sólo puedo divertirme si me intereso. No hace falta añadir que ninguno de estos relatos habría sido escrito sin que yo me interesara por ellos" (*Cuando* 11) ("... I can only write something if I'm enjoying myself and I can only enjoy myself if I find the project interesting. It goes without saying that none of these stories would have been written if I had felt no interest in them" [*When* vii]).

It is also the case that Marías's style and general approach to the writing of fiction—e.g., slow, deliberate, digressive in both time and space, packed with indeterminacies—often seems better suited to the novel and, quite literally, to the space that it provides. While Marías has demonstrated an engaging talent for writing brief narratives (from his hundreds of newspaper columns to the sketches in *Vidas escritas* and *Miramientos*), his novels clearly form the core of his work. Yet it is possible to discern in his stories, in one form or another, many of the elements that are threaded throughout his long fiction—in subject matter (e.g., ghosts); recurrent thematic concerns (e.g., the role of violence in society); the intertextual base of writing (e.g., with Shakespeare in particular); dialogues with popular culture (e.g., Hollywood movies); the appearance of characters who are given life in a story and then more fully developed in a novel (e.g., Esteban Custardoy and John Gawsworth); the importance of storytelling and its social impact (e.g., the futile attempt to control the content or even tone of a story as it gains social circulation and is retold by others).

The role of violence, often attached to other matters explored in his writing, is especially pronounced in many of Marías's short stories, as it is in much of his fiction. He often portrays explicit violence in his novels, from the Hollywood style murder and bloodshed found in *Los dominios del lobo* to the

---

(New York: New Directions, 2000). All references to the work in English are to this edition. In the prologue Marías provides the date and place of the original publication of each story, and offers details about why he wrote several of the pieces.

[10] Javier Marías, *Mientras ellas duermen* (Barcelona: Anagrama, 1990); *While the Women are Sleeping*, trans. Margaret Jull Costa (New York: New Directions, 2010). The two pieces from *El monarca del tiempo* are not included in the English translation of *Mientras ellas duermen*. *El monarca del tiempo* (Madrid: Alfaguara, 1978).

violent beating of characters that constitutes lengthy segments of *Tu rostro mañana*, with works such as *Corazón tan blanco* and *Mañana en la batalla piensa en mí* in between, offering incidents of murder and suicide, though with the less explicit portrayal of violent actions. In many of his short stories, Marías represents acts of brutality—sometimes as a component of interpersonal relations (e.g., in "La herencia italiana" "The Italian Legacy," where a woman is abused by her young husband), other times as a key component in the plot of a mystery (e.g., "Sangre de lanza" "Spear Blood"), and still others as a structural device to create analogous tensions in different but parallel plots within a story, as in "Tiempo indeciso" ("In Uncertain Time"). In other stories violence appears unexpectedly but, when it does occur, it derives from the spiraling of the plot toward circumstances in which violence suddenly seems inevitable when at the beginning of the story it seemed immaterial, even illogical. For example, in the long story *Mala índole* (*Bad Nature*),[11] the first-person narrator (who is eventually identified as Ruibérriz de Torres) tells of his brief working relationship with Elvis Presley on the movie *Fun in Acapulco* in 1963. Ruibérriz narrates the story many years later, after reading on the soundtrack of the movie that all of the filming had taken place in Los Angeles, and that Presley in fact had never been to Acapulco.

The story begins with Ruibérriz commenting on the odd and complicated nature of living in fear because of being pursued by someone ("Cuando uno es así perseguido tiene la sensación de que sus cazadores no hacen más que perseguirlo y buscarlo las veinticuatro horas del día: uno está convencido de que no duermen ni comen, no beben ni tan siquiera se paran, sus pasos envenenados son incesantes o infatigables y no hay ningún alto" (*Mala* 16) ("When you're being hunted down like that you feel as if your pursuers do nothing but search for you, chase you twenty-four hours a day: you're convinced that they don't eat or sleep, they don't drink or stop even for one second, their venomous footsteps are incessant and tireless and there is no rest" [*Bad* 4]). Such a feeling eventually transforms the person being pursued into a fugitive whose life can never be settled once and for all. In this case, the narrator's dilemma, as he points out, grows entirely from his relationship with Elvis Presley, for whom he worked as a translator during the film of *Fun in Acapulco* and with whom, he assures us, he spent ten days in Acapulco despite public reports that insisted on Presley's absence from on-location

---

[11] This is a stand-alone publication, not included in the two collections of stories. *Mala índole* (Barcelona: Plaza & Janés Editores, 1998). Translated by Esther Allen as *Bad Nature, or With Elvis in Mexico* (New York: New Directions, 2010).

filming. As the story unfolds, Presley visits Mexico City accompanied by the narrator, which becomes the source of Ruibérriz's problem and also the impetus for him to advance one of the recurrent concerns expressed in Marías's fiction as a whole: the way in which stories are told and retold, and with each new telling, how parts of the story are transformed and meanings accumulated that were never intended or imagined in the first place. As Ruibérriz notes here:

> Esa fue la versión oficial del paso de Presley por México o más bien de su falta de paso; aún perdura, por lo que veo, y hasta cierto punto es comprensible. O quizá es más simple, quizá es que nunca hay manera de borrar lo dicho, sea verdadero o falso, una vez que se ha dicho: las acusaciones y las invenciones, las calumnias y los cuentos y las fabulaciones, desmentir no es bastante, no borra sino que se añade, antes habrá mil versiones contradictorias e imposibles de un hecho que la anulación de ese hecho una vez relatado; los mentís y las discrepancias conviven con lo que refutan o niegan, se acumulan, se agregan y jamás lo cancelan, en el fondo lo sancionan mientras se siga hablando, lo único que borra es callar, y callar prolongadamente. (*Mala* 25–26)

> That was the official version of Presley's sojourn in Mexico, or rather his lack of a sojourn; it's still around, I see, which to some extent is understandable. Or perhaps it's simpler than that, perhaps it's just that there is never a way of erasing what's been said, true or false, once it's been said: accusations and inventions, slanders and stories and fabrications, disavowal is not enough, it doesn't erase but adds; once an event has been recounted there will be a thousand contradictory and impossible versions long, long before the event is annihilated: denials and discrepancies coexist with what they refute or deny, they accumulate, add up, they never cancel anything out but only end up sanctioning it for as long as people go on talking, the only way to erase is to say nothing, and go on saying nothing for a very long time. (*Bad* 9)

Two critical components of Marías's novels thus gain deep traction in *Mala índole*: first, the unwieldy and uncontrollable nature of stories, and thus their potential danger for those whose lives are affected by them; second, the assertion here, as at the beginning of *Tu rostro mañana*, that gives foundational meaning to the work, that one should never tell anyone anything (or as the narrator puts it here, "lo único que borra es callar, y callar prolongadamente").

For the narrator, the story line seems to produce the violence that circles back to his fear of being pursued. As Presley's translator, Ruibérriz travels with him to Mexico City for nights out on the town along with other of

Presley's friends. While much of the narrator's story has to do with his admiration for Presley—his friendly nature, his colorful outfits, or his enormous talent that was squandered in increasingly bad movies—Ruibérriz tells of the incident that precipitates his murder of a Mexican thug and thus the fear of retaliation that lingers so many years later. In other words, he is "haunted" by an act of violence, not unlike the narrators in novels such as *Corazón tan blanco*, *Mañana en la batalla piensa en mí*, and *Tu rostro mañana*. The violence itself seems oddly dislocated for Ruibérriz. He was plucked from Hollywood for the film, to translate for Presley, because he uses the "zeta" in his pronunciation; he is a witness in Mexico City to an incident at a nightclub that involves Presley and his entourage, after which (and after Presley himself is whisked away to avoid trouble) the narrator finds himself in the center of a group of gangsters. In self-defense he kills the man who is intent on killing him—and the description of the violence clashes with the general tenor of the story and with the friendly nature of the narrator as we know him through his own narration:

> ... soy yo ahora quien agarra un pico y corro con él alzado para clavárselo en el pecho al gordo que está caído y no puede levantarse rápido, como si fuera un escarabajo, las manchas de sudor me indican dónde debo golpear con el pico, allí hay carne y allí hay vida y tengo que acabar con ellas. Y clavo el pico una y dos y tres veces con un ruido como de chapoteo, lo mato, lo mato, lo estoy matando, cómo puede ser cierto, está sucediendo y es irreversible y lo veo. ... (*Mala* 117–18)

> ... and now I'm the one who grabs a pick and runs with it raised over my head to dig it into the chest of the fat man who has fallen and can't get up quickly enough, as if he were a beetle, the dark sweat stains tell me where to strike with the pick, there is flesh there and life there and I must finish both of them off. And I dig the pick in, one and two and three times, it makes a kind of squelch, kill him, I kill him, I am killing him, how can it be true, it is happening and it is irreversible and I see him. ... (*Bad* 55)

Much like Jaime Deza, the main character and narrator of *Tu rostro mañana*, Ruibérriz is both astonished and disconcerted by his capacity for violence. And while its justification is clear in this instance (self-preservation), its gross brutality and abruptness haunt the narrator thirty-three years later as he tells the story about it.

One of the recurrent concerns woven through much of Marías's fiction has to do with coming to know something previously unknown about the past, and whether gaining such knowledge might lead to unhappiness or unwanted change in one's life that would otherwise have been avoided. This occurs most acutely in *Corazón tan blanco*, where the narrator seeks not to know what happened to his father's first wife and why his father's second wife, his mother's sister, committed suicide. In the title story of *Cuando fui mortal*, Marías turns to one of his favorite literary figures, the ghost, to explore the anguish experienced by the narrator (the ghost) for whom there is no escape from knowing. In an oft-repeated gesture in Marías's writing, the title of the story calls for an intertextual connection to Shakespeare's *Richard III*: the ghost of Henry VI haunts Richard, along with his other victims, and accuses the King of murder: "When I was mortal, my anointed body / By thee was punched full of deadly holes."[12] Mortality certainly has its benefits, as Marías purposefully demonstrates in his story of the ghost who now lives outside of the passage of time and returns to see places and people he knew when he was mortal. Above all, however, he has lost the ability to forget; in other words, he becomes engulfed by memory. He thus has lost the ability not to know things, which has long provided "mortals" with refuge from the past while clearing a psychological path for existential sufficiency in the future. As he notes, "... la maldición consiste en recordarlo *todo*, los minutos de cada hora de cada día vivido, los de tedio y los de trabajo y los de alegría, los de estudio y pesadumbre y abyección y sueño, y también los de espera, que fueron la mayor parte" (*Cuando* 58) ("... the curse consists in remembering *everything*, the minutes of each hour of each day lived through, the minutes and hours and days of tedium and work and joy, of study and grief and humiliation and sleep, as well as those of waiting, which formed the greater part" [*When* 44]).

However, as the narrator notes, remembering everything pales in the degree of suffering that it causes when placed alongside an even more pernicious condition of immortality: a hyperrealism that emerges from awareness of one's surrounding in the past as well as the present—the knowledge of things which the narrator knew nothing about before but which now overwhelm him: "... es que ahora no sólo recuerdo lo que vi y oí y supe cuando fui mortal, sino que lo recuerdo completo, es decir, incluyendo lo que entonces no veía ni sabía ni estaba a mi alcance, pero me afectaba a mí o a quienes me importaban y acaso me configuraban" (*Cuando* 58) ("... now I not only remember what I saw and heard and knew when I was mortal, but I remember it in its entirety, that is, including what I did not see or know or hear, even things that were beyond my grasp, but which affected me or those

---

[12] William Shakespeare, *Richard III*, ed. Peter Holland (New York: Penguin, 2000), p. 146.

who were important to me, and which possibly had a hand in shaping me" [*When* 44]).

Marías has proposed throughout his writing that the story of one's life (and implicitly, the life story of someone who is mortal) can be little more than a gloss of the authentic life that one has led. Indeed, he has asserted on many occasions that telling distorts, twists, and configures the real rather than represents it. But in this instance, the dilemma is even more cruel: the possibility of knowing everything that abides in immortality also annuls telling the story about it. Such intense knowledge resists being framed within a story whose significance might be perceived and understood. Yet at the same time, this kind of hyperrealism easily engenders pain and despair. For the narrator, it is the discovery that his father, in order to avoid going to prison for being a Republican sympathizer during and after the Civil War, gave the narrator's mother to the man who threatened to turn his father in to the police—that is, he allowed the man to use her sexually until he grew tired of her. Every detail and memory, every act both noble and vile lingers and haunts the ghost after his death. It is a haunting more torturous than occurs in mortal life because the sheer mass of it suffocates. As the narrator notes, "Casi todo se olvida en la vida y todo se recuerda en la muerte, o en este estado de la crueldad en que consiste ser un fantasma" (*Cuando* 65) ("You forget almost everything in life and remember everything in death, or in this cruel state which is what being a ghost is" [*When* 51]).

In much of his fiction Marías is enamored of ghosts of various kinds. For example, they may appear as disembodied figures of the dead, who now live again (his fondness for Joseph Mankiewicz's film *The Ghost and Mrs. Muir* comes to mind, or his short story in *Mientras ellas duermen*, "La dimisión de Santiesteban" ("The Resignation Letter of Señor de Santiesteban"), in which a young school teacher grows obsessed with discovering the ghost who haunts his school). Ghosts may emerge, as well, as metaphorical figures who keep the past alive for those things that need to linger on in the present so that the story may be completed, as occurs in *Corazón tan blanco* and *Mañana en la batalla piensa en mí*. Yet as the narrator of "Cuando fui mortal" sees it, and as he laments, the immortality that we often desire, if realized, compels a kind of knowing about the past that we are unable to endure. The weight of time bears heavily on life—and it is mortality itself that allows us to sustain and understand its importance. As he notes, "Yo no puedo hablar ahora de noches o días, todo está nivelado sin necesidad de esfuerzo ni de rutinas, en las que puedo decir que conocí sobre todo la tranquilidad y el contento: cuando fui mortal, hace ya tanto tiempo, allí donde todavía hay tiempo" (*Cuando* 68) ("I cannot speak now of nights and days, everything has been levelled out without resort to effort or routine, a routine in which I can say that I knew, above all, peace and contentment: when I was mortal, all that time ago, in that place where there still is time" [*When* 55]).

Time also plays a critical role in *El monarca del tiempo*, published during a period when Marías was working intensely on the translation of Sterne's *Tristram Shandy* into Spanish. The fragmented and hybrid nature of *Monarca*—Marías himself refers to it somewhat hesitantly as a novel—is no doubt indebted to some extent to Marías's immersion in Sterne's text and the English author's strategy of progression through digression. *Monarca* consists of five loosely connected sections—three stories, a dramatic dialogue with extensive narrative description, and an essay on Shakespeare's *Julius Caesar*. The essay, as Marías himself has pointed out, serves as a pretext for discussing the importance of present time in our perception of truth in the past, as well as the more complicated idea of how the past can be known in the present in the first place. Equally important, the essay serves as a reflection on the use of the present indicative tense in narration and how this technique shapes perception. Marías's thinking in the essay is then given more concrete form and structure in the remaining pieces of *Monarca*, which are intended to embody his theoretical considerations.

While the five parts of *Monarca* cohere somewhat tenuously to form the novel, Marías himself hints that *Monarca* may not really be a novel at all. He permitted two of the short stories ("Portento, maldición" and "El espejo del mártir") to stand alone outside of *Monarca* in *Mientras ellas duermen*, and included the essay from the work, "Fragmento y enigma y espantoso azar," in his book of columns, *Literatura y fantasma*. It thus seems clear that the generic association of *Monarca* with the novel grew at least in part from the marketing side of the publishing industry, which promoted the work somewhat hyperbolically as "quizá el venablo más audaz lanzado en los últimos años por un escritor de lengua castellana" ("perhaps the most audacious javelin thrown in recent years by a writer in the Spanish language") (*Monarca*, inside flap).

Like many of Marías's stories in *Cuando fui mortal* and *Mientras ellas duermen*, the stories of *Monarca* are most propitiously viewed in the context of his longer fiction. "Portento, Maldición," the second story of the work, serves to make the point, especially in its narrative perspective and technique. It is written in the first person, as are all of Marías's novels beginning with *El hombre sentimental* (1986); it also uses the present tense to convey the narrator's point of view as he records his relationship with his godson, who one day comes to live with him after the apparent death of his family (though we never learn why he is now an orphan). As the narrator sees it, the sudden and unwanted arrival of his godson interrupts and encumbers every aspect of his own life. At first glance, the story appears to focus on the godson. We learn that he is overweight, that he is uncoordinated physically and frequently falls, and that he seems to have no friends or talent to do anything at all. The narrator scrutinizes his godson's every move, and he views the boy with a mixture of disgust and irritation.

Over the course of three years, however, the boy begins to interact with others his own age. He hosts parties for friends in his room in the narrator's house and, much to the narrator's surprise, begins to demonstrate a keen talent for singing, eventually becoming an accomplished opera performer. But what stands out, as often occurs in Marías's longer fiction, is the self-revealing nature of the narrator's story, which ostensibly is meant to describe the personality of the boy. In other words, the tension that grows between the two characters has little to do with any comment made or action taken by the boy (his perspective is never offered in the story), and everything to do with what the narrator feels as he increasingly isolates himself from the world while his godson grows ever more open to it. In the end, his godson moves out of the house, leaving the narrator alone but free from having to care for him—precisely what the narrator had been hoping for over the previous three years. Yet the narrator soon realizes that his solitude and discontent stem from his own shortcomings rather than from the intervention in his life of the young boy. It is not what he had expected, but what he must now endure. There is no irony in this realization, however—only the despair of his own alienation.

It is difficult to pin down the possible unity of Marías's short fiction. The stories themselves were written at disparate times (up to fifteen years apart in *Mientras ellas duermen*, from 1975 to 1990; in the late 1970s for *El monarca del tiempo*; during a five-year period in *Cuando fui mortal*, 1991–1995). Only *Monarca* was conceived as a single volume, though, as we have seen, it is held together less by the stories themselves than by an essay on time and truth around which they are constructed. While some critics have discerned a certain thematic unity in the collections of short stories, it is clearly more incidental and tenuous than premeditated and tightly constructed.[13] Ghosts, violence, adultery, intertextuality, and metaliterary framing devices are found in many of these stories, whose importance to Marías's writing is largely synecdochic—to a large degree they are representative of the whole of

---

[13] Irene Andres-Suárez, for example, sees a special unity of the stories of *Cuando fui mortal* through the representation of "relaciones interpersonales" ("interpersonal relations") which are "amorosas, amistosas o profesionales" ("amorous, friendly or professional") in nature. "Los cuentos de Javier Marías o las múltiples caras de la realidad," *Cuadernos de Narrativa: Javier Marías* (Madrid: Arco/Libros, 2005), pp. 197–215.

Marías's fiction, and on occasion, as with "Viaje de novios" in *Cuando fui mortal*, they form the parts that engender the whole, the seed of an idea briefly narrated grows into a full-length novel (here, into *Corazón tan blanco*). Much like his sketches of other authors, Marías sees oddly and perceptively in his short fiction, which on the whole reinforces the overall nature of Marías's writing as a bold implementation of the authority of storytelling. As Gonzalo Navajas perceptively writes, "los diversos narradores de Marías ven y oyen más allá de lo habitual y convierten esta capacidad de observación en un instrumento no sólo de conocimiento sino también de poder sobre las figuras y acontecimientos que los afectan, tanto de manera directa como circunstancial" ("the diverse narrators of Marías see and hear beyond the habitual and transform this capacity for observation into an instrument not only of knowledge but also of power over the figures and incidents that affect them, directly as well as circumstantially").[14] For Marías, the authority granted to narrators and embodied in texts leads not to the immutability of truth, but rather to its slipperiness. His narrators perceive, scrutinize, reflect, and digress, never laying claim to a single truth about the real but instead celebrating its elusiveness through the creative impulse to imagine it.

---

[14] Gonzalo Navajas, "Javier Marías: el saber absoluto," in *Foro Hispánico* 20 (2001): 39–50.

Suggested Further Reading

Given the international recognition and critical acclaim that Marías has received (and in particular, beginning with the publication of *Todas las almas* in 1989), the relatively small amount of critical study devoted to his work is somewhat unexpected. Much of the work is in Spanish, but because of the growing number of his novels translated in English, and especially because of his strong reception in Great Britain and Ireland, critical reading in English has become increasingly relevant to Marías studies over the past decade.

For readers wishing to place Marías in his Spanish context, but who are not familiar with post-Franco Spain, the subsequent transition to democracy, and the paroxysm of cultural and social change that quickly followed, several collections of essays exist that explore various aspects of contemporary Spain. Two of the best that cover much of the cultural terrain are *Spanish Cultural Studies: An Introduction*, ed. Helen Graham and Jo Labanyi, and *Contemporary Spanish Cultural Studies*, ed. Barry Jordan and Rikki Morgan-Tamosunas. In addition to placing Marías in the cultural landscape of Spain, readers may also want to locate his fiction historically within the development of the Spanish novel from the late Franco years to the twenty-first century. This is especially pertinent to the understanding of Marías's writing. With the exception of novelists such as Cervantes in the seventeenth century, Leopoldo Alas in the nineteenth century, and a handful of writers (including his principal mentor, Juan Benet) in the twentieth, he has publicly and frequently rejected nearly the entire body of canonical fiction in Spain. For an overview and general history of the novel in Spain during the Franco and post-Franco eras the selection available in English is quite small. The most useful is *A Companion to the Twentieth-Century Novel*, ed. Marta E. Altisent. Robert Spires's *Post-Totalitarian Spanish Fiction* offers insightful readings of several Spanish novels of the 1970s and 1980s, including a well-wrought piece on Marías's 1989 novel, *Todas las almas*. For an excellent introduction to the cohort of writers that began to publish in the 1990s, and thus who share two decades of writing with Marías (but who stand radically apart from him in focus and style), see *Generation X Rocks*, ed. Christine Henseler and Randolph D. Pope. In Spanish, the best history of the

Spanish novel during the latter part of the twentieth century continues to be Gonzalo Sobejano's *Novela española de nuestro tiempo*, along with Ignacio Soldevila Durante's *Historia de la novela española (1936–2000)*.

Several books in English explore certain thematic aspects of the novel during the Franco and post-Franco years. See, for example, Samuel Amago's *True Lies* on the self-conscious novel of the later twentieth and early twenty-first centuries; *The Scripted Self: Textual Identities in Contemporary Spanish Narrative*, ed. Ruth Christie, Judith Drinkwater and John Macklin, which offers individual essays on several Spanish novelists, including Marías; and my own book on history and the novel in Spain during the Franco regime and early tradition to democracy, *Narrating the Past*. In a more general vein and with an emphasis on film as well as the novel, see *Spanishness in the Spanish Novel and Cinema of the 20th–21st Century*, ed. Cristina Sánchez-Conejero (this volume contains an interesting essay by Stephen Miller on the role of the historical past in Marías's novels). In Spanish, Carmen Moreno-Nuño's *Las huellas de la Guerra Civil* is an excellent study of how the Civil War is portrayed in the post-Franco novel (it also includes a very useful chapter on Marías), while Santos Alonso's *La novela en la transición* gives a brief, but early look at the novel during the first years of the transition to democracy from 1977 to 1981.

The body of critical work devoted specifically to Marías is on the whole very strong. The sole book on Marías written in English is Alexis Grohmann's *Coming Into One's Own: The Novelistic Development of Javier Marías*, which focuses on Marías's novels through *Mañana en la batalla piensa en mí*. Grohmann's study is very helpful for those seeking a general introduction to Marías's fiction, his literary thinking, and the ways in which he has progressed as a writer from his first novels in the early 1970s to the late 1990s. In Spanish, Isabel Cuñado's *El espectro de la herencia. La narrativa de Javier Marías*, covers a specific aspect of Marías's fiction through volume one of *Tu rostro mañana*: what she sees as the specter of Spain's past that runs throughout his writing. Two collections of essays on Marías, one in *Foro Hispánico* (ed. Maarten Steenmeijer) and the other in *Cuadernos de Narrativa* (ed. Irene Andres-Suárez and Ana Casas) contain articles on various aspects of Marías's work, including his literary theory, short fiction, and newspaper columns. Both offer detailed bibliographies of Marías's writing as well as criticism written about it. For readers interested in *Tu rostro mañana*, the collection of essays edited by Steenmeijer and Grohmann (*Allí donde uno diría que ya no puede haber nada. Tu rostro mañana de Javier Marías*) offers in-depth and sophisticated readings that explore nearly every aspect of Marías's three-volume masterpiece. Of particular interest here is a remarkable piece by Antonio Iriarte (with the help of

Marías himself), " 'Cito a menudo para mis adentros': citas y alusiones en *Tu rostro mañana* de Javier Marías," which cites nearly 250 textual allusions in *Rostro* to other works of literature (some quite obvious but others esoteric and obscure).

Biographical information about Marías has generally come out in small pieces and in different venues and formats. Marías himself has been helpful and (most often) reliable. In his hybrid text *Negra espalda del tiempo* he reveals much about his association with the Kingdom of Redonda and also about his family. He also discusses his youth and family in the collection of columns *Aquella mitad del tiempo*, while *Donde todo ha sucedido. Al salir del cine* collects many of his columns on the importance of movies in his personal and artistic formation. A great deal of insight into Marías's past and his thinking on a number of literary and personal matters can be garnered from several of his interviews. Two stand out in particular: one with Paul Ingendaay in *BOMB Magazine* in the Fall of 2000, the other with Sarah Fay in *The Paris Review* in 2006. The semi-official webpage for Marías, http://www.javierMarías.es/ (sanctioned, but not run by him), also provides a wide range of information about the author, as well as a very useful blog that carries his weekly columns from *El País Semanal*. See this same website for a list of literary prizes that Marías has won, beginning in 1979, when he was awarded the National Tanslation Prize for his translation of Laurence Sterne's *Tristram Shandy*.

Bibliography

Books by Javier Marías

Novels

Corazón tan blanco. Barcelona: Anagrama, 1992. *A Heart So White.* Trans. Margaret Jull Costa. New York: New Directions, 2000.
El hombre sentimental. México: Alfaguara México, 2000. *The Man of Feeling.* Trans. Margaret Jull Costa. New York: New Directions, 2003.
El siglo. Barcelona: Seix Barral, 1983.
El siglo. Barcelona: Anagrama, 1995.
Los dominios del lobo. Madrid: Alfaguara, 1999.
Mañana en la batalla piensa en mí. Barcelona: Anagrama, 1994. *Tomorrow in the Battle Think on Me.* Trans. Margaret Jull Costa. New York: Harcourt Brace, 1996.
Negra espalda del tiempo. Madrid: Alfaguara, 1998. *Dark Back of Time.* Trans. Esther Allen. New York: New Directions, 2001.
Todas las almas. Barcelona: Anagrama, 1989. *All Souls.* Trans. Margaret Jull Costa. New York: New Directions, 1992.
Travesía del horizonte. Madrid: Punta de Lectura, 2001. *Voyage Along the Horizon.* Trans. Kristina Cordero. San Francisco: Believer Books, 2006.
Tu rostro mañana I: Fiebre y lanza. Madrid: Alfaguara, 2002. *Your Face Tomorrow: Fever and Spear.* Trans. Margaret Jull Costa. New York: New Directions, 2005.
Tu rostro mañana II: Baile y sueño. Madrid: Alfaguara, 2004. *Your Face Tomorrow: Dance and Dream.* Trans. Margaret Jull Costa. New York: New Directions, 2006.
Tu rostro mañana III: Veneno y sombra y adiós. Madrid: Alfaguara, 2007. *Your Face Tomorrow: Poison, Shadow and Farewell.* Trans. Margaret Jull Costa. New York: New Directions, 2009.

Short Fiction

Cuando fui mortal. Buenos Aires: Debolsillo, 1996. *When I Was Mortal.* Trans. Margaret Jull Costa. New York: New Directions, 2000.
El monarca del tiempo. Madrid: Alfaguara, 1978. (Contains 3 stories, an essay, and a dramatic dialogue.)
Mala índole. Barcelona: Plaza & Janés Editores, 1998. *Bad Nature, or With Elvis in Mexico.* Trans. Esther Allen. New York: New Directions, 2010.
Mientras ellas duermen. Barcelona: Anagrama, 1990. *While the Women are Sleeping.* Trans. Margaret Jull Costa. New York: New Directions, 2010.

No más amores. Madrid: Alfaguara, 1997. (Audio book.)
Una noche de amor. Madrid: H. Kliczkowski, 2005. (Contains four stories published previously in *Cuando fui mortal* and *Mientras ellas duermen*.)

Short Fiction Edited by Javier Marías
Cuentos únicos. Madrid: Siruela, 1987.

Collections of Columns by Javier Marías
A veces un caballero. Madrid: Alfaguara, 2001.
Aquella mitad del tiempo. Barcelona: Círculo de Lectores, 2008.
Demasiada nieve alrededor. Madrid: Alfaguara, 2007.
Donde todo ha sucedido. Al Salir del cine. Barcelona: Círculo de Lectores, 2005.
El oficio de oír llover. Madrid: Alfaguara, 2005.
Harán de mí un criminal. Madrid: Alfaguara, 2003.
Literatura y fantasma. Madrid: Alfaguara, 2001.
Mano de sombra. Madrid: Alfaguara, 1997.
Pasiones pasadas. Madrid: Alfaguara, 1999.
Salvajes y sentimentales. Madrid: Aguilar, 2000.
Vida del fantasma. Madrid: Alfaguara, 2001.

Other Non-Fiction
Miramientos. Madrid: Alfaguara, 1997.
Vidas escritas. Madrid: Ediciones Siruela, 1992. *Written Lives*. Trans. Margaret Jull Costa. New York: New Directions, 2006.

Major Translations by Javier Marías (English to Spanish)
Browne, Thomas. *Religio Medici. Hydriotaphia*. Madrid: Alfaguara, 1986.
Conrad, Joseph. *El espejo del mar*. Madrid: Hiperión, 1982.
Dinesen, Isak. *Ebrengard*. Barcelona: Bruguera, 1984.
Faulkner, William. *Si yo amaneciera otra vez*. Madrid: Alfaguara, 1997.
Hardy, Thomas. *El brazo marchito y otros relatos*. Madrid: Alianza, 1974.
Nabokov, Vladimir. *Desde que te vi morir*. Madrid: Alfaguara, 1999.
Sterne, Laurence. *La vida y las opiniones del caballero Tristram Shandy. Los sermones de Mr Yorick*. Madrid: Alfaguara, 1999.
Stevens, Wallace. *Notas para una ficción suprema*. Valencia: Pre-Textos, 1994.
Stevenson, Robert Louis. *De vuelta del mar*. Madrid: Hiperión, 1980.
Yeats, William Butler. *El crepúsculo celta*. Madrid: Alfaguara, 1985.

Non-Fiction Essays/Columns by Javier Marias Cited in the Text
"Autobiografía y ficción." *Literatura y fantasma*. Madrid: Alfaguara, 2001. 70–78.
"Botellón de encapuchados." *Demasiada nieve alrededor*. Madrid: Alfaguara, 2007. 192–94.
"Contar el misterio." *Literatura y fantasma*. Madrid: Alfaguara, 2001. 117–23.
"Cuéntale el cuento." *Literatura y fantasma*. Madrid: Alfaguara, 2009. 268–69.
"Desde una novela no necesariamente castiza." *Literatura y fantasma*. Madrid: Alfaguara, 2009. 51–69.

"Eight Questions for Javier Marías." *Voyage Along the Horizon*. Trans. Kristina Cordero. San Francisco: Believer Books, 2006. 175–82.
"El camino de nuestra lengua." *Demasiada nieve alrededor*. Madrid: Alfaguara, 2007. 300–02.
"El hombre que pudo ser rey." *Pasiones pasadas*. Madrid: Alfaguara, 1999. 197–201.
"El terreno sin confines." *Vida del fantasma*. Madrid: Alfaguara, 2001. 417–20.
"Epilogue: Something Unfulfilled." *The Man of Feeling*. Trans. Margaret Jull Costa. New York: New Directions, 2003. 179–82.
"Errar con brújula." *Literatura y fantasma*. Madrid: Alfaguara, 2001. 107–10.
"¿Es usted el santo fantasma?" *Harán de mí un criminal*. Madrid: Alfaguara, 2003. 139–41.
"Falsificaciones literarias." *Pasiones pasadas*. Madrid: Alfaguara, 1999. 185–90.
"Imaginar para creer." *Literatura y fantasma*. Madrid: Alfaguara, 2001. 211–15.
"La fama de la fama." *Mano de sombra*. Madrid: Alfaguara, 1997. 99–201.
"La negra espalda del no venido." *Literatura y fantasma*. Madrid: Alfaguara, 2001. 369–70.
"Lo que no se ha cumplido." *El hombre sentimental*. México: Alfaguara México, 2000. 171–74.
"Los malditos detalles." *Mano de sombra*. Madrid: Alfaguara, 1997. 325–27.
"Mala noticia miserable." *Vida del fantasma*. Madrid: Alfaguara, 2001. 329–34.
"¿Mande?" *Demasiada nieve alrededor*. Madrid: Alfaguara, 2007. 114–16.
"Nota previa." *Mano de sombra*. Madrid: Alfaguara, 1997. 13–16.
"Noticias de mis favoritas." *Seré amado cuando falte*. Madrid: Alfaguara, 1999. 192–94.
"Productos podridos." *Demasiada nieve alrededor*. Madrid: Alfaguara, 2007. 27–29.
"Prólogo." *Pasiones pasadas*. Madrid: Alfaguara, 1999. 13–14.
"Shakespeare indeciso." *Literatura y fantasma*. Madrid: Alfaguara, 2001. 363–68.
" 'Sobre la dificultad de contar': Javier Marías y el sillón R de la RAE (discurso íntegro)." http://blogs.periodistadigital.com/electroduende.php/2008/05/26/javiermarias-rae-sillon-88935.
"Todas las farsantas son iguales." *A veces un caballero*. Madrid: Alfaguara, 2001. 291–94.
"Todos los días llegan." *Donde todo ha sucedido*. Barcelona: Círculo de Lectores, 2005. 27–33.

Books and Edited Books of Criticism on Marías

Andres-Suárez, Irene and Ana Casas, eds. *Cuadernos de Narrativa: Javier Marías*. Madrid: Arco/Libros, 2005.
Cuñado, Isabel. *El espectro de la herencia: La narrativa de Javier Marías*. Amsterdam and New York: Rodopi, 2004.
Grohmann, Alexis. *Coming Into One's Own: The Novelistic Development of Javier Marías*. Amsterdam and New York: Rodopi, 2002.
Grohmann, Alexis and Maarten Steenmeijer, eds. *Allí donde uno diría que ya no puede haber nada. Tu rostro mañana de Javier Marías*. Amsterdam and New York: Rodopi, 2009.

Steenmeijer, Maarten, ed. *El pensamiento literario de Javier Marías.* Special number of *Foro Hispánico* 20 (2001).

Articles and Book Chapters Cited on Marías's Work

Alberca, Manuel. "Las vueltas autobiográficas de Javier Marías." *Cuadernos de Narrativa: Javier Marías.* Ed. Irene Andres-Suárez, and Ana Casas. Madrid: Arco/Libros, 2005. 49–72.

Andres-Suárez, Irene. "Los cuentos de Javier Marías o las múltiples caras de la realidad." *Cuadernos de Narrativa: Javier Marías.* Madrid: Arco/Libros, 2005. 197–215.

Baugen, Carmen. "Autor real y ficción en *Todas las almas, Corazón tan blanco, Mañana en la batalla piensa en mí* y *Negra espalda del tiempo*." *Foro Hispánico* 20 (2001): 105–12.

Benet, Juan. "Ningún terreno clausurado." Epilogue. *El hombre sentimental*, by Javier Marías. Mexico: Alfaguara Mexico, 2000. 169–70.

Berger, James. Review of *Written Lives.* http://www.sfgate.com/cgi-bin/article.cgi?f=/c/a2006/03/26/RVG97HQ0Q1.DTL

Blanca, Inés. "Ficción autobiográfica en la narrativa española actual: *Todas las almas* de Javier Marías." *Actas de Congreso en homenaje a Rosa Chacel.* Ed. Martínez Latre and María Pilar. Logroño: Universidad de la Rioja, 1994. 215–22.

Christie, Ruth. "Nostalgia for a Prescribed Identity in *Todas las almas* by Javier Marías." *The Scripted Self: Textual Identities in Contemporary Spanish Narrative.* Ed. Ruth Christie, Judith Drinkwater, and John Maklin. Warminster: Aris & Phillips, 1995. 15–29.

———. "Self-Writing and 'lo que pudo ser' in *Corazón tan blanco* by Javier Marías." *The Scripted Self: Textual Identities in Contemporary Spanish Narrative.* Ed. Ruth Christie, Judith Drinkwater, and John Maklin. Warminster: Aris & Phillips, 1995. 135–52.

Cuñado, Isabel. "Realidad y ficción en *El hombre sentimental*." *Foro Hispánico* 20 (2001): 95–103.

———. "*Tu rostro mañana* y la ética de la memoria." *Allí donde uno diría que ya no puede haber nada. Tu rostro mañana de Javier Marías.* Ed. Alexis Grohmann and Maarten Steenmeijer. Amsterdam and New York: Rodopi, 2009. 23–49.

De Azúa, Felix. "Lanzas, espadas, rostros y nada." *Allí donde uno diría que ya no puede haber nada. Tu rostro mañana de Javier Marías.* Ed. Alexis Grohmann and Maarten Steenmeijer. Amsterdam and New York: Rodopi, 2009. 49–54.

De Maeseneer, Rita. "Sobre la traducción en 'Corazón tan blanco' de Javier Marías." *Espéculo. Revista de Estudios Literarios.* http://www.ucm.es/info/especulo/numero14/jmarias.html. np.

Edemariam, Aida. "Words and Meaning." http://www.theage.com.au/news/books/words-and-meanings/2005/07/08/1120704543379.html. np.

Fay, Sarah. "Javier Marías: The Art of Fiction," Interview with Javier Marías. *The Paris Review* 179 (2006). http://www.theparisreview.org/interviews/5680/the-art-of-fiction-no-190-javier-Marías. np.

Grohmann, Alexis. "La literatura como paradoja." *Allí donde uno diría que ya no*

puede haber nada. Tu rostro mañana de Javier Marías. Ed. Alexis Grohmann and Maarten Steenmeijer. Amsterdam and New York: Rodopi, 2009. 161–69.
Ingendaaly, Paul. Interview with Javier Marías. http://bombsite.com/issues/73/articles/2345, pp. 150–58.
Kercher, Dona. "Children of the European Union, Crossing Gendered Channels: Javier Marías's Novel, *Todas las almas*, and Gracia Querejeta's *El último viaje de Robert Rylands*. Cine-Lit 3 (1997): 100–12.
Logie, Ilse. "La traducción, emblema de la obra de Javier Marías." *Foro Hispánico* 20 (2001): 67–76.
Marías, Javier. On-line question and answer session with BBC Estudio Abierto, June 22, 2007. http://news.bbc.co.uk/hi/Spanish/forums/newsid_6687000/6687353.stm.
Marías, Miguel. "El arte de recordar." *Donde todo ha sucedido: Al salir del cine*, by Javier Marías. Ed. Inés Blanca and Reyes Pinzás. Barcelona: Galaxia Gutenburg, 2005. 13–20.
Miller, Stephen. "Graphic-Lexical Dialogue in Marías and Rivas." *Romance Quarterly* 51 (2004): 97–110.
Scarlett, Elizabeth. "Victors, Villains, and Ghosts: Filmic Intertextuality in Javier Marías's *Mañana en la batalla piensa en mí*." *Revista Canadiense de Estudios Hispánicos* 28 (2004): 391–410.
Simonsen, Karen-Margrethe. "*Corazón tan blanco*—a Postmodern Novel by Javier Marías." *Revista Hispánica Moderna* 52 (1999): 193–212.
Steenmeijer, Maarten. "Javier Marías, columnista: el otro, el mismo." *El columnismo de escritores españoles (1975–2005)*. Ed. Alexis Grohmann and Maarten Steenmeijer. Madrid: Editorial Verbum, 2006. 79–96.
Wood, Gareth J. "Literary Allusion in Javier Marías's *El siglo*." *Bulletin of Hispanic Studies* 84 (2007): 589–607.

Other Works Cited

Alonso, Santos. *La novela en la transición*. Madrid: Puerta del Sol, 1983.
Altisent, Marta E., ed. *A Companion to the Twentieth-Century Spanish Novel*. Woodbridge: Tamesis, 2008.
Amago, Samuel. *True Lies*. Lewisburg, PA: Bucknell University Press, 2006.
Bakhtin, Mikhail. *Problems of Dostoevsky's Poetics*. Trans. Caryl Emerson. Minneapolis: University of Minnesota Press, 1984.
Bauman, Zygmunt. *Postmodernity and Its Discontents*. Cambridge: Polity, 1997.
Benet, Juan. "Incertidumbre, memoria, fatalidad y temor." *En ciernes*. Madrid: Taurus, 1976. 43–61.
———. *La inspiración y el estilo*. Barcelona: Seix Barral, 1973.
———. *Volverás a Región*. Madrid: Destino, 1967.
Brombert, Victor. "Opening Signals in Narrative." *New Literary History* 11 (1980): 489–502.
Burke, Kenneth. "Literature as Equipment for Living." *Modern Criticism: Theory and Practice*. Ed. Walter Sutton and Richard Foster. New York: Odyssey Press, 1963. 242–47.
Cameron, Ian, ed. *The Book of Film Noir*. New York: Continuum, 1993.
Cassuto, Leonard. *Hard-boiled Sentimentality: the Secret History of American Crime Stories*. New York: Columbia University Press, 2009.

Cohn, Dorrit. *Transparent Minds: Narrative Modes for Presenting Consciousness in Fiction*. Princeton, NJ: Princeton University Press, 1978.
Commager, Henry Steele. *The Search for a Usable Past and Other Essays*. New York: Knopf, 1967.
Docherty, Thomas. *Alterities*. Oxford: Oxford University Press, 1996.
——. *Reading (Absent) Character*. Oxford: Oxford University Press, 1983.
Empson, William. *Seven Types of Ambiguity*. London: Chatto & Windus, 1947.
Graham, Helen and Jo Labanyi, eds. *Spanish Cultural Studies: An Introduction*. Oxford: Oxford University Press, 1995.
Hamlin, Cyrus. "The Conscience of Narrative: Towards a Hermeneutics of Transcendence." *New Literary History* 13 (1982): 205–29.
Hanson, Helen. *Hollywood Heroines. Women in Film Noir and the Female Gothic Film*. London: I.B. Tauris, 2007.
Hazlitt, William. *The Miscellaneous Works of William Hazlitt*. Vol. 2. New York: Derby & Jackson, 1859.
Henseler, Christine and Randolph D. Pope, eds. *Generation X Rocks*. Nashville: Vanderbilt University Press, 2007.
Intonti, Vittoria. " 'The Figure in the Carpet' as an Allegory of Reading." *Henry James Against the Aesthetic Movement*. Ed. David Garrett Izzo and Daniel T. O'Hara. Jefferson, NC, and London: McFarland, 2006.
Irwin, John T. *Unless the Threat of Death is Behind Them: Hard-boiled Fiction and Film Noir*. Baltimore: Johns Hopkins University Press, 2006.
Jordan, Barry and Rikki Morgan-Tamosunas. *Contemporary Spanish Cultural Studies*. London: Edward Arnold, 2000.
Kaplan, E. Ann, ed. *Women in Film Noir. New Edition*. London: British Film Institute, 1998.
Labanyi, Jo. "History and Hauntology; or, What Does One Do with the Ghosts of the Past? Reflections on Spanish Film and Fiction of the Post-Franco Period." *Disremembering the Past: The Politics of Memory in the Spanish Transition to Democracy*. Ed. Joan Resina. Amsterdam and Atlanta: Rodopi, 2000. 65–82.
Lyotard, Jean-François. *The Postmodern Condition*. Trans. Geoff Bennington and Brian Massumi. Minneapolis: University of Minnesota Press, 1984.
Martín Gaite, Carmen. *El cuarto de atrás*. Barcelona: Destino, 1981.
Moore, Marianne. *The Complete Poems of Marianne Moore*. New York: Macmillan/Viking Press, 1967.
Moreno-Nuño, Carmen. *Las huellas de la Guerra Civil. Mito y trauma en la narrativa de la España democrática*. Madrid: Ediciones Libertarias, 2006.
Poulet, Georges. *Studies in Human Time*. Trans. Elliott Coleman. Baltimore and London: Johns Hopkins University Press, 1956.
Ricoeur, Paul. *Memory, History, Forgetting*. Trans. Kathleen Blamey and David Pellauer. Chicago and London: University of Chicago Press, 2004.
——. *Time and Narrative*. Trans. Kathleen Blamey and David Pellauer. Vol. II. Chicago: University of Chicago Press, 1985.
Rubin, Martin. *Thrillers*. Cambridge: Cambridge University Press, 1999.
Sánchez-Conejero, Cristina. *Spanishness in the Spanish Novel and Cinema of the 20th–21st Century*. Newcastle: Cambridge Scholars Publishing, 2007.
Shadoian, Jack. *Dreams and Dead Ends. The American Gangster Film*. Oxford: Oxford University Press, 2003.

Shakespeare, William. *Othello*. Oxford: Oxford University Press, 2006.
Sobejano, Gonzalo. *Novela española de nuestro tiempo*. Madrid: Editorial Prensa Española, 1975.
Sobejano-Morán, Antonio. *Metaficción española en la postmodernidad*. Kassel: Edition Reichenberger, 2003.
Soldevila Durante, Ignacio. *Historia de la novela española (1936–2000)*. Madrid: Cátedra, 2001.
Spacks, Patricia Meyer. *Novel Beginnings. Experiments in Eighteenth-Century English Fiction*. New Haven and London: Yale University Press, 2006.
Spires, Robert. *Beyond the Metafictional Mode. Directions in the Modern Spanish Novel*. Lexington, KY: University Press of Kentucky, 1984.
———. *Post-Totalitarian Spanish Fiction*. Columbia and London: University of Missouri Press, 1996.
Thomas, Ronald R. "Detection in the Victorian Novel." *The Cambridge Companion to the Victorian Novel*. Ed. Deirdre David. Cambridge: Cambridge University Press, 2001. 169–91.
Todorov, Tzvetan. *The Fantastic: A Structural Approach to a Literary Genre*. Trans. Richard Howard. Ithaca, NY: Cornell University Press, 1975.
Whiteside, Anna and Michael Issacharoff, eds. *On Referring in Literature*. Bloomington and Indianapolis: Indiana University Press, 1987.
Wimsatt Jr., W. K. and Monroe C. Beardsley. "The Intentional Fallacy." *Modern Criticism: Theory and Practice*. Ed. Walter Sutton and Richard Foster. New York: Odyssey Press, 1963. 248–57.

Index

Alas, Leopoldo, 31, 229
Alonso, Santos, 230
Amago, Samuel, 230
Altisent, Marta, 230
ambiguity, 63–4, 70, 132–3
Armstrong, Terrence *see* Gawsworth, John
Azúa, Félix de, 180

Benet, Juan, 2, 5, 31, 33–5, 38, 64, 71n.1, 87, 121n.13, 168, 170, 229
biography (vs.) fiction, 106, 106–7n.7, 107, 108n.9, 121–5, 127, 129–32, 134
Borges, Jorge Luis, 40, 218
Brombert, Victor, 186–7
Browne, Robert, 85
Browne, Sir Thomas, 40
Burke, Kenneth, 182

Cabrera Infante, Guillermo, 38–9
censorship, 18–19
Cervantes, 2, 31, 229
Christie, Ruth, 230
Civil War (Spanish), 73, 77–8, 202–4, 225
  memory of, 11–12, 162n.19
Conan Doyle, Sir Arthur, 58n.16, 61n.20, 63
Conrad, Joseph' 2, 9, 40, 58n.16, 214
Cuñado, Isabel, 161n.17, 198, 230

Díaz Migoyo, Gonzalo, 120–1n.13
de Wet, Oloff, 127–9

Dinesen, Isak, 214
dreams, 87–93
Durante, Ignacio, 230

Eliot, T. S., 214
El Semanal, 17–19, 231
El último viaje de Toby Rylands see Querejeta, Elías and Gracia
ethics, 152, 160, 172, 200–10
Ewart, Wilfred, 127, 135

fantastic, 64n.24
Faulkner, William, 2, 40
Fay, Sarah, 231
Franco, Dolores, 3, 6, 128
Franco, Jesús, 5–6

Gawsworth, John, 14, 106, 118–19, 128
Generation X, 13
ghosts *see* haunting
Graham, Helen, 229
Grien, Hans Baldung, 181
Grohmann, Alexis, 182, 230

haunting, 161, 161n.17, 162–3, 165, 167, 169, 172–3, 176–7, 223, 225
Hazlitt, William, 101
Henseler, Christine, 229
hermeneutic consciousness, 124–5, 124–5n.18, 127, 134, 137, 182
Herzberger, David, 230

Igendaay, Paul, 231
Iriarte, Antonio, 230

James, Henry, 2, 58n.16, 63–5
  figure in the carpet, 65, 67–68
Jordan, Barry, 229
Joyce, James, 215–16

Labanyi, Jo, 162, 169, 229
living (vs. telling), 28–31, 108–9, 186, 196, *see also* storytelling
Love Story, 39n.26
Lowry, Malcolm, 214

Machen, Arthur, 118, 118n.12, 128
Madrid, 22–3, 94
Mankiewicz, Joseph, 2, 22, 164, 225
Marías, Javier
  life, 3–7
  newspaper columns (collections)
    Aquella mitad del tiempo, 231
    A veces un caballero, 26
    Demasiada nieve alrededor, 22–3n.10, 24–5, 40n.27
    Donde todo ha sucedido. Al salir del cine, 20–2, 231
    El oficio de oír llover, 23n.11
    Harán de mí un criminal, 19, 26, 40n.27
    Literatura y fantasma, 29–32, 35, 37–44
    Mano de sombra, 17, 19n.4, 22–3, 25, 37
    Pasiones pasadas, 28, 40n.28
    Seré amada cuando falte, 22
    Vida del fantasma, 17, 19n.4, 23–4
  newspaper columns (individual)
    "Ausencia y memoria en la traducción poética", 41
    "Autobiografía y ficción", 33n.18
    "Botellón de encapuchados", 22–3n.10
    "Cabezas llenas", 38
    "Caso crítico", 21
    "Contar el misterio", 29n.17, 30
    "Cuéntale el cuento", 39
    "Desde una novela no necesariamente castiza", 31–2
    "El camino de nuestra lengua", 40n.27
    "El fantasma y la señora Muir", 22
    "El oficio de oír llover", 23n.11
    "El terreno sin confines", 17
    "El viejo truco del grito en el cielo", 25
    "Emblema y caso", 19n.3
    "Enemigos de la libertad", 25
    "Errar con brújula", 38
    "¿Es usted el santo fantasma?", 40n.27
    "Falsificaciones literarias", 40n.28
    "Ficciones bastardas", 19–20n.4
    "La casa en semiorden", 19n.3
    "Ladrones mayores", 19n.4
    "La fama de la fama", 19n.4
    "La huella del animal", 30, 38, 43–4
    "La infancia recuperada", 17
    "La intromisión que no para", 24
    "La venganza y el mayordomo", 28
    "Las bromas divinas", 31
    "Locuacidades ensimismadas", 23n.11
    "Los malditos detalles", 37
    "¿Mande?", 40n.27
    "Mi libro favorito", 40–1
    "Mala noticia miserable", 19n.4
    "Malos tragos", 22
    "Noticias de mis favoritas", 22n.9
    "Paridas o paridos", 26
    "Posdata", 19n.3
    "Productos podridos", 40n.27
    "Qué hace falta", 23–4
    "Si no han visto el río", 22n.8
    "Todas las farsantes son iguales", 26n.12
    "Todos los días llegan", 20–1
    "*Un inédito censurado*: Creed en nosotros a cambio", 19n.3

newspaper columns (individual) cont.
  "Una explicación y un adiós", 19
  "Una invitación", 35
  "Una pobre cerilla", 35
  "Una proposición muy razonable", 23
  "Volveremos", 33, 37
novels
  Corazón tan blanco, 14, 139–59, 221, 223, 225, 228
  El hombre sentimental, 14, 87–102, 106
  El siglo, 71–87, 87n.17
  Los dominios del lobo, 9, 46, 47–58, 59, 71, 119, 180, 220
  Mañana en la batalla piensa en mí, 14, 139, 159–78, 179, 184, 221, 223, 225
  Negra espalda del tiempo, 14, 36, 37n.25, 43–4, 103–4, 107, 109, 120–38, 180, 185–6, 231
  Todas las almas, 14, 103, 104–20, 122–4, 130–1, 133, 137, 142, 179, 186
  Travesía del horizonte, 2, 9, 46, 58–70, 71, 180
  Tu rostro mañana, 14, 75n.10, 103n.1, 106, 108n.8 109, 179–211, 221, 223
other writings (non-fiction)
  Miramientos, 180, 212, 216–19
  Vidas escritas, 180, 212, 213–16, 219
political views, 23–26
short fiction (collections)
  Cuando fui mortal, 219–20, 224–28
  El monarca del tiempo, 220, 226–7
  Mala índole, 221–3
  Mientras ellas duermen, 28, 219–20, 226–7
theory of reading, 42–5, 53–4, 66–8, 70, 134–8, 149, 156, 171, 175, 211

theory of writing, 29–31, 32–9, *see also* storytelling
Marías, Julián, 3, 4, 74n.7, 170
Martín Gaite, 54, 109
memory, 91–2, 161, 167, 224
Milton, John, 85–6
Miranda Warning, 188–9
Moore, Marianne, 182
Moreno-Nuño, Carmen, 73n.5, 230
movies, 2, 6, 19–22, 166, 166n.23, 175–6, 176n.20, 178, 221
  in *Los dominios del lobo*, 49, 50n.8, 50n.9, 53–5, 57

newspaper columns, 17–45
  narrative voice in, 27–8
novel in Spain, 7–9, 31–2, 48–9

Oxford (city), 110–14, 116–17
Oxford University, 122–4, 131

Pérez-Reverte, Arturo, 18
Pope, Randolph, 229
postmodern, 125–6, 153n.11, 153–7, 180, 182, 187
Presley, Elvis, 221–3

Querejeta, Elías and Gracia, 104n.2

Redonda (Kingdom of), 3, 106n.6, 118, 127n.19
Rimbaud, Arthur, 214

Sánchez-Conejero, Cristina, 230
Sartre, Jean-Paul, 109
Shakespeare, William, 13, 13–14n.14, 97, 121n.13, 159, 224, 163–4n.21
  in *Corazón tan blanco*, 139–41, 146–7, 149–51
  in *Mañana en la batalla piensa en mí*, 163, 163n.20, 164–5, 176, 178, 178n.30
  in *Tu rostro mañana*, 194–5, 195n.21, 197, 224

Sobejano, Gonzalo, 230
social realism, 7–9
Spires, Robert, 110, 133n.22, 181n.7, 229
Steenmeijer, Maarten, 230
Sterne, Laurence, 2, 10, 38–9, 41, 215–16, 231
Stone, Ralph and Gillian, 130–1
storytelling, 15, 28–31, 222, 225
   Corazón tan blanco, 132–8, 147–8, 151–8
   El hombre sentimental, 89, 92–3, 99
   El siglo, 72, 75, 81–5
   Los dominios del lobo, 50–3
   Mañana en la batalla piensa en mí, 165, 168, 170–8
   Todas las almas, 105–6, 108–9
   Travesía del horizonte, 60–1, 65–70

Tu rostro mañana, 181–92, 203, 206, 208, 210–11

thread of continuity, 163, 166, 175–6, 179
time, 79–81, 152, 166–9, 225–6
Todorov, Tzvetan, 64
translation, 9–11, 39–42
   list of Marías's translated authors, 39n.26
Turandot, 98
Turgenev, Ivan, 214

Valle-Inclán, Ramón del, 2, 31, 217–18
Verdi, Giuseppe (*Othello*), 96–8
violence, 56–7, 184, 194–210, 220–1, 223

www.ingramcontent.com/pod-product-compliance
Lightning Source LLC
Chambersburg PA
CBHW070759230426
43665CB00017B/2424